EFFECTIVE TEACHING AND SUCCESSFUL LEARNING

The overall aim of this reader-friendly book is to enable current and prospective teachers as well as other education professionals to improve practice, leading to more successful learning for all students. Drawing on her extensive experience as both a high school teacher and a university professor, Inez De Florio provides an evidence-informed and value-based approach to teaching and learning that takes the personality and the accountability of teaching professionals into account. Students' needs and interests are the primary focus of an evidence-informed teaching model, the MET (Model of Effective Teaching), which is described and exemplified in detail. In order to allow for informed decisions and suitable applications of the steps of the MET, the book furthermore provides a succinct and comprehensible introduction to the main features and types of educational research, especially newer findings of evidence-based education such as presented in John Hattie's research.

Inez De Florio is a professor in the Department of Humanities at the University of Kassel.

Effective Teaching and Successful Learning

BRIDGING THE GAP BETWEEN RESEARCH AND PRACTICE

Inez De Florio
University of Kassel

CAMBRIDGE
UNIVERSITY PRESS

University Printing House, Cambridge CB2 8BS, United Kingdom

One Liberty Plaza, 20th Floor, New York, NY 10006, USA

477 Williamstown Road, Port Melbourne, VIC 3207, Australia

314-321, 3rd Floor, Plot 3, Splendor Forum, Jasola District Centre, New Delhi - 110025, India

103 Penang Road, #05-06/07, Visioncrest Commercial, Singapore 238467

Cambridge University Press is part of the University of Cambridge.

It furthers the University's mission by disseminating knowledge in the pursuit of education, learning and research at the highest international levels of excellence.

www.cambridge.org
Information on this title: www.cambridge.org/9781107112612

© Inez De Florio 2016

This publication is in copyright. Subject to statutory exception and to the provisions of relevant collective licensing agreements, no reproduction of any part may take place without the written permission of Cambridge University Press.

First published 2016

A catalogue record for this publication is available from the British Library

Library of Congress Cataloging in Publication data
Names: De Florio-Hansen, Inez.
Title: Effective teaching and successful learning : bridging the gap between research and practice / Inez De Florio.
Description: New York, NY : Cambridge University Press, 2016. | Includes bibliographical references and index.
Identifiers: LCCN 2016000952 | ISBN 9781107532908 (Paperback) | ISBN 9781107112612 (Hardback)
Subjects: LCSH: Educational psychology. | Learning, Psychology of. | Effective teaching. | Education–Research–Methodology. | BISAC: PSYCHOLOGY / General.
Classification: LCC LB1051 .D362 2016 | DDC 370.15–dc23 LC record available at http://lccn.loc.gov/2016000952

ISBN 978-1-107-11261-2 Hardback
ISBN 978-1-107-53290-8 Paperback

Cambridge University Press has no responsibility for the persistence or accuracy of URLs for external or third-party internet websites referred to in this publication, and does not guarantee that any content on such websites is, or will remain, accurate or appropriate.

Science is simply common sense at its best, that is, rigidly accurate in observation, and merciless to fallacy in logic.

THOMAS HUXLEY

Contents

Preface .... page xi

    Introduction 1
    1. Premises 1
    2. Aims 2
    3. Structure 2

1 Main Features of Scientific Research on Education 8
    1.1 A Conference Talk 8
    1.2 Science and Research 10
    1.3 Jean Piaget (1896–1980): Major Contributions to Developmental Psychology 12
    1.4 Lev Vygotsky and Jerome Bruner: Going Beyond Piaget 16
        Lev S. Vygotsky (1896–1934) 16
        Jerome Bruner (born 1915) 19
    1.5 Educational Science and Educational Research 22
    Review, Reflect, Practice 25

2 Important Types of Scientific Research on Education 27
    2.1 Main Types of Research: Description and Explanation 27
    2.2 Theories, Hypotheses, and Models 28
    2.3 Research Design and Methodology 32
    2.4 Psychometrics 35
    2.5 Experiments (RCTs), Quasi-Experiments, and Correlation Studies 37
    2.6 A Presentation of John Dewey's Main Ideas 41
    Review, Reflect, Practice 43

3 Main Features of Evidence-based Research on Education 45
  3.1 Evidence-based Medicine and Evidence-based Education 45
  3.2 A Question of Age 47
  3.3 Essential Features of Evidence-based Research 49
  3.4 Potential and Pitfalls of Randomized Controlled Trials 51
  3.5 The Measurement of Interventions in Teaching and Learning .. 54
  3.6 Assumptions about *What Works* 56
  3.7 How to Deal with Results of Evidence-based Research 58
  Review, Reflect, Practice 62

4 Meta-Analyses on Education 63
  4.1 Meta-Analyses and Effect Sizes 63
  4.2 A Critical Look at Research on Teaching Effectiveness 69
  4.3 Thinking without Thinking 71
  4.4 A Theory-based Meta-Analysis of Research on Instruction 73
  Review, Reflect, Practice 77

5 A Synthesis of Over 800 Meta-Analyses Relating to Achievement ... 79
  5.1 Hattie's Study *Visible Learning* 80
  5.2 "Know Thy Impact" 83
  5.3 Shortcomings of *Visible Learning* 84
  5.4 Hattie's Resource Book *Visible Learning for Teachers* 87
  5.5 An *International Guide to Student Achievement* 90
  Review, Reflect, Practice 92

6 Scaffolding Effective Teaching and Successful Learning 94
  6.1 Hattie's Model of Direct Instruction (DI) 95
  6.2 Links between Facts and Values 100
  6.3 Premises of Effective Teaching 102
  6.4 MET – A Model of Effective Teaching and Successful
      Learning 110
  6.5 Research Evidence and Teacher Expertise 113
  Review, Reflect, Practice 117

7 Planning and Starting the Lesson 118
  7.1 A Thoughtful Review of Effective Teaching 119
  7.2 Planning the Lesson 121
  7.3 The Realm of the Smartest 128
  7.4 Starting the Lesson 130
  Review, Reflect, Practice 136

Contents

8 Presenting Knowledge and Skills – Assertive Questioning 137
   8.1 Classroom Management and Classroom Climate 139
   8.2 Presenting Knowledge and Skills 143
   8.3 The Impact of an Expert Peer 149
   8.4 Assertive Questioning and Interactive Dialogue 151
   Review, Reflect, Practice 155

9 Guided and Independent Practice 157
   9.1 Summary of the Preceding Steps of the MET 157
   9.2 Types of Practice 158
   9.3 Planning Guided Practice 164
   9.4 Even Good Things Can Be Improved 170
   9.5 Independent Practice 170
   9.6 All's Well that Ends Well 173
   Review, Reflect, Practice 174

10 Cooperative and Project-based Learning 175
   10.1 Cooperative vs. Collaborative Learning 175
   10.2 The Message of John Dewey 176
   10.3 Basics of Learning in Small Groups 178
   10.4 Newer Research into Cooperative Learning 179
   10.5 Major Forms of Cooperative Learning 182
   10.6 A Joint Venture: *Othello* 190
   10.7 PBL – Project- and Problem-based Learning 191
   10.8 Newer Research into Problem-based Learning 195
   Review, Reflect, Practice 196

11 Feedback – Reciprocal and Informative 198
   11.1 Newer Research into Feedback 199
   11.2 The Feedback Model of Hattie and Timperley 202
   11.3 Feedback Given by Teachers to Students 204
   11.4 Peer Feedback 208
   11.5 Love is Not Always Blind 211
   11.6 Feedback Given by Students to Teachers 212
   Review, Reflect, Practice 214

   Concluding Remarks: Standards Need More Evidence 215

References 221
Index 231

Preface

During the past years, I have dedicated much time to gaining better insights into educational research and the implementation of its results. Among other things, I read many scientific research studies on education and the social sciences, watched a great amount of videotaped teaching, tried to make sense of lesson transcripts, and consulted textbooks as well as lesson plans. More and more the picture of a land of milk and honey came to my mind.

Even though a host of scientific studies on education, as well as research textbooks and teacher guides, do not meet the criteria of serious scientific endeavor, educators can draw on a rich and helpful body of literature in their field – at least in the English-speaking countries. The more my readings and my searches proceeded, the more I began asking myself questions like the following:

- How may busy teachers find the time to read at least the most important studies regarding their teaching context?
- How can they evaluate the quality of educational research?
- According to which criteria will they decide whether an intervention program or a teaching strategy is adequate for their students?
- Furthermore, by which means are they enabled to adapt science-based interventions to their classroom, as they are always confronted with the warning that the evaluated "tools" don't work in every context in the same way?
- How will they be able to distinguish useful research-based teacher guides from the recipe books of self-proclaimed education gurus?

As time went by, another association crossed my mind: I saw Pieter Bruegel the Elder's well-known painting of the Land of Cockaigne before my inner eye. The protagonists on the ground show in a striking manner what it means to cope with abundance. In my opinion, the fact that even countries with a remarkable body of education research don't perform well in international achievement studies may depend to a certain degree on the plethora of advice which is lavished on teachers. To avoid misunderstandings, international studies such as TIMSS or PISA are only one small indicator for the proper functioning of a school system, and other factors, for example teacher training and opportunity standards such as public funding, are of even greater importance than the overabundance of scientific findings.

For all these and many other reasons, my overall aim is to provide teachers in training and in service, as well as other education professionals, with a comprehensible, concise, and critical overview of current scientific research on education. I don't focus on a particular country but rather address teachers all over the world who are willing to improve their everyday practice to the benefit of all their students. My aim is to help teachers find their way to a more reflective practice on their own or in interaction with colleagues without further resources. This will be made possible by looking at scientific research and the implementation of its findings through the eyes of teachers.

Inez De Florio

Introduction

In this introduction the starting point and the aims of the book are briefly stated, followed by the chapter summaries.

1. PREMISES

In the past decades, more rigid concepts of research gathered momentum in the social sciences, and subsequently in scientific approaches to teaching and learning. What is undoubtedly a gain per se may have unexpected and undesirable consequences for teachers and learners:

- Many important aspects of teaching and learning are beyond experimental research; others still wait to be investigated.
- In general, there is too much emphasis on Randomized Controlled Trials (RCTs), often considered as a panacea for all educational problems.
- On the other hand, important results from the social sciences are neglected or even considered as unscientific: for example, studies on intuition and teacher personality, as well as research into different ways to make ideas and learning stick.
- Standards-based education is not sufficiently aligned with evidence-informed teaching and learning.
- For educators and students alike it is often difficult to find their way through the maze of scientific results, that is to say, to select those procedures that are most appropriate for the learners in a specific context.
- There are too many guides and "cookbooks" that indiscriminately propagate, not to say preach, dozens of techniques and strategies

without helping teachers and learners to sort the wheat from the chaff.
- Even though many suggestions may be suitable for many learning contexts, what to adopt and adapt is the choice of the teacher. Otherwise the professionalism of educators is at risk, reducing them to puppets on a string.

2. AIMS

Effective teaching and successful learning are quite possible if we look at research through the eyes of educators who want to obtain the best results for all their learners. To do so, this book aims to:

- concentrate on the foundations of different approaches to research;
- enable teachers to understand the most important scopes and pitfalls of scientific research into education;
- look at the premises of effective teaching practices that lead to successful learning;
- focus on important techniques and strategies to apply during different parts of the lesson;
- exemplify teaching practices for different grades and various subject matters;
- take care of the accumulation of competencies in the longer term;
- help teachers to cope with standards, tests, and evaluation;
- strengthen teacher personality as a means to promote the joy of teaching and learning.

Using research to improve practice means choosing adequate tools and adapting them to a special learning context determined not only by goals, standards, and objectives, but also by unique teachers and learners. Many parts of this book are inspired by my experiences as a school teacher and a university professor specializing in empirical research on language teaching as well as in intercultural communication. My considerations about effective teaching and successful learning are based on a large amount of prior publications (mostly in German and English), particularly on De Florio-Hansen (2014a, 2014b, 2015).

3. STRUCTURE

In Chapter 1, the main features of scientific research are described in a succinct way, including recent developments and current accepted knowledge. Science and research are defined so that their interrelationship becomes evident. The examples of three outstanding educational psychologists of the past century help (prospective) teachers and other education professionals to understand that the approaches of scientists often are different, even though they arrive at comparable findings. Furthermore, the results of Piaget, Vygotsky, and Bruner – in part closely related; in part in contrast to each other – form the basis of contemporary views of teaching and learning, not only in the English-speaking countries.

A closer look at education and educational research will lead to a better understanding of the shortcomings of certain teacher guides.

In Chapter 2, basic knowledge of scientific research is further developed, explaining and defining the most important types of research, such as descriptive and explanatory studies. After focusing on the fundamental differences between theories, hypotheses, and models on the one hand, and research design and methodology on the other, we will move forward to the main aspects of psychometrics indispensable for experimentation, such as RCTs, quasi-experiments, and correlation studies. All features are explained using examples from the field of education. The obsolete distinction between qualitative and quantitative research and other critical issues are problematized. The chapter is completed by a conversation between two undergraduate students who are preparing a presentation about Dewey's contributions to scientific inquiry and educational research.

Chapter 3 deals with the main features of newer scientific approaches to educational research influenced by evidence-based medicine. Starting with a discussion of similarities and differences between medicine and education, the role of treatments in both fields – drugs in the one case, pedagogical interventions in the other – is of particular interest. Essential features of evidence-based research, such as empirical evidence, grades of evidence, and the difference between effectiveness and efficiency, are illustrated in order to show the potential and the pitfalls of controlled experiments (RCTs). In this context a well-designed RCT, in the form of a natural experiment, is presented. It is argued that learning outcomes are not directly influenced but rather are stimulated by teaching; that is to say, student achievement is not the output of teaching, but the consequence of learning. Therefore findings of evidence-based research into educational issues should be considered in an unorthodox way. Results of evidence-based research are to be taken as an important source for teachers to reconsider their educational practices. It is for the expert, adaptive, evidence-informed teacher to decide whether to adopt and in which way to adapt a certain intervention to his or her own educational context.

In **Chapter 4**, before looking at examples of meta-analytic research, the main features of this research design are defined and described so that teachers can benefit from the results. As the main findings of meta-analyses are indicated in an averaged measure of synthesized outcomes – the so-called effect size – a comprehensible explanation of this highly relevant term is given and exemplified. On the basis of this knowledge, two relevant meta-analyses are critically appraised in order to further inform teachers about the potential and the limits of meta-analyses in the complex field of education. The scholarly studies are first and foremost presented with the intention of helping teachers to make informed decisions about improving the learning of all their students. The limits of meta-analytic research lead to the advice to be cautious before putting evidence-based research findings into practice.

Chapter 5 deals extensively with John Hattie's mega-analysis, a synthesis of more than 800 meta-analyses of research on achievement.

The design and the main findings of Hattie's study are analyzed and critically examined. This critique refers partly to the methodological procedure of a mega-analysis per se, which potentiates the shortcomings of meta-analytic research. Hattie's unorthodox attitudes toward empirical and especially experimental research are detected and noted so that teachers and the whole education profession might be well aware of how to deal with Hattie's results. The merit of Hattie's enormous research endeavor is mostly seen in the teaching model that he presents in *Visible learning* (2009) and in more detail in *Visible learning for teachers*, a resource book that shows once more the curse of knowledge. An important, and perhaps the most criticized, outcome of Hattie's study is the low effect that he attributes to class size. In the *International guide to student achievement*, a useful handbook edited together with Eric Anderman (Hattie & Anderman, 2013), Hattie himself is eager to correct his previous views and to underscore the importance of small-sized classes.

N.B. In the following chapters I refer to the effect sizes indicated in Hattie's study of 2009: First, because effect sizes of different primary studies and meta-analyses are not comparable; second, because Hattie's ranking of 138 factors is widely known in the scientific world.

Chapter 6 presents a comprehensive teaching model, the MET (Model of Effective Teaching), based on experimental research – mostly on the detailed research findings of Hattie, Marzano, and Wellenreuther (2004, 2014). The MET is in some ways comparable to Hattie's model of Direct

Instruction, which draws explicitly on the DISTAR model of Siegfried Engelmann and implicitly on the Lesson Plan Design of Madeline Cheek Hunter. My own compilation, the MET, is however intended as a scaffold for practitioners. There is no claim that all thirty steps must be followed. Teachers may equally profit from important analyses of single teaching and learning strategies that will enable them to choose adequate interventions and translate them into locally adapted applications. Therefore, the thirty steps will be discussed on the basis of research findings and illustrated by examples referring to different grades and subject matters (see Chapters 7–11). The MET is intended to help teachers to question teaching traditions and personal habits so that they can make informed decisions to the benefit of their students. My overall aim, besides presenting newer research findings, is to strengthen the personality of teachers in order to avoid their de-professionalization.

Chapter 7 illustrates the steps of **planning and starting a lesson**, including several practical examples. **The planning phase** comprises five steps, the most important of which is the choice of challenging goals in accordance with the needs and interests of the students. In order to build on previous knowledge, teachers must know where their learners stand with regards to subject matter knowledge, skills, and related attitudes. Furthermore, they have to make efforts to gain insights into the world knowledge of their students based on maturation and the influences of students' families and wider living contexts. Both aspects – didactic knowledge and knowing about the world – are illustrated in this chapter. As there are great differences between learners regarding the aforementioned issues, teachers have to be prepared for alternative activities if students' misconceptions call for re-teaching.

Starting the lesson includes the following steps: giving the students a clear idea of the goals, the learning intentions, and the success criteria; making the value of the learning objectives transparent; confirming students' expectations regarding their ability to meet the goals; and building commitment and engagement in the learning tasks. To start well, teachers should think of a motivating and inspiring hook in order to focus student attention on the following lesson.

Chapter 8 deals with empirical research into **explaining, presenting, and modeling new content**. The premise is **classroom management and classroom climate**. No teaching or learning will be effective if the teacher is unable to create a favorable classroom atmosphere, which is mainly determined by efficient classroom management with clear rules and routines. Introducing content or skills through effective teaching means comprehensible explanations or demonstrations of the content, enriched by illuminating examples related to students' lives. Teacher clarity is of utmost importance. In many cases, further illustration of the content through pictures, graphics, figures, and audio-visual examples taking recourse to the new media can be significant. The presentation phase is interrupted and followed by assertive questioning. These questions from the teacher and the students allow for checking if and how the students have understood the new learning content. During all steps, teachers have to display a positive attitude towards misconceptions and mistakes. If learning results turn out to be insufficient, teachers have to be prepared to repeat part of the lesson.

Chapter 9 shows how to conceptualize **guided and independent practice** on the basis of newer research. As important as the presentation of input may be, the following steps of practice are indispensable. Guided practice consists of graded tasks and worked examples including explanation of the solution steps. Whereas guided practice is closely supervised by the teacher, with formative feedback and short explanations for single students, independent practice is often accompanied by peer feedback and concluded by formative assessment through tests. Thoroughly planned, varied, and decontextualized tasks aim at the reinforcement and transfer of the content or skills to other relevant situations. The final step, the closure part, brings the lesson to an appropriate conclusion.

In **Chapter 10** we will look at the ample research findings regarding **cooperative learning and PBL used interchangeably for project- and problem-based forms of learning**. Dewey's thoughts and claims are illustrated as they are one of the foundations of a democratic education based on mutual support. Furthermore, "learning by doing" is another characteristic of cooperative forms of learning. Newer research illustrates that group cohesion contributes more than competition or individualistic learning to the success of overlearning as deliberate practice. Five major forms of cooperative learning are defined and exemplified. In order to embed learning content in the long-term memory and make it easily retrievable for appropriate application, deliberate practice is essential. To encourage teachers to integrate cooperative learning and PBL into their practice, selected examples are explained in detail.

Chapter 11 is dedicated to **feedback as formative (and summative) assessment**. From research findings, the following suggestions are deduced: Feedback should be informative and not generic. Praise and extrinsic rewards have to be avoided. Feedback is most successful when it is reciprocal, which is to say it should not be one-track but should lead to a dialogue between teachers and students. Three different forms of feedback in the classroom – in my view, the most important aspect of teaching and learning in an institutional setting – are discussed on the basis of Hattie and Timperley's feedback model. The main questions are: How can teachers provide adequate feedback to their students? How can students give effective feedback to their peers? How can teachers elicit feedback about their teaching from the students? Important issues of reciprocal and informative feedback are exemplified.

In the **Concluding Remarks**, conjectures are made about possible relationships between standards-based and evidence-based teaching and learning. Important questions to be answered are: What does standardization of schools mean? What are educational standards? What are performance standards used for? Which standards may further teaching in such a way that student learning is initiated and improved? Is there a relationship between education systems that are based on performance standards and students' test scores in international assessment studies? How can educational standards be assessed? Are standards in accordance with significant results of evidence-based education? Provisional answers are meant as an opportunity for further debate.

1

Main Features of Scientific Research on Education

Before being able to see learning processes and their results through the eyes of the students (Hattie, 2009, 2012), educators and teachers should take a closer look at relevant findings of scientific research on education. Why is it necessary to spend a certain amount of time and effort in studying research when you, as a teacher, are more or less satisfied with the learning outcomes of your students?

In a complex field like education it is always useful to question habits and conventions in the light of newer and newest research findings. Furthermore, as part of the debate on accountability, we have to answer to ourselves as to whether we choose the best possible teaching and learning activities with regard to our individual learners.

The following statements and explanations are a succinct introduction to the main features of scientific research on education. The overall aim of these introductory remarks is to enable teachers in training and in service to appraise research findings. If an educator concludes that a research proposal may work better as usual practices, new strategies as well as whole intervention programs may be tried out. Don't forget that even highly recommended tools must be adapted to your specific teaching and learning context. Nevertheless they still might be revealed as inappropriate, for various reasons.

1.1. A CONFERENCE TALK

Sarah and Kate, both ELA high-school teachers, meet just once a year at their state's annual curriculum conference. During the year, they keep in loose email contact, exchanging ideas and sometimes teaching materials. Recently, they participated in the same webinar.

This time more than ever before, the focus of the conference is on evidence-based education. During the breaks Sarah and Kate come together in the hallway:

SARAH: You don't look very happy. Is there something wrong?
KATE: No, no, but I can't hear it anymore, evidence-based teaching, evidence-based learning, evidence-based everything ...
SARAH: But don't you think it's a good thing that we are invited to question our teaching habits?
KATE: Sure, but you can't analyze the whole teaching and learning process through experimental research.
SARAH: That's true. But there are many aspects of teaching and learning that I considered in a certain way without questioning either the premises or the consequences. The results of scientific research showed me that I wasn't aware of certain details.
KATE: Don't misunderstand me. I'm not against research into education, not at all. What bothers me is the fact that experiments or quasi-experiments are considered a cure-all.
SARAH: I agree with you, sure. There are other types of research of equal importance. It depends on what you are looking for.
KATE: Without saying it openly, some scholars devalue older studies that didn't include rigid experimentation. What about great thinkers on education like Piaget, Vygotsky, Bruner, or Dewey?
SARAH: From my point of view their influence on teaching and learning is not contested at all; it continues. But there are strategies – for example, *reciprocal teaching* or *concept mapping* – that weren't in the focus of those great thinkers. In these cases, evidence-based research can be of help. Don't you think so?
KATE: Yes, but sometimes the results of evidence-based research are not reliable, and even when this is the case, I don't have the time to read all the details about the context in which the strategy or the tool worked well.
SARAH: You mean, an evidence-based result is nothing more than an invitation to consider the strategy as a possible means to improve teaching and learning?
KATE: Yes, that's why I'm in favor of research-based education that is influenced by the thoughts of great educationalists. They did not prescribe everything in detail, but suggested ... how shall I put it? ... a certain mindset. Furthermore, their work has proven its value over decades and even centuries.
SARAH: You are right. When I think about it, an amazing fact comes to my mind: Most of the authors that report results of recent evidence-based research quote ancient philosophers such as Socrates, Plato, and Aristotle to underline their new findings.

KATE: Oh, yes; therefore I think the expression "evidence-based education" isn't acceptable. We can't base our teaching only on the results of experimental research.

SARAH: I see ...

KATE: In my opinion, research-based education consists of a mixture of useful older research and newer studies which still have to prove their practical benefits. Therefore I prefer the term evidence-oriented or rather evidence-informed teaching and learning.

SARAH: Let's go back and talk with others about our views.

KATE: Oh, no; I'm afraid I'm not an expert. During my teacher training, research was not the center of attention. Qualitative research, quantitative research, ok, but I don't know the exact difference between a theory and a hypothesis, and I have only vague ideas about research design and methodology ...

1.2. SCIENCE AND RESEARCH

The word *science* is derived from Latin *scientia*, which means knowledge. You might object that not every type of knowledge is science. In fact, the knowledge you accumulated during your time at high school in a subject matter such as physics or history is not considered science, even though knowledge of school subjects is based on scientific results. If all knowledge was considered as science, every educated person would be a scientist. So what is the relationship between the two terms?

> **Science** is a systematic endeavor that builds and organizes knowledge. The knowledge generated and accumulated through the systematic work and effort of scientists has to be in accordance with certain criteria. Scientific knowledge is supposed to offer explanations and predictions about different kinds of phenomena in a testable and replicable way.

Imagine the following situation: One of your colleagues has, several times in different classes – let's say in grade 9 and in grade 10 – tried using advance organizers to inform his or her students about the objectives of a lesson or a teaching unit. An advance organizer is a structured overview of the following text or content that aims at facilitating the students' learning processes. The U.S. psychologist D. P. Ausubel introduced this strategy into educational psychology in the 1960s.

Even though the positive outcomes of your colleague's intervention were higher in grade 10 than in grade 9, he or she is convinced that the positive effects of advance organizers outperform other forms of pre-information provided to the students about objectives and learning activities. As he or she talks enthusiastically about the progress made by his or her learners, you decide to give advance organizers a try in one of your own classes. To do so, you must have a great deal of information: In what form did your colleague conceive the advance organizers? To what length and in what detail were they written? Did he or she expose them on the black/whiteboard or on a work sheet? Were there any differences as regards the structure of the advance organizers assigned to the students in grade 9 and those in grade 10?

There is nothing wrong with the idea of giving a successful strategy or a technique applied by others a try; on the contrary, if you have gathered sufficient information, you might find it useful to adapt the procedure to your special teaching context and then try it out, with equal or even better results. Yours and your colleague's work may lead to a scientific project. Why are the results of your efforts not considered to be scientific knowledge? Remember that your colleague did not indicate the exact effect of the intervention, nor did he or she offer an explanation of the phenomenon. And what about the aforementioned claim "in a testable and replicable way"? In the paragraph about experiments, quasi-experiments, and correlation studies (see Section 2.6), we will discuss this example further.

The systematic endeavor to generate knowledge that corresponds to certain criteria is considered as research. Thus, science and research are inextricably entwined. As in the case of science, there are numerous definitions of research. How science and research are defined depends on the perspective of the researcher: that is to say, the ways in which he or she conceives the nature and scope of knowledge. For our purpose, the following definition is viable.

Research is the systematic investigation of a topic or an issue for the advancement of knowledge. It is a process of steps used to collect and analyze data in order to discover and interpret facts. Other purposes of research are the revision of existing theories in the light of new facts and the practical application of these new or revised theories.

Before looking at the field of education, that is to say educational psychology and educational research, I conclude these introductory remarks with a quote from Shavelson and Towne (2002, p. 2):

"At its core, scientific inquiry is the same in all fields. Scientific research, whether in education, physics, anthropology, molecular biology, or economics, is a continual process of rigorous reasoning supported by a dynamic interplay among methods, theories and findings. It builds understanding in the form of models or theories that can be tested."

1.3. JEAN PIAGET (1896–1980): MAJOR CONTRIBUTIONS TO DEVELOPMENTAL PSYCHOLOGY

At the beginning of the millennium, Palmer (2001) edited a two-volume anthology about eminent educationalists from ancient times to the present. The second volume is dedicated to *Fifty Modern Thinkers on Education: From Piaget to the Present Day.*

Of the fifty thinkers on education presented in the articles of this second volume, I have chosen Jean Piaget, Lev Vygotsky, and Jerome Bruner on whom to focus our attention. They are considered the most influential psychologists and educationalists of the twentieth century (for Vygotsky & Bruner see Section 1.4). Furthermore, the three researchers – or, at least, many of the results of their scientific research – are well known among teachers and other education professionals.

On the one hand, their influence on today's teaching and learning is beyond doubt. On the other, their research endeavors comprise not only educational issues, but also broader aspects of human development and behavior. Furthermore, the findings of Piaget, Vygotsky, and Bruner are somewhat interrelated and thus allow for a more integrative but also differentiated view of scientific research on education. Even though some of their research findings did not pass without criticism, their theories are still valid.

The enormous worldwide impact of Piaget's theories was due to a variety of reasons, for example:

- Piaget was the first psychologist that engaged in the systematic study of cognitive development, preparing the ground for developmental psychology (Piaget, 1952).
- His model of cognitive development explains features of human knowledge that weren't taken into account by other researchers before him (Piaget, 1970, 1971).
- Piaget was opposed to the behaviorist orientation of psychology of his time and opted for research designs that allowed for introspection.
- Even though his research methods did not correspond to the requirements of rigid experimentation, his original model of cognitive development, as well as other Piagetian findings, have proven to be remarkably robust.

Piaget's main focus was on children and cognitive development, not on learners and acquiring knowledge and skills in general. Nevertheless, it is difficult to overestimate his impact on teaching and learning.

Before engaging in research into cognition, Piaget, a Swiss psychologist, worked with Binet at Paris-Sorbonne University. Perhaps the construction of intelligence tests with which he was engaged under the guidance of Binet induced him to investigate further into the development of knowledge and intelligence. He was interested in discovering the differences in the cognitive structures underlying qualitative development of knowledge. How do children from birth to adolescence gradually conceive of the world in more and more sophisticated ways? At what age are they capable of formal reasoning, that is to say thinking about thoughts and considering the consequences of their behavior without acting it out?

According to Piaget, infants dispose of a basic mental structure which is the foundation of further cognitive development. The child passes from a sensorimotor stage (from birth to age two), dominated by movements and the five senses, to the preoperational stage, which starts when the child learns to speak and continues until the age of seven. During this second stage the child is not yet able to reason logically and to manipulate information in the mind. In the third of the four stages, the stage of concrete operations (from ages seven to eleven), children begin to think logically, but they don't go beyond what they can physically manipulate. The development of abstract reasoning takes place in the formal operational stage, the last of Piaget's stages. Children and adolescents (from age eleven onward) are capable of using metacognition.

It is not worthwhile to discuss whether these stages are more or less gradual or quite distinct. According to Piaget, the assumption of these four stages and their development are based on genetic factors; that is to say, they are more or less the same in every cultural context. Even though Piaget can show, through interesting and intriguing experiments, how children and adolescents behave and, most notably, reason in the different stages, he does not deduce transitions toward abstract thinking from his experimentation. As the universality of the stages is considered a genetic presupposition, his experiments serve to confirm what he already presupposes.

If not stimulated by impulses from the external world, especially by those of their environment, why should children move from one stage to another? Piaget answers this important question by introducing the need for equilibration. Every individual tries to adapt incoming information to his own mental structures in order to feel comfortable. This adaption occurs through two different processes: assimilation and accommodation. In this context, *assimilation* means that children incorporate new ideas or pieces of information into their knowledge and transform them so that they can use them effectively. *Accommodation* means adjusting to or accepting external factors transforming part of their own mental structures or creating new ones.

Another basic component of Piaget's stage model is the concept of schema, which goes back to the German philosopher Immanuel Kant. According to Piaget, schemata are the basic building blocks of intelligent behavior. These units of knowledge relate to different aspects of the world. Let's take an example: eating in a restaurant is considered a schema. On the basis of your experience in a given culture, you have internalized concepts of how a visit in a restaurant proceeds, from entering the place and consulting the menu to ordering and paying the bill. If it comes to an experience in a cultural context quite different from your own, you will have to adjust your restaurant-schema. What is not very difficult for an adult can cause problems for a child.

What can we deduce from Piaget's overall findings for teaching and learning?

- Students are active learners that construct knowledge on their own, and not recipients to fill with information.
- The challenging task for teachers consists of providing learning activities that stimulate and support the development of mental structures such as schemata.
- Based on the assumption of biological maturation of the four stages, readiness is an important prerequisite of teaching and learning. Only when students have reached the appropriate stage should they be taught certain concepts.
- An eminent focus is on discovery learning, as, according to Piaget, skills of problem-solving cannot be taught, but must be discovered.
- Teachers should focus on the processes of learning, not on the end product.
- Piaget's research results underscore the importance of interaction in classrooms.
- Collaborative as well as individual activities further learning processes.
- Creating disequilibrium through appropriate tasks can stimulate the restructuring of knowledge.

- As the Piagetian approach is child-centered, teaching and learning activities should take place in an atmosphere of reciprocal respect.

Later on (see Chapters 3 and 5), we will examine the extent to which these pieces of advice from Piagetian findings are in accordance with the results of recent studies, for example strong experimental research such as Randomized Controlled Trials (RCTs; see Section 2.5). In any case, it is not difficult to understand why Piaget is praised as a precursor of radical constructivism and artificial intelligence.

As previously mentioned, Piaget's assumption of the genetic universality of the four stages of cognitive development did not pass without criticism. Piaget, however, was criticized much more for his research methods, which he changed or at least adjusted several times during his long life span. Observation and experimentation were combined with forms of interviews used for psychiatric clinical examination and psychoanalysis. During his research processes Piaget increasingly rejected this form of clinical interview, not so much due to the pressure of critics, but rather because they were revealed to be too suggestive and not sufficiently empirical. As Piaget considered standardized methods to be counterproductive with regard to the overall aims of his research, the changes, however, were not substantial. Furthermore, Piaget conducted his research with very small sample sizes, mostly his own three children.

Despite shortcomings in the assumptions and the research methods, **Piaget's findings are still influential.** Because his ideas were widely propagated only from the 1960s onward, many results of his research had already been modified by contemporary and subsequent scientists, for example Vygotsky and Bruner. What should we retain?

- The concept of readiness of the student for certain concepts is valid to a certain point.
- Cognitive development is determined much more by external (cultural) factors than by maturation.
- Language as a developmental trigger is at least as influential as thought. Both are closely interrelated.
- Cognitive development is a gradual process that differs a great deal with regard to individual learners.
- Teachers and instructors have a greater impact on learners than Piaget's pedagogic pessimism makes us believe.

1.4. LEV VYGOTSKY AND JEROME BRUNER: GOING BEYOND PIAGET

Among the great number of psychologists and educationalists influenced by Piaget's work are Vygotsky in Russia and Bruner in the United States, both of whom take the Piagetian model of cognitive development, with its related research findings such as adaptation and schemata, as starting points for their own research endeavors.

While both somewhat opposed to Piaget's notions of cognitive development, it is not only the case that their research results differ from Piaget's findings; also, Vygotsky and Bruner each arrive at quite different conclusions about the processes underlying or determining cognitive development. In my view, it is particularly significant for teachers and educators to consider that three eminent scientists focusing mainly on the same aspects arrive at different views, theories, and models of cognition, which nevertheless together exert great influence on teaching and learning in today's schools and classrooms.

Lev S. Vygotsky (1896–1934)

Vygotsky, a psychologist and educationalist from Belarus, is known worldwide for his contributions to developmental and educational psychology. He started with a doctoral thesis about the psychology of art, considering the aesthetic reaction of the reader or viewer as an essential criterion in the social construction of art work. Looking at theories and practices in our classrooms, we can easily recognize his eminent influence on teaching and learning activities in subject matters such as English Language Arts (ELA), especially literature, and art studies in general.

Vygotsky's theory of social construction, known as the cultural-historical theory of cognitive development, goes far beyond his early engagement with art and is directly opposed to Piaget's conviction regarding underlying genetic factors (Vygotsky, 1978). Through observation and experimentation, Vygotsky found out that interaction between very young children and their caretakers is crucial for the development of cognition and higher mental functions. In interacting with the environment, the child constructs the mental tools of his culture. At the beginning, the infant depends to a very large extent on impulses from the external world, most of all on the language of the caretaker. Even though Vygotsky takes into consideration other tools in this process of internalization, he sees language as a major influence (see his most popular work, *Thought and Language*, published in 1934 and again in 1999). According to him, the processes of internalization are not linear but are characterized by different stages. Contrary to Piaget, the psychologist arrives at the conclusion that mental structures develop gradually depending on the stimulation children receive from their (cultural) environment.

What, according to Vygotsky, is based on interpersonal and external processes in the beginning becomes more and more an internal, intra-psychological tool of the mind that the child uses on his or her own. Thought and language become increasingly independent. Children are increasingly able to construct their own socio-cultural environment and to influence it. These considerations are also valid for the development of meaning. Through experiments, Vygotsky could show that lexical items and their meaning are not stable, but develop in close relationship under the influence of external cultural factors. Not only basic tools of the mind but even complex mental processes are acquired through social interactions.

Vygotsky's theories, summarized under terms such as social constructivism or sociocultural theory, exert great influence on teaching and learning in today's classrooms. This does not mean there haven't been many other philosophers and educationalists – for example, Bruner – that expanded on the research of the psychologist, but the roots of sociocultural theory date back to Vygotsky. Unfortunately, Vygotsky died at the age of thirty-eight, leaving behind many threads of his ample studies for his colleagues A. R. Lurija and A. N. Leontiev, with whom he spent five years in collaboration in a research program at Moscow University's Institute of Psychology. It was not only Vygotsky's premature death that meant many of his scientific studies were left unaccomplished; additionally, Stalinism limited and hindered his work. It became more and more difficult to publish the results of his research because his considerations were termed "decadent" and not in line with communist materialism. Some of his research was published later on by his assistants and students, but the bulk of his work remained undiscovered until the 1960s. It was only in the late 1970s that Vygotsky's work came to be published and appreciated in the western world.

What is less known is Vygotsky's research into defectology, an older term for special education. In accordance with his emphasis on social construction, his attitude toward children or students with special needs goes beyond inclusive education of disabled and non-disabled students in the same class. For him, blindness as a psychological fact is not to be considered a disaster; it is the social fact, namely how society reacts to a blind person, that leads to misfortune.

It is obvious that we as teachers and educators benefit from his findings when we put major emphasis on cooperative and project-based learning. We should also consider Vygotsky's reflections on instruction itself. Whereas young children stretch their cognition to a large extent by playing with others, older children and adolescents do not only construct knowledge, skills, and attitudes through cultural artifacts such as books and art work; adequate instruction from teachers and other experts is of great help for students when it comes to the development of higher mental functions, for example conceptual learning and critical thinking (see Chapter 5).

After this brief introduction to the main features of Vygotsky's research it is quite easy to understand how the psychologist arrived at his best known theory, which compares the actual development of a child or an adolescent to their level of potential development. The Zone of Proximal Development (ZPD) states what a learning individual cannot achieve alone, but can achieve with the help of a teacher, an adult, or more competent peers.

Let's take the example of a child playing with shapes. The child knows that the blocks have to be put into the holes, but does not succeed in doing so. His elder sister explains to him how to do it successfully. Perhaps she shows him once or twice how the blocks fit into the holes. After this, most children are able to do it successfully on their own. Vygotsky's theory presupposes that we know the level of actual development: The child is not engaged in discovering something completely new, but has already grasped the sense of the toy. Furthermore, we must have an idea of this particular child's level of potential development.

ZPD theory entered lesson planning and instructional design some decades ago under the term *scaffolding*, which goes back to Bruner and his team. This useful teaching and learning strategy is often mistaken by considering every type of support as scaffolding in accordance with the ZPD. The scaffold has to fit within the ZPD and is removed as soon as the student is able to do things on his or her own.

Why is it so difficult and time-consuming to create adequate scaffolds for students in a classroom? Whereas the sister in the earlier example knows quite well the actual level of development of her little brother, and moreover has probably observed him coping with the blocks, it is an enormous challenge for teachers to determine the point from which their students start and to understand what is beyond reach for most of the students. In other words, it is very difficult to reach every student's ZPD. A good way to do so is to assess students' capabilities when trying to accomplish a task on their own and compare it to the learning outcome(s) when the learners work together with one or more competent individuals (see Chapter 6 for practical advice).

Although we don't know very much about the exact research design and methodology of **Vygotsky**, it is undeniable that he provides multiple applications to general and special education, in part developed by later generations. A well-known and corroborated theory refers to the **Zone of Proximal Development**:

- The understanding of complex concepts is limited at a given age. These limits can be partly surpassed with the help of an expert.
- All learning, especially the development of higher mental functions, arises from social interaction.

Jerome Bruner (born 1915)

Like Piaget and Vygotsky, the U.S. scientist Jerome Bruner is a psychologist widely known for his research into cognition. He is one of the eminent figures in the so-called cognitive revolution. Initially he engaged in studies of human perception, soon becoming interested in the development of cognition, especially in young children. His assumptions with regard to cognitive development are – as we will see – in contrast to those of Piaget and even to those of Noam Chomsky (born in 1928). The latter assumes an innate ability to reach more and more complex cognitive structures depending on specific capacities, for example an innate Language Acquisition Device (LAD).

In addition to the work of Piaget and Vygotsky, which is circumscribed by developmental psychology, a main focus of Bruner's studies was education itself, a field to which he made great contributions, especially from the 1950s. His books *The Process of Education* (1960) and *Toward a Theory of Instruction* (1996) were widely read and influenced teaching and learning not only in the United States but also in many other countries all over the world. In contrast to Piaget's genetic stages of cognitive development, Bruner attributed great importance to environmental and experiential factors. Children and adolescents are active learners who can understand difficult content and solve complex tasks if they are confronted with them by the teacher or an expert in an adequate way. This relates to Bruner's idea of the spiral curriculum: "A curriculum as it develops should revisit these basic ideas repeatedly, building upon them until the student has grasped the full formal apparatus that goes with them" (Bruner, 1960, p. 13).

From my point of view, it is useful for teachers and education professionals to reflect on the following of Bruner's considerations about classroom teaching and learning:

- Learning goes far beyond the memorizing of facts and other information. A teacher's main challenge is to enable the students to get an idea of the structure in the sense of deeper learning, an objective to be reached by going on in spiral order (discussed later).
- In contrast to Piaget, Bruner is convinced that there is nothing like readiness. No subject or concept is too difficult. If the teacher is able to present even complex content in a form that reaches the individual learner, any child at any developmental stage can grasp any subject.
- Bruner's view of education is widely determined by intuitive and analytical thinking. Intuition is a key feature of productive and creative thinking. With his research on the role of reflection, Schoen (1984) puts a major emphasis on intuition not only in teaching and learning, but also in many other professional contexts (see Chapter 4).
- Theories of motivation as are now set forth by scientists such as Dweck, namely the role of natural curiosity and the wish to learn instead of external remunerations, had already been emphasized by Bruner (and other educationalists before him). A main task of the teacher is to arouse interest in the subject matter and the specific content of the lesson.

As a result of the attention and recognition Bruner attracted with the results of his studies in education, and especially in schooling, he was invited to take an active part in various educational projects funded by the federal government, as well as by different states. He did not limit himself to scientific advice but elaborated a social studies program, *Man: A Course of Study* (MACOS), a comprehensive curriculum. According to Bruner, the program tries to answer three important questions:

- What is uniquely human about human beings?
- How did they get that way?
- How could they be made more so?

Although it was considered a landmark in curriculum design by many experts and influenced a number of young researchers, such as Howard Gardner (born in 1943), MACOS was not really implemented, being too elaborate for ordinary teachers and in disaccord with the political convictions of many Republicans.

In the early 1970s, Bruner left his position at Harvard University to teach at the University of Oxford for several years. From then until his return to the United States in 1979, he devoted a great deal of his research to children's language. In Bruner's stage model, which comprises three modes of mental representation, the different stages are not neatly age-related (as in Piaget's model), but more or less integrated. In the third mode of representation, the symbolic stage, information is stored mostly in the code of language. From the age of seven years onward, children are increasingly able to deal with abstract concepts.

Influenced by the ideas of Vygotsky, Bruner became more and more aware of the fact that the cognitive turn was incomplete. In accordance with the psychologist, cognitive and constructivist scholars consider language to be an important feature in mental development. Like Vygotsky, Bruner emphasizes the role of the social environment and especially that of scaffolding, mentioned earlier, a term introduced by Wood, Bruner, and Ross (1976). Simplifying, one can compare Bruner's concept of scaffolding to Vygotsky's ZPD. Both are based on the interaction between a learner and an expert – the teacher or a more competent peer – that helps the student to achieve a specific goal.

Following Vygotsky's ideas, from the 1960s, Bruner began to attach increasing importance to culture. He opted more and more for a cultural turn in psychology. In his publication of 1996 entitled *The Culture of Education*, Bruner describes what cultural psychology implies for education. With regard to his changed views, it is culture that shapes the mind and helps us not only to construct the world around us; moreover, culture provides us with the very conception of our selves (Bruner, 1996, pp. X–XI).

According to **Bruner**, cognitive development is a continuous process that occurs not in fixed stages but gradually. An important reason for cognitive growth is the use of language in social interaction. As the environment in which a child grows and is educated has an enormous impact, cultural aspects play an eminent role in the development of mental structures not only in the early years but also during schooling (as well as during one's whole life span).

Learning can be accelerated through scaffolding. This term is often used interchangeably with Vygotsky's Zone of Proximal Development. Using the instructional technique of scaffolding, a teacher or another expert bridges the gap between what a learner knows and what he or she is able to achieve with the help of a more competent person.

1.5. EDUCATIONAL SCIENCE AND EDUCATIONAL RESEARCH

> **Educational science** is the type of knowledge that relates to all facts of human learning. **Educational psychology** and **educational research** aim at generating scientific results for the purpose of enhancing educational activities related to instructional design, classroom management, and assessment. Educational science is in close relationship with other disciplines, especially psychology, sociology, and philosophy.

The criteria for scientific research on education are quite the same as for any other field of science. At this point you may have serious questions about the utility of teacher guides or other books that diffuse advice for teachers. In general, the authors of such "cookbooks" pretend they will improve the learning processes of most students, if teachers follow their recipes. Here, too, a differentiated view of a very complex reality is indispensable. Let us have a closer look at two examples.

At the end of her inspiring report on her first year as a teacher in an elementary school entitled *Educating Esmé* (Raji Codell, 1999, 2009), the author gives a list of "Advice for New Elementary School Teachers." Point no. 21 invites you as a teacher to be consistent: "It means you do what you say and you say what you mean," telling the students: "This is the way we do things around here" and sticking to articulated rules, procedures, and consequences without walking right into the trap of "inflexibility" (ibid., p. 244). There is nothing wrong with this advice, because Raji Codell in no way recommends the use of educational science. However, it would be very difficult to submit her advice to scientific scrutiny "in a testable and replicable way."

Things are different when the author of a teacher guide claims that his advice is research-based, but offers at best teacher-tested procedures. A typical example is the resource book by Lemov, which is representative of many other "cookbooks" in the field. Lemov published a guide entitled *Teach Like a Champion: 49 Techniques that Put Students on the Path to College* in 2010, reedited in 2015 to offer sixty-two techniques. I selected this guide because it represents many others in the field. In general the techniques illustrated by the author follow the course of a lesson, but there is no weighing of more or less useful techniques. His procedure refers to the overabundance I mentioned in the preface of this book; it may limit teachers in their choice. Even if teachers with all good will try two of the forty-nine or sixty-two techniques per week, it will take approximately one school year until they come to the end of the book, which, in the 2015 edition, amounts to 500 pages.

How did Lemov select the numerous techniques described in the guide? In the introduction to his book, the author presents some of his "champion teachers" and explains how he arrived at the best working techniques:

> So how did I choose the teachers I studied and the schools I frequented? And what does it mean to say they were successful in closing the achievement gap? Because my primary measure was state test scores, it is worth addressing some misconceptions about their use, if only to underscore how exemplary the work of the teachers who informed this book is. (In some cases, I also used other testing instruments such as [...] internal diagnostic tools we use at Uncommon Schools to surpass or complement the measurement range of state assessments.) (Lemov, 2010, p. 17)

Lemov observed and videotaped a great amount of lessons in about a dozen private Charter Schools, mostly Uncommon Schools, in the states of New York and New Jersey. The laudable goal of Uncommon Schools – Lemov is a member of the leading board – is to put children of underprivileged families, mostly African-Americans, "on the path to college."

Lemov's reasoning is as follows: If these schools were so successful that their students outperformed even the New York State white students (SWA = Student White Average; see figure I.1 and I.2, ibid., p. 21), it had to be the impact of the teachers that produced these noteworthy effects. So he focused mainly on the teaching procedures of preselected teachers at Uncommon Schools. He calls their ways of behaving and teaching techniques, not strategies. The latter are overarching the whole educational enterprise, whereas techniques are steps to greater efficiency – for example, how to distribute worksheets without losing precious time for teaching and learning. My critique of Lemov's approach is at least threefold:

- As previously mentioned, there is no weighing of the different techniques. All forty-nine or sixty-two, respectively, are presented with equal emphasis. Thus, he does not provide his readers with tools of reflection or critical thinking about when and how to use which technique.
- Lemov does not present his findings in a testable and replicable way. He presupposes that what works will work in every teaching and learning context. But his findings are in no way to be generalized.

- What is, in my opinion, worse than the lack of generalizability is the fact that Lemov allows his audience to think his champion teachers' techniques are the cause of their students' gains in achievement.

The last point deserves further consideration because Lemov's approach can be considered a classic example of confusing correlation and cause. A correlation is a mutual relation of two or more things. The advocates of religious schools often assert that Catholic schools are a better choice than public schools. Ample research has shown that the reasons why the students of these private schools reach higher scores are not found in these schools per se. Similarly, the gains in achievement of African–American children in Lemov's Uncommon Schools may depend on a number of other facts:

- The better performance may be caused not only by the numerous teaching techniques (or by some of them), but also by the result-driving strategies that, according to the author, have to be used in concert with the techniques. These four superior strategies are: teaching assessed standards, using data, higher-level lesson planning, and content and rigor (ibid., 2010, pp. 9–13). In comparison to the forty-nine/sixty-two techniques, these strategies may be much more relevant. Lemov should have investigated if there is a causal effect between them and the achievement of the students.
- There may also be a causal relationship between the engagement and the passion of the (preselected) teachers and their preparation or training for service in Uncommon Schools.
- Positive effects on student learning and achievement may be due to the fact that the teachers at Uncommon Schools work together in stable teams and are supported by their principals and other members of the school administration.
- As in the case of religious schools, parents' attitudes toward education and the particular school attended by their children contribute to the success of the learners.

Guides like this, which illustrate at best teacher-tested techniques, should not be used as the basis of college courses for prospective teachers. Nevertheless, in the context of educational psychology governed by science and research in the above sense, they may serve as examples of more or less unscientific approaches to teaching and learning. In my view it is an illuminating and instructive activity for (pre-service) teachers to find out which of the techniques are really research-based, and in which way they can become useful tools in particular classrooms.

In the social sciences and especially in the field of education, researchers and scholars not only point to the general fact that all scientific results are tentative (see Section 2.2 *Theories, Hypotheses, and Models*), but also advise educators to be careful with direct transfer of the findings of educational research to another context, because they may not be applicable in every time and place. Whereas the phenomena of nature are mostly the same over time, concepts of education are subject to many changes. This historical dimension, in combination with the contextual factors that shape education, makes the study of human learning inherently complex. What Shavelson and Towne state with regard to the U.S. education system is true of schooling in many countries in the western world.

Education is multilayered, constantly shifting, and occurs within an interaction among institutions (e.g., schools and universities), communities, and families. It is highly value-laden and involves a diverse array of people and political forces that significantly shapes its character. These features require attention to the physical, social, cultural, economic, and historical environment in the research process because these contextual factors often influence results in significant ways. Because the U.S. education system is so heterogeneous and the nature of teaching and learning so complex, attention to context is especially critical for understanding the extent to which theories and findings may generalize to other times, places, and populations (Shavelson & Towne, 2002, p. 5).

Furthermore, there are significant differences between the interests of scientists and those of practitioners and policy makers: The main motivation of a scholar is to find out what is possible, whereas policy makers, educators, parents, and the wider public want to know what is practical, affordable, desirable, and credible.

REVIEW, REFLECT, PRACTICE

1. Why is it always a good idea to take the findings of scientific research on education into account? (see Section 1 introduction, 1.1, 1.2) Discuss your answers with other students or with colleagues.
2. What is the difference between research-based and research-informed teaching and learning? (see Chapter 1.2)

3. What messages of Piaget, Vygotsky, and Bruner would you retain as helpful for teaching and learning in today's classrooms? (see Chapter 1.3 and 1.4) Try to find out if and up to what point textbook units in your subject matter correspond to the overall ideas of the three educationalists.
4. Imagine you have received knowledge about the positive effects of a certain teaching strategy, for example presenting worked examples. What concrete information would you like to have about the strategy before trying it out in your own classroom? (see Chapter 1.5) Discuss your results with other students or with colleagues.

2

Important Types of Scientific Research on Education

2.1. MAIN TYPES OF RESEARCH: DESCRIPTION AND EXPLANATION

In general, researchers distinguish between two essential approaches: that is, between descriptive research and explanatory research. Descriptive research tries to answer questions such as: What is going on? What is happening? For example, you want to know how much time your students pass with social networking every day, because you suppose that some of your low-performing learners do not spend sufficient time on homework or independent reading. A look at official questionnaires will help you conceive a written survey to find out the exact amount of time your students spend on social networking per day. This example demonstrates that descriptive research is not always qualitative. Qualitative research findings are mostly written up in a report, but descriptive research can also consist of quantitative results, which means the findings are expressed in numbers.

Let us return to our example. You find out that your low-performing students indeed spend more time on social networking than your successful learners. This does not at all mean that there is a causal relationship between the students' achievement and the hours spent on social networking. There may only be a correlation, a mutual relationship between the two, as in the case of the aforementioned example of Lemov's techniques.

Continuing with our imaginary research project, we now move to explanatory research. You must seek an answer to the question if the time spent on social networking really causes the respective students' insufficient achievement. There may be other reasons for their unacceptable performance; for example, the lack of a place at home where they can study, or their exaggerated engagement in sports. The questions to answer are the following: Does x cause y? Is there a systematic effect between social networking and low achievement? You rightly think that answering questions regarding systematic effects is not as simple as finding out how much time your students spend on social networking. That is not all: If you obtain results that show systematic effects between the two phenomena, there is another important twofold question: How and why does social networking cause a deterioration of cognitive achievement?

> Scientific studies can be descriptive and/or explanatory.
>
> The findings of **descriptive research** show what is happening or what is going on in the context of inquiry.
>
> The results of **explanatory research**, which often starts from descriptive findings, answer questions of causal relationship such as: Does x cause y? Is there a systematic effect of x on y? How and why does x affect y?
>
> The results of descriptive as well as of explanatory research can assume **qualitative** and/or **quantitative** formats.

2.2. THEORIES, HYPOTHESES, AND MODELS

In everyday language, theory is opposed to practice. We say, for example, "It is a long way from theory to practice" or "In theory, there is no difference between theory and practice, but in practice, there is." Theory in everyday language means something suggested but not proven as a reasonable explanation for facts, a condition, or an event. When words or expressions of common language become scientific terms, their meaning often changes in some way. So what are scientific theories, hypotheses, and models? The following definitions are based on a recent publication by Gorard (2013, passim), whose overall focus is on *Creating robust approaches for the social sciences*.

> Theories are types of abstract or generalizing thinking. A **scientific theory** is a tentative explanation. It provides an explanatory framework for some observation. Theory does not equal hypothesis.
>
> From the assumptions of a theory follow a number of possible **hypotheses** that can be tested in order to provide support for or challenge the theory. Thus, a hypothesis is a supposition to be tested.
>
> Theories are often viewed as **scientific models**. A model is a logical framework intended to represent reality, for example a geographical map.

Models are created to show the particular, whereas theories refer to more general conjectures. Although models try to come as close to the truth as possible, they don't represent reality.

Only if theories, hypotheses, and models are **falsifiable**, that is to say if they can be proven as false, are they considered scientific ideas.

A still influential scientific theory in the aforementioned sense is the dual-coding theory which was introduced into cognitive science in the 1970s by Paivio, a Canadian psychologist (Paivio, 1969, 1971). His main focus was on the question of how to enhance learning through memory. He hypothesized that verbal information is not stored in the brain in the same way as images. His conjecture that there are different representations of verbal and visual information led him to the hypothesis that the formation of mental images aids in learning: a conjecture that dates back to antiquity. Paivio and other scientists carried out extensive experimental research to prove and underscore the importance of imagery in cognitive operations.

Let us take the example of vocabulary learning: If you want to remember a lexical item or an expression, it is often useful to memorize not only the wording but also a mental image. For example, if you want to learn the French word *garçon* (English: waiter), it is helpful to memorize this verbal information by additionally evoking the picture of a waiter before your inner eye. It further enhances memory and retrieval if this visual information represents a waiter you met personally, perhaps in France. There are many expansions of this theory. Absurd mental images are even better retained than simple ones: for example, that of an egg in a shoe when you try to memorize the two French lexical items *chaussures* (English: shoes) and *œuf* (English: egg).

To date there has been no falsification of the dual-coding theory, but many researchers find it insufficient. Paivio's theory does not take into account that there might be other forms of mental representation besides words and images. You can easily imagine that sounds also may stimulate memory and recall. This is underlined by the increasing claim for enhancing students' audio-visual literacy in different subject matters. Furthermore, the theory loses its importance if associations between lexical items and images can't be formed, as in the case of many abstract nouns. Nevertheless, dual-coding theory is still valid, as it has not been falsified over the course of decades.

Why is it so essential to find competing hypotheses that may falsify a theory? Falsifiability marks the essential difference between a scientific and a religious worldview. There is no possibility to test religious faith as right or wrong: Religious truth is in the mind of the beholder.

Scientific findings, on the contrary, must withstand every sensible test. Furthermore, if a scientific theory did not grant exemption and all conjectures, once proven, rest valid, there would be no progress with regard to our knowledge. For example, the geocentric model of the solar system, which was supported by scientific research over centuries, was later abandoned for a heliocentric model.

Knowledge grows when certain hypotheses and even whole theories prove to be insufficient or completely wrong. A well-known example is the theory that all swans are white. At the moment that you see the first black swan, the theory is falsified. Therefore, theories and hypotheses must be stated in clear, unambiguous, and empirically testable form (Shavelson & Towne, 2002, p. 19), so that they allow for rival plausible hypotheses (de Vaus, 2001).

> *The Provisional Nature of Support for Theories*
>
> Even where the theory is corroborated and has survived attempts to disprove it, **the theory remains provisional**. [...] There always may be an unthought-of explanation. We can't anticipate or evaluate every plausible explanation. The more alternative explanations that have been eliminated and the more we have tried to disprove our theory, the more confidence we will have in it, but we should avoid thinking that it is *proven*. (de Vaus, 2001, p. 15; author's emphasis)

How does a scientist come to a theory? The philosopher K. R. Popper, to whom we owe the claim that all scientific conjectures have to be falsifiable (Popper, 1963), sustains that the act of finding a valuable theory does not follow a scientific or even a logical path. In most cases it depends on the intuition and the creativity of the researcher. Sometimes scientists make a series of observations that leads them to meaningful conjectures; under other circumstances, a researcher might have already formulated a more or less valid theory which he or she wants to submit to further scrutiny.

With the aim of answering the questions of explanatory research – does x cause y? Is there a systematic effect of x on y? How and why does x affect y? – research proceeds broadly in two ways, either by a theory-building or by a theory-testing approach. The empirical level from which a theory-building approach starts is a series of observations. Through induction, that is to say by advancing from the particular (the observation) to the general, the research process moves on to the more abstract level of concepts, that is to say a theory. If, on the contrary, there already exists a theory on the conceptual–abstract level to start with, the scientist passes on to the empirical level of particular observations. The latter procedure is known as deduction (see Figure 2.1).

The two methods of reasoning – from the particular to the general, or vice versa – are often part of lesson plans and/or instructional design. As teachers, we often prepare for our learners a series of meaningful examples to start from. We give them, for example, two or three summaries of narrative texts recently read in class to let them find the main points of a summary on their own. Guided by appropriate questions, they state that a summary is a concise version of the most important facts of the original text, formulated in a neutral tone and in their own words. After a short discussion in class, the students are now able to formulate guidelines on how to write a good summary. Hereafter, they write a summary of another story or novel on the basis of their guidelines. In this case, they are proceeding by induction.

Until recently, deduction was rejected by teachers and educationalists as being too theoretical. It is increasingly being rehabilitated, especially in second and foreign language pedagogy, in the wake of the dictum *form follows function*. First, the learners are confronted with a series of texts exemplifying a certain perspective of the speaker or writer on the narrated events. After having discovered in what way the speaker or writer conceives of the events, they try to find out by which forms of the verb or by what tense(s) the narrator expresses his or her perspective.

Returning to the basic features of research: At what point of the two approaches does the aforementioned intuition and creativity of the scientist play its role in the research process? Is it in inductive and/or deductive

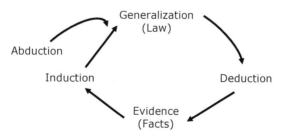

FIGURE 2.1: Induction, Deduction, and Abduction

reasoning? McComas (1998, p. 9, figure 5) offers "a more accurate illustration of the knowledge generating process in science. Here the creative leap (sometimes called abduction) is shown as a necessary element leading from evidence to the generalization."

Another essential question is about the preference between research-building and research-testing approaches. In his monograph about *Self-Concept*, Hattie seems to privilege deduction, as he states:

> Science does not progress this way, and little is gained from inducing meaning and theories from observations. Rather, science proceeds from formulating a theory and then assessing the adequacy of that theory to bring order and meaning to sets of observations. Thus, research on self-concept must begin with a theory or model that will begin to provide order and aid in explaining observations. (Hattie, 1992, p. 2)

It is obvious that an expert in psychometrics, that is to say psychological measurement, will place emphasis on deduction (see Chapter 5 for Hattie's newer research; Hattie, 2009, pp. 46–47, d = 0.43, rank 60). Another reason for Hattie's preference may be the subject of his research. Self-concept is one of the most complex issues on which to carry out empirical research. It would be very complicated to start from observations of the multifaceted expressions of self.

2.3. RESEARCH DESIGN AND METHODOLOGY

In order to understand and evaluate scientific results so that the findings help to improve teaching and learning practice, all educational practitioners should have sufficient knowledge of research methodology. Even if professional cooperation is established, it is for the single teacher to decide on the validity and applicability of a teaching strategy or another intervention. A good foundation of quantitative (and qualitative) theoretical underpinning is necessary to answer questions such as: Is the research finding reliable? Is the examined strategy or technique really what I intend when using the same term? Is the learning context in which the study was carried out comparable to my own classroom? Is the result transferable to my subject matter?

Quite often, teachers who have had no occasion to deepen their knowledge and skills in the field of educational research are impressed by the quantity of study participants, by the inspiring narrations of a researcher, and especially by the methods used to conduct a particular research project. Methodology is an important factor in research, but methods are determined by the research design. It is crucial for teachers to have a closer look at the intentions of the scientist, which may differ widely from the needs and interests of their students. In a world determined by measurability and accountability, teachers have to make great efforts to gain sufficient knowledge of research, namely of research design and methodology.

Research design is the term for the framework of a scientific study. It consists of the single steps to be conducted during a research process, from finding relevant hypotheses to start from, to choosing the sampling that might represent the population, to designing the single steps to carry out when gathering and analyzing the data. Methodology, by contrast, refers to the body of research methods and their analysis.

Quite often research design is confounded with scientific methods. What is even worse is the fact that many readers of research reports equate the two different features and judge the findings of a study with an overemphasis on the methods used by the researcher. A useful simplification to underscore the difference between research design and methods is that of an architect who decides on the materials to be used before knowing what type of building is to be constructed.

Research not only influences teaching and learning, as well as education in general, by its findings; often the proceedings of scientific research also have a great impact on how we plan and prepare lessons. No expert teacher should decide first on the methods to use, for example strategies or techniques. Methods in our example of the architect correspond to the construction materials.

Lesson planning and instructional design start by fixing the goals, standards, and objectives to aim at – that is to say, the type of building to be constructed – before choosing instructional methods. This way of structuring an educational curriculum is known as backward design: First, you identify the results your students should reach, and then you fix the success criteria by which you and your learners see that/if they attained the desired results. Finally, you prepare learning activities that will lead the students to achieve the goals.

Research design is the overarching framework of a research project conceptualized to answer the research questions in the most unambiguous way possible. Design specifies the cases to be studied and their attribution to subgroups, as well as the timing and the sequence of the data collection. In the case of experimental research, the number and the type of interventions are planned.

Research methods come into play after the structure of the project has been thoroughly defined. On the basis of the design following the logic of inquiry, precise techniques or procedures are chosen and the adequate methods of data collection and analysis are fixed. In recent international research the overemphasis on qualitative or quantitative methods has been abandoned in favor of multimethod approaches.

The following succinct overview can facilitate a better use of research findings to improve teaching and learning (University of Western Cape, Cape Town, South Africa; www.uwc.ac.za/Students/Postgraduate/Documents/Research_and_Design_I.pdf; last accessed August 2015).

Research design	Research methodology
Focuses on the end-product: What kind of study is being planned and what kinds of results are aimed at.	Focuses on the research process and the kind of tools and procedures to be used.
Point of departure (driven by): Research problem or question.	Point of departure (driven by): Specific tasks (data collection or sampling at hand).
Focuses on the logic of research: What evidence is required to address the question adequately?	Focuses on the individual (not linear) steps in the research process and the most 'objective' (unbiased) procedures to be employed.

Simplifications like the above juxtaposition are useful to grasp the main differences, but they lead to the risk of underestimating the difficulties of empirical research conducted in the social sciences and in education. The following quote from Shavelson and Towne gives the reader an impression of the multiple requirements to be met by educational scientists:

> The features of education, in combination with the guiding principles of science, set the boundaries for the design of scientific education research. The design of a study does not make the study scientific. A wide variety of legitimate scientific designs are available for education research. They range from randomized experiments of voucher programs to in-depth ethnographic case studies of teachers to neurocognitive investigations of number learning using positive emission tomography brain imaging. To be scientific, the design must allow

direct, empirical investigation of an important question, account for the context in which the study is carried out, align with the conceptual framework, reflect careful and thorough reasoning, and disclose results to encourage debate in the scientific community. (Shavelson & Towne, 2002, p. 6)

It is interesting that the authors (ibid., passim) call several times for long-term partnerships between research and practice in order to accomplish useful scientific research in education.

2.4. PSYCHOMETRICS

In the context of research design and research methods it is indispensable to look at psychometrics, a vast field that is related to most sub-disciplines of psychology, and also to the social sciences and education. Psychometrics refers to the measurement of psychological phenomena, for example personality, behavior, and learning. Measurement in the social sciences means the assignment of numerals to objects or events.

Sir Francis Galton, a British scholar at the time of Darwin, might be considered as the founder of psychometrics, as he was the first to show interest in measuring certain traits of human beings. Over the centuries, mathematical models and statistics gathered considerable momentum in psychological research. At the beginning of the twentieth century, a well-known scholar in the field of psychometrics was the French psychologist Binet, who created the first intelligence tests. Another renowned researcher that added to the growing field of psychometrics was Thurstone, a U.S. engineer and psychologist. He is known for factor analysis, a statistical method for taking unconsidered (latent) variables into account (Thurstone, 1925).

More recently psychometrics has focused on the measurement of attitudes as well as educational outcomes. International studies such as TIMSS (*Trends in International Mathematics and Science Study*) and PISA (*Program for International Student Assessment*) have contributed to publicizing psychometrics. The results of these studies led to a worldwide discussion on whether cognitive achievement in different countries can be tested using the same tasks.

Psychometrics, an influential field of psychology, refers to the theory and technique of psychological measurement. Its overall aim is the construction and validation of assessment instruments. During the past decades,

> mathematical models and statistics have prevailed more and more in the field of psychology, so that nowadays only experts in statistics are able to conduct research that comprises the respective methods. Recent developments of psychometrics which have contributed to a large extent to educational theory and practice include the measurement of academic achievement.

In spite of the incontestable merits of psychometrics, there are important points of criticism. First of all, skeptics express serious doubts about the feasibility of measuring psychic phenomena. But the question of whether these phenomena are measurable or not is posed too broadly. A general distinction is to be made between psychology as a behavioral science that addresses objective cognitive or motoric reactions on the basis of physiological or neuronal processes and the measurement of inner states of mind. Undoubtedly, feelings and moods, as well as needs, attitudes, and personal traits, cannot be easily and exactly measured.

Many scientists outside the inner circle of psychometrics criticize what they call the reduction of subjective mental phenomena and psychological characteristics to numbers. The equation of psychometrics with the measuring of human beings is often connected with general social criticism. Nevertheless, teachers and educators need to have a differentiated view on these controversial issues in order to benefit from the results of psychometric findings without neglecting the necessary adaptation to their special school and lesson contexts in order to improve teaching and learning.

Another problem inherent to psychometrics and closely related to education is scaling. Scaling is not only about the assignment of objects to numerals according to a rule; it is also about how to get numbers which are meaningful for the phenomenon that is measured, for example intelligence or achievement. Furthermore, scaling includes the fixing of cutting points. Simply put, this is about questions such as: What (numeric) quotient of intelligence relates to intellectual giftedness? When is a child to be considered a student with special needs? As you can imagine, or know from your teaching experience, it is very difficult to apply psychometric findings to practice, because numbers quite often don't tell you anything about the reasons for lower or higher achievement. It is even more difficult for teachers and educators to deduce adequate strategies or intervention programs from psychological measurement (see Chapter 3).

2.5. EXPERIMENTS (RCTS), QUASI-EXPERIMENTS, AND CORRELATION STUDIES

In the introductory conference talk in Chapter 1, Kate is annoyed by the debates about evidence-based education because, according to her, it is not possible to analyze the whole teaching and learning process through experimental research. She is quite right, and many teachers and educationalists are of the same opinion. Why is empirical educational research more and more in vogue? What can we learn from the findings based on these research methods?

As international studies such as TIMMS and PISA displayed insufficient results of student achievement in basic knowledge and skills in many western countries, policy-makers and educators as well as students and their parents tried to find out the reasons for what they called the failure of the educational system. Funding and resources apparently did not furnish sufficient explanations. A country like Poland, for example, with a relatively low budget spent on public education, outperforms the United States of America in the PISA rankings. Quite soon policy makers, supported by public opinion, imagined they had found the real culprits: the teachers, whose impact on students is often estimated to be much greater than it is in reality. What Palmer states about U.S. teachers holds true for the members of the teaching profession in many countries all over the world.

> Teachers make an easy target, for they are such a common species and so powerless to strike back. We blame teachers for being unable to cure social ills that no one knows how to treat; we insist that they instantly adopt whatever "solution" has most recently been concocted by our national panacea machine; and in the process, we demoralize, even paralyze, the very teachers who could help us find our way. (Palmer, 2007, pp. 3–4)

What has been "concocted" during the past two decades is education based on experimental evidence; that is, teaching and learning strategies whose positive (or negative) effects are considered as proven by results of quantitative research. In this way, the reasoning of great thinkers on education seems to count less than the results of experimental or at least quasi-experimental studies. To express in numbers what works in the classroom seems more important than the findings of great educationalists, even though they have not expressed unfounded opinions.

The main focus of newer educational research is on quantitative approaches. Experiments are considered to be the gold standard for research in the social sciences, and especially in education. We all have an idea of what is called an experiment in everyday language: for example, we can observe children carrying out experiments to understand the foundations of gravity. In the field of science, an experiment is a systematic investigation conducted to discover more details of a phenomenon in order to advance knowledge.

Most experiments try to answer the questions: Does x cause y? Is there a systematic effect of x on y? Experiments are carried out to verify or to falsify a cause-and-effect relationship. In this order of thought, x and y are called variables. In our example of the colleague who works with advance organizers to pre-inform his students about the objectives and the success criteria of the knowledge and/or skill to be acquired (see Chapter 1.2), the two variables are the advance organizers and the learning outcome of the students.

The first is the independent variable, which is hypothesized to have an influence on the dependent variable: in our case, better understanding and learning. In other words: The dependent variable represents the effect, whereas the independent variable consists of the input expected to cause a change. It is often not sufficiently underlined that, besides the independent and the dependent variables, there are many other variables that may interfere in an experimental design so that the results are biased.

As an experiment is a systematic procedure conducted to verify or refute one or more assumptions about a phenomenon, scientists have established certain rules to which experiments have to correspond. The two most discussed quality criteria for experimental research are validity and reliability.

Validity means that the experiment really measures what it claims to measure. Moreover, the measured event has to correspond to the real world. Is it really the advance organizer that caused the improvement in the students' learning outcomes in the earlier example? There may be other factors that contributed to the learning effects, for example a greater engagement of the teacher and/or the students because they worked toward an important test. Reliability, on the other hand, means that the results are always the same when the experiment is repeated under the same conditions. Reliability thus refers to the consistency of the measurement. If an experiment leads to valid as well as reliable measures the results can be considered well-founded, albeit not certain.

A **scientific experiment** is a systematic procedure to measure the effect of an **independent variable**, for example a special strategy or intervention program, on the **dependent variable**, in our case the learning outcomes. A **valid experiment** measures what it pretends to measure without being biased by other variables. It is considered a **reliable experiment** if the measured effects are exactly the same when the experiment is replicated. **Validity** and **reliability** are the most important quality criteria for experimental research.

The main problem with which any educationalist has to cope is avoiding invalid interferences. That is particularly true for experimental designs. Is the observed effect really caused by the intervention or are there other influences to be taken into account? Imagine that our experiment about the effect of advance organizers is carried out by a scientist. Taking his own observations in different classrooms as a starting point, he has extensively reviewed the literature, analyzing and interpreting a great amount of data with regard to the effects of advance organizers on student achievement in various learning contexts (see Chapter 3 for an extensive discussion of these and the following issues).

He decides to find out the exact impact of a certain type of this graphic organizer in grade 10. His sample, which should represent the entire population, is about 700 tenth-graders attending eight different schools. How can he be sure that the participants do not differ notably in their learning experiences and their achievement? How is it possible to exclude or control variables beyond the independent and the dependent variables?

To minimize the biases of experimental research, a particular type of experiment denominated the Randomized Controlled Trial (RCT) was introduced into scientific research, probably by R. A. Fisher in the first half of the twentieth century. Over decades, RCTs have proven to be valid in the sciences and, more recently, in applied fields like medicine and agriculture. The use of RCTs in the social sciences is controversial, even though this type of experiment is increasingly commonly conducted to evaluate educational interventions.

Researchers that favor RCTs divide their samples into two halves by chance. In this order of thought, randomization is considered a means to minimize or even avoid distorting interferences. One half, the experimental group, is exposed to the intervention – for example, advance organizers presented by their teachers at the beginning of the lesson. The other half, the control group – thus the term RTC – follows the same lessons without advance organizers.

Before and after the teaching, the students' performance is assessed by a test developed by the scientist. In many RCTs pre- and post-test are more or less the same. In analyzing the obtained data, the scientist tries to deduce the effect of the specific organizer on the experimental group in comparison to the control group. Is there any impact? How large is the effect? Is it worthwhile for teachers to spend effort and time in the development of advance organizers?

> In a **Randomized Controlled Trial (RCT)**, the sample is divided by the researcher randomly into two groups of the same size. The experimental group is exposed to some sort of intervention, whereas the control group is not. The results of the same pre- and post-test measuring the achievement of all participants are compared in order to make valid and reliable statements about the potential effect of the intervention.

Despite doubts about their usefulness in the field of education, RCTs are on the whole considered the gold standard of scientific research, followed by quasi-experiments and correlation studies. Shavelson and Towne (2002, pp. 112–116) illustrate how causal relationships can be established when randomization is not feasible. School classes often cannot be freely chosen, which may lead to a selectivity bias caused by unmeasured prior existing differences. In these cases, quasi-experiments are a good option:

> In some settings, well controlled quasi-experiments may have greater "external validity" – generalizability to other people, time, and settings – than experiments with completely random assignment. [...] It may be useful to take advantage of the experience and investment of a school with a particular program and try to design a quasi-experiment that compares the school that has a good implementation of the program to a similar school without the program (or with a different program). (Shavelson & Towne, 2002, p. 114)

> **Quasi-experiments** share with experiments and RCTs the aim to measure an intervention's causal impact on a specific population. Quasi-experiments lack randomization, namely the random assignment to an experimental and a control group. There are different ways in which researchers try to control interfering variables.

Correlation studies are designed to explore whether two variables are correlated, that is to say whether they increase or decrease contemporarily in the sample under investigation. Correlations do not imply causal relationships.

In sum, scientific knowledge is gained through various forms of research. Therefore, wider debates about what counts as research and for whom, in relation to the increasing influence of "what works" approaches building on RCTs and other forms of experimentation, are imperative.

2.6. A PRESENTATION OF JOHN DEWEY'S MAIN IDEAS

Matthew and Bharat are attending the same undergraduate course of a teacher training program. Among the assignments proposed by their lecturer, they chose to give a presentation of Dewey's research into education. They have divided the texts assigned by the lecturer more or less equally. Matthew is the expert on Dewey's thoughts about inquiry, whereas Bharat has focused on the role of education in a democratic society.

MATTHEW: For me, it's quite difficult to decide which aspects of Dewey's extensive research findings we should incorporate into our presentation. What do you think?

BHARAT: It's the same with me. As our course is dedicated to scientific research on education, we will have to concentrate on those aspects that in some way are related to research in general.

MATTHEW: Yes, so let's start our presentation with a short overview of the main philosophical assumptions. I think it's indispensable to mention Dewey's key role in pragmatism.

BHARAT: Well, in some way it's linked to the rest of his findings. And we should say something about his engagement with democracy. It's clear that education contributes to form future citizens.

MATTHEW: Sure, but Dewey also claims for democratic forms of living together in families, at the workplace, and in classrooms.

BHARAT: On the internet I found other important points, for example the exploration of thinking and reflection. Look here: "His concern with interaction and environments for learning provides a continuing framework for practice."

MATTHEW: Ah, learning by doing!

BHARAT: Yes, but it's too easy to limit Dewey to what teachers always quote when thinking of him. It's the same with child-centered education.

MATTHEW: I always thought of Dewey as an advocate of progressive education. So he isn't, is he?
BHARAT: No, he considered this approach as too free. According to him, freedom must be useful in education. I think it's important to underline the role of experience when talking about Dewey's educational concepts.
MATTHEW: What does experience mean? Hands-on activities? Project-based learning?
BHARAT: For Dewey, experience is something more general, it is based on the relationship between continuity and interaction. (reads) "Continuity is that each experience a person has will influence his or her future, for better or for worse. Interaction refers to the situational influence on one's experience. In other words, one's present experience is a function of the interaction between one's past experiences and the present situation."
MATTHEW: For lesson planning that means that a student's past experiences influence his perception of the new learning content. Thus, the teacher must know quite well where every student stands in order to plan and arrange the learning activities.
BHARAT: Exactly. As the teacher takes the past experiences of the students into account, he has to decide about the amount of freedom and discipline for the individual learner.
MATTHEW: And what about practice? I wonder if there were many teachers in Dewey's time who tried out his model of democratic education based on experience.
BHARAT: I don't know, but together with his wife, Dewey himself founded in the 1890s a school at the new University of Chicago, the so-called laboratory school. Unfortunately, they left after a few years because they didn't get along with the school administration.
MATTHEW: Now I understand better why our lecturer seems to see a link between Dewey's thoughts about education and his theory of inquiry. The starting point is a problematic situation to solve.
First, the researcher or the student has to identify the details of the problem. What follows is a process of reflection about the possible solutions ending in a practice test.
BHARAT: You think that also a child does inquiry in Dewey's sense?
MATTHEW: The theory of inquiry presupposes active individuals. Look here: "... the world is not passively perceived and thereby known; active manipulation of the environment is involved integrally in the process of learning from the start."
BHARAT: I would suggest that we start with his theory of inquiry and then apply it to education. What do you think?

MATTHEW: I fully agree with you; to me it seems logical. But we should also involve the others in some debate. Did you think about that?
BHARAT: Not really, but we can take two or three quotes from Dewey's writings and invite the others to discuss them.
MATTHEW: That's a good idea. In his book *Logic: The Theory of Inquiry* I found some interesting sentences about the role of language and culture that are still valid. There is also a whole paragraph on the provisional nature of knowledge and science.
BHARAT: Yes, I read it too, but I think it is a bit too complex. What about this one? (reads): "Evidence does not supply us with rules for action but only with hypotheses for intelligent problem solving. And for making inquiries about our ends in education."
MATTHEW: Very well. Where did you find it?
BHARAT: I don't remember exactly, I have to look it up.
MATTHEW: So, next time, we will prepare our slides.
BHARAT: Fine, we have enough time. See you next Thursday.
MATTHEW: Okay. Bharat...
BHARAT: Yes?
MATTHEW: Don't you think that our collaboration is quite good?
BHARAT: Sure, we are a real dream team.

REVIEW, REFLECT, PRACTICE

1. Why does descriptive research often precede explanatory research? (see Section 2.1)
2. What does falsifiability mean? Why is it a *sine qua non* of scientific research? (see Section 2.2)
3. What is more important, research design or research methods? Why? Discuss your arguments with other students or with colleagues. (see Section 2.3)
4. Why do many educationalists criticize psychometrics as the measuring of human beings? Do you think their position is justified? Why? Why not? Discuss your answers with others. (see Section 2.4)
5. Why is it very difficult to conduct Randomized Controlled Trials (RCTs) in schools? (see Section 2.5)
6. Why are correlation studies often rejected? Compare your answer to that of others. (see Chapter 2.5)
7. Read the following quotes from Dewey's book *Logic: The Theory of Inquiry* (1938) and reflect on the impact they have on education today. Compare your outcomes to those of other students or colleagues.

Language in its widest sense – that is including all means of communication such as, for example, monuments, rituals, and formalized arts – is the medium in which culture exist and through which it is transmitted. (ibid., p. 20)

... any sentence isolated from place and function is logically indeterminate. (ibid., p. 135)

It is commonplace that every cultural group possesses a set of meanings which are so deeply embedded in its customs, occupations, traditions and way of interpreting the physical environment and group-life, that they form the basic categories of the language-system by which details are interpreted. (ibid., p. 62)

3

Main Features of Evidence-based Research on Education

The main purpose of this chapter is to provide an introduction to evidence-based teaching and learning in order to enable (prospective) teachers and education professionals to make informed and reasoned decisions about the findings of evidence-based educational research. As education is multi-layered and complex (see Section 1.5), nobody should expect recipes to follow. Practices of teaching and learning cannot be based on one single approach to research. There are no ready-made examples, but teachers who have gained insights into evidence-based education undoubtedly are more adequately prepared for enabling their students to reach the desired learning outcomes.

3.1. EVIDENCE-BASED MEDICINE AND EVIDENCE-BASED EDUCATION

First, I shall describe some important reasons that led to the use of evidence-based approaches in medicine. It was not long until there was a paradigm shift to evidence-based research into many fields of the social sciences, including teaching and learning. As a consequence of the success of empirical evidence in medicine, health care, agriculture, and management, evidence-based education gathered momentum during the past three decades.

As early as 1793, G. Fordyce, a Scottish physician, published an article entitled *An Attempt to Improve the Evidence of Medicine* in a specialized journal (*Medical and Chirurgical Transactions*). Even though there had been various attempts to establish evidence-based methods in medicine since the beginning of the twentieth century, the official introduction of evidence-based medicine did not come until the 1990s. The foundation of the Cochrane Collaboration in 1993, named after Cochrane, a British professor of epidemiology who is considered the founder of evidence-based medicine, was a milestone. In 1972 Cochrane published the book *Effectiveness and Efficiency: Random Reflections on Health Services*, the influence of which goes far beyond medicine (see Section 3.3).

The Cochrane Collaboration is an independent organization whose motto is: *Working together to provide the best evidence for health care.* More than 31,000 volunteers in more than 120 countries conduct systematic reviews of RCTs of medical interventions published in the Cochrane Library. Information about medical research is thus gathered in a systematic way in order to provide health professionals, patients, policy makers, and the wider public with all information available about health interventions.

At the beginning of the new millennium, an organization similar to the Cochrane Collaboration was founded at the University of Pennsylvania, named after Campbell, an U.S. psychologist. The Campbell Collaboration promotes the accessibility of systematic reviews in fields such as criminal justice, social policy, and education. Nevertheless, to date evidence-based education can only draw partly on the results of RCTs conducted according to the principles of evidence-based research.

Why is there a need for systematic research reviews? Imagine a colleague tells you that she read an interesting article in an educational review which propagates cooperative learning and reports on an experiment conducted with incredible success in the school of the two authors. How could you exclude that the positive learning outcomes of the students were due to other factors, for example the engagement of the teachers, the positive attitudes of the students toward learning, or the inspiring activities discussed during the group work? Wouldn't it be better to compare other results of cooperative learning to the outcomes described in the article? What if you could read a systematic review of all available findings about group work?

When evidence-based education came to the fore, a great number of educationalists and educators pointed out the great differences between medicine and education. They simplified by underscoring that the effects of medication, for example drug A and drug B or drug A and a placebo, are easy to compare. But, as is often the case, things are more complicated for insiders. First, every patient is different, and medication often has adverse effects. Second, evidence-based medicine conducts research in more complex fields than medication. Drug A versus drug B is a convenient example for those who tend to reduce the variability in professional fields other than their own. Third, even strong evidence from RCTs in the field of medicine is seen as supplementary information. What counts more is the expertise of the respective doctor. The triad is completed by the patient, whose needs and wishes are the ultimate court of judgement.

Treatments in a complex field such as education, however, are much more difficult to define, and the outcomes in form of achievement are much less under the control of teachers and/or researchers. Thus, far from underestimating the differences between medicine and education, there is an important similarity: Both fields would undergo severe restrictions if professionals – physicians on the one hand, and teachers on the other – were to base their professional engagement only on their own experience, without taking external evidence into account.

The measuring of human beings of which some educationalists accused psychometrics (see Section 2.4) finds its counterpart in doctors and other medical professionals that advocate human-based medicine as a biopsychosocial field. In my view, statements like these are caused by a misunderstanding: Medicine and education, as well as many other social sciences that refer to evidence-based research, are above all human-based because they are in search of the best possible treatments for those for whom they are responsible.

Evidence-based results of educational research are an additional opportunity to improve teaching and learning. While comparable to other scientific disciplines such as medicine, education differs a great deal when it comes to the application of research findings. Furthermore, using research to improve practice requires not only findings beyond reasonable doubt, based on strong evidence, but also dissemination of the results in a user-friendly way, as well as sufficient means for possible implementation.

3.2. A QUESTION OF AGE

William Laird teaches history in the final two grades of a high school, and Olivia Anderson is in her first year of teaching. Quite often she does not know how to cope with what she calls "rookie problems," but there is William. Most of the time he seems cheerful and does not feel bothered by her questions.

Today Olivia is quite concerned because she has heard that during the next staff meeting they will discuss newer results of evidence-based teaching and learning. She has mixed feelings about it, as her lecturers during teacher training focused mostly on qualitative research.

OLIVIA: Hi, William, how are you doing? Fine, I suppose.
WILLIAM: Yes, it is summer, the sun is shining and you are near.
OLIVIA: Oh, William ... But I have a serious question.
WILLIAM: So, out with it! I'm all ears.
OLIVIA: What about evidence-based teaching ...?
WILLIAM: Oh, you are speaking about the staff meeting. But that's at the end of next week.
OLIVIA: I know, but I am worried because I didn't learn very much about it at college.
WILLIAM: Why ever not? I thought you were waiting for an opportunity to explain to us the main points and to help us implement our evidence-based curriculum.
OLIVIA: Not at all! If I have got it right, colleagues want to introduce evidence-based teaching and learning, hopefully not in history or geography.
WILLIAM: I can't really follow you. I have already been waiting for a long time to consider evidence-based results for our school curriculum and I'm eager to see changes come about before I retire.
OLIVIA: I don't understand you. Aren't you satisfied with the outcomes of your lessons? The students like you and they respect you. And Nelly told me that you were elected teacher of the year some time ago.
WILLIAM: You must be kidding. You can always reach better results for the students, and research based on evidence and not on the more or less unfounded opinion of some expert is a good means to this end. For me, it is always worthwhile to take robust evidence into consideration.
OLIVIA: But my favorite lecturer told us not to focus on research, at least not on experimental research, because human behavior cannot be measured.
WILLIAM: It depends what you mean by behavior. Achievement can be measured. The opinion of your lecturer has nothing to do with research; that's the advice of an authority.
OLIVIA: But at my own high school we always followed the same lesson plan, and that was quite good for me.
WILLIAM: Perhaps your classmates would have learned more if your teachers had accepted external evidence and used more varied instructional designs. Teaching habits have nothing to do with evidence.
OLIVIA: When I think about it, you may be right. Two of my classmates left high school in the eleventh grade even though we all knew that they could have made it. They didn't get along with the methods of our teachers.
WILLIAM: That's what I mean. External evidence is a chance to reach more students and support them in their learning.

OLIVIA: When you say chance, you mean I'm not forced to use the tools some researchers propagate?
WILLIAM: It is always your decision. Otherwise it would be quite undemocratic.
OLIVIA: If so, it would not be bad to have a look at some results.
WILLIAM: Welcome to the community of evidence-based education. If you want, we can get together one afternoon and I will tell you what I know about evidence-based teaching and learning.
OLIVIA: That would be fine. If you have got some examples, could you bring them with you, please?
WILLIAM: Sure, no problem.
OLIVIA: Thank you so much.
WILLIAM: For nothing, because I told most of our colleagues that a young teacher like you coming straight from college will be a driving force behind our evidence-movement. It is a question of age.
OLIVIA: Oh, William ...

3.3. ESSENTIAL FEATURES OF EVIDENCE-BASED RESEARCH

In order to help teachers and education professionals to gain the necessary insights into this particular research design and its scientific methods, the essential features are defined and described: The meaning of empirical evidence, grades of evidence, the difference between effectiveness and efficiency, and appropriate ways to reach evidence.

In ancient Greece, when highly renowned philosophers such as Plato, Socrates, and Aristotle communicated their wisdom to groups of elected young men, their teaching was not only inspired by their sublime thoughts. We know that Socrates used methods of observation and some form of experimentation in order to arrive at what we call today *Socratic inquiry*. Empirical evidence means that scientific findings are not exclusively based on reasoning but include concrete experience. This confrontation with real-world experience does not automatically include experimentation.

Empirical evidence refers to the endeavors of scientists to come as close to the truth as possible using a research design and scientific methods appropriate for testing the hypothesis under scrutiny. We should not forget that there are even educationalists who apply the term "evidence-based" not only to quantitative research, but also to qualitative studies that correspond to certain scientific quality criteria (Davies, 1999). A multilayered and complex field like education requires a much greater variety of designs and methods than simply RCTs, which seem to be favored especially by policy makers and often don't reach the practice level. That is what Berliner (2002, p. 18) underscores in the following quote: "But to think that this form of research [RCTs] is the only scientific approach to gaining knowledge – the only one that yields trustworthy evidence – reveals a myopic view of science in general and a misunderstanding of educational research in particular."

As previously mentioned (see Section 2.5), RCTs are not always possible to use and/or meaningful in the field of education. But also, when it is possible to carry out strong experimentation, the results, often indicated in numerals, are not easily transferable into teaching and learning strategies. Moreover, to date, teachers and education professionals cannot draw on a systematic set of RCTs in important fields of teaching and learning. How could a busy teacher engage in searching of the relevant literature?

The research findings obtained through thoroughly planned and conducted RCTs can have an important impact on education, but other research approaches may be of equal influence. High-quality research of whatever type enables reflective teachers to make professional judgements. What is most needed to promote teaching and learning is a set of principles and practices apt to alter the way people think about education, not a set of ready-made solutions (Davies, 1999).

In the fields of medicine, agriculture, and other sciences that favor evidence-based research, no serious researcher excludes findings based on methods other than experimental ones. The Oxford Center of Evidence-based Medicine mentions *Outcome Research* and *Ecological Studies* as well as *Individual Case-Control Studies* as sources of scientific results. Even expert opinion without explicit critical appraisal is not completely excluded (www.cebm.net/oxford-centre-evidence-based-medicine-levels-evidence-march-2009/; last accessed July 2015). With regard to education, we should be aware of the pyramid of grades of evidence (see Figure 3.1).

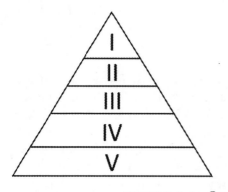

FIGURE 3.1: Grades of evidence

Furthermore, the aims of practitioners and policy makers aren't the same. Teachers are mostly interested in results that help them increase the effectiveness of the learning processes and the outcomes of their students. The intervention program or a set of strategies should produce the desired results. By contrast, policy makers are looking above all for efficiency, that is to say avoiding undue effort, money, and time in reaching the desired results.

Empirical evidence is reached when the research endeavors, using whatever systematic type of scrutiny, come as close to the truth as possible.

There are **grades of evidence** favoring experimental research, especially RCTs. Even though the results of strong experimental research are important, they tend to abstract from concrete aspects of teaching and learning, making it difficult for teachers and other practitioners to draw on these findings.

In a multilayered, complex field such as educational research, **a variety of research designs and methods** can produce valid and reliable results.

Whereas **effectiveness** is the principal aim of teachers, policy makers often base their decision on **efficiency**; that is to say, they look for unambiguous results promising the highest outcome combined with low cost.

3.4. POTENTIAL AND PITFALLS OF RANDOMIZED CONTROLLED TRIALS

As previously mentioned, Randomized Controlled Trials (RCTs; see Chapter 2.5) are considered the gold standard of quantitative–empirical research.

By means of an example concerning class size, the potential of strong experimentation is emphasized. On the other hand, the pitfalls will be discussed – that is to say, limitations caused by the researcher and/or the study participants. Furthermore, we will have a closer look at particular restrictions caused by classroom interventions – entire programs or single teaching and learning strategies – in a rich and varied field like education.

RCTs are an indispensable means to gain insights into the effects caused by particular interventions in most scientific fields, and thus also in educational research (see Section 2.5). Strong experimentation allows for a comparison between the effects of different interventions. The potential of this scientific method is best illustrated by an example.

The Tennessee Study of Class Size in the Early Grades, presented in an influential paper by Mosteller (1995), was standard-setting for its research quality as well as for its results. Tennessee legislators interested in reducing class size in different urban and rural contexts of the state were looking for a cost-effective option. They wanted researchers to find out through an RCT the effects of three different types of classes on student achievement: "(1) small, 13–17 pupils; (2) regular size, 22–25 pupils; and (3) regular size with a teacher's aide" (Mosteller, 1995, p. 116). The research project was carried out as follows.

The Tennessee Class Size Project

The Tennessee project on the effectiveness of small classes and teachers' aides had three phases.

> **Phase 1**
> 1985–1989. Tennessee's education system carried out a four-year experiment, called Project STAR (for Student–Teacher Achievement Ratio), to assess the effectiveness of small classes compared with regular-sized classes, and of teacher's aides in regular-sized classes, on improving cognitive achievement in kindergarten and in the first, second, and third grades.
>
> **Phase 2**
> 1989–. The Lasting Benefits Study (LBS) was an observational study of the experimental program's consequences for children when they came to attend regular-sized classes in the fourth, fifth, and sixth grades and beyond. This research phase asked whether the children who started in the smaller classes performed better in later grades. Only students who had been in the experiment (Phase 1) could contribute data to the second phase.
>
> **Phase 3**
> 1989–. Project Challenge implemented the small classes in kindergarten and in first, second, and third grades in the seventeen districts of Tennessee where children are at a high risk of dropping out early. The districts have the lowest average incomes in the state. (Mosteller, 1995, p. 16)

Kim presented the STAR Project and the results of the Tennessee Study in his paper *The Influence of Class Size Research on State and Local Education Policy*, which even in 2006 remained the point of reference:

> In 1985, the legislature provided $ 12 million for the study on "Student– Teacher Achievement Ratio" (Project Star) and gave the Tennessee Department of Education authority to carry out the evaluation, which

was ultimately completed by researchers at four Tennessee Universities. Ultimately, the Star experiment involved over 6,000 students in 79 elementary schools, and the study has been celebrated as a landmark in American education.

The Star findings have been amply documented by researchers [...], but the most noteworthy findings were as follows: small class sizes of 13 to 17 students improved student achievement by approximately .20 standard deviations, or 4 national percentile ranks; effect sizes were nearly twice as large for minority students as white students; test score gains were largest in Kindergarten and first grade; and long-term effects persisted on a variety of academic outcomes in middle and high school. The Star findings have been replicated in quasi-experimental results from Wisconsin, and the study has motivated numerous empirical and theoretical studies on the effect of class size. (Kim, 2006, p. 10)

The study's success was due not only to the results but also, and above all, to the scrupulously elaborated research design, with a sufficiently large number of classes. Quite often RCTs suffer from samples too small to allow for generalizability. As class size is always a crucial question, we will come back to the STAR Project when we discuss the results of Hattie (2009, 2012) on the same subject. (For *effect size* and *standard deviation* see Section 3.8). Last but not least, to my view Mosteller's paper is a benchmark; without doubt, its comprehensible structure and its clear layout contributed to the success of the study.

At first sight, RCTs seem to guarantee a high degree of objectiveness. In practice, experiments are seldom as successful as in the case of the Tennessee Class Size Project. In general, a RCT is subject to the same pitfalls as other research methods. The problems are not only caused by the aforementioned interfering variables; other pitfalls we have to take into account are the requirements concerning the integrity and the impartiality of the researcher.

Imagine the following example: An educationalist has observed various times that a certain strategy seems to bring about very good student achievement results. Classroom observation as well as interviews with students and teachers showed him that in reading comprehension, multiple-choice tests yield much better results than answering questions about the text. Multiple-choice tests seem not only to lead to better understanding, but also to enhance memory with regard to the most important aspects of the text. On this basis he decides to carry out a RCT with random distribution of a great number of tenth-grade students across three different schools. Convinced of the substantial positive effect of multiple-choice tasks in comparison to questions and answers, he thoroughly prepares the multiple-choice test which the teachers will use in the experimental groups. The distractors – that means the incorrect options in each sequence – are meticulously matched with the text so that the right choices are easy to make for students who have read the text attentively.

Informing the teachers of the experimental groups, the researcher underscores the importance of their contribution to the groundbreaking study and invites them to a training session in order to guarantee that they will perform well using the new strategy in their classes. In most cases the teachers will talk about the importance of the scientific research to their students, inviting them to reread the text and to do their best. On the other side, the teachers of the control groups are told to teach as usual.

The results of this RCT – although it corresponds to the external quality criteria of research – are biased. Hopefully other educationalists who examine the results will have doubts about the objectivity – another indispensable research feature – of the RCT in question and replicate the experiment in order to come closer to the truth.

> If **properly conducted, RCTs** (as other research methods) can yield important results. That does not imply their successful implementation, as it may be difficult to re-contextualize the findings. Numeral effects that abstract too much from teaching and learning in a school context cannot be easily transformed into teaching and learning strategies. Furthermore, besides interfering variables, RCTs can be biased by the more or less conscious partiality of the researcher.

3.5. THE MEASUREMENT OF INTERVENTIONS IN TEACHING AND LEARNING

Strong experimentation is based on the conviction that the treatment to be measured has a direct influence on the participants of the study. But every expert teacher knows there is a gap between what is taught – even through the most appropriate and motivating activities – and what different students in the same classroom learn from the offer made by the teacher or by peers. Is it possible to treat learners as doctors treat their patients?

Very often people, especially policy makers, are convinced that interventions, at least if they are appropriate, have a positive impact on teaching and learning, in the same way that medication or other medical treatments influence diseases. What is true in general needs to be specified. Whereas there is a direct effect between the medication and the patient, things are very different in education. There is no direct link between a teaching or learning strategy and the outcome reached by different learners.

When we compare interventions in two different fields like medicine and education, we must be very careful about predictions of the impact that our teaching may have on individual learners. We all know that our well-planned lessons quite often don't reach all learners. Furthermore, what we try to transmit to our students reaches every single student in a different way. In other words: the outcome differs to a great extent between individual learners. Even though the same drug does not have exactly the same effect on all patients, variance is much lower than in education. Why are there such huge differences between the effect of a medication and a teaching intervention?

As mentioned several times before, education is a complex field influenced by many factors, such as teaching and learning contexts, and a great number of interactions between aspects that govern schools and classrooms. Those responsible for medical treatment may object that patients are very different too, thinking about previous diseases and adverse effects of drugs. Nevertheless, there is a crucial difference. Teaching and learning strategies do not influence students in the same way that drugs operate on patients.

Let's take an example (Herzog, 2013, p. 45): If you fill a coffee machine with a certain amount of coffee and water, you will have a pre-established number of cups of coffee. You influence the built-in algorithm of the machine through the amount of coffee and water with which you fill the machine. In other words, you regulate the output of the machine. Asking now for the outcome – that is to say, the effect of a cup of coffee on someone who drinks the coffee – we have to state that there is no direct influence between the algorithm that governs the machine and the effects on the coffee drinker. Nevertheless, we can't deny some sort of relationship between the output of the machine and the outcome. If you add more coffee to the same amount of water, the coffee will be stronger and the effect on the consumer will be greater, or at least different. But that does not mean that you control the outcome, because it occurs in a different system.

The earlier mentioned comparison is incomplete: The coffee drinker starts the machine because he or she wants to have some coffee. The student isn't the agent of teaching or learning activities in the same sense. Therefore you may compare the teaching interventions in a classroom as offers of a teacher of which individual learners make different use. How they benefit from the teacher's offer depends on a myriad of factors. "Any teaching behavior interacts with a number of student characteristics, including IQ, socioeconomic status, motivation to learn, and a host of other factors" (Berliner, 2002, p. 19). Besides the complexities of educational contexts and interactions, teachers and other education professionals have to take the frequent changes in the social environment into consideration.

> **The measurement of interventions in teaching and learning** is useful, but numbers are nothing more than an indication that a certain intervention program or a single strategy may have an influence on student achievement. The effects of schooling are not directly caused by teaching; they are a consequence of learning. Therefore no orthodox view is ever advisable.

3.6. ASSUMPTIONS ABOUT *WHAT WORKS*

Another problem of educational research, closely related to the aforementioned limitations, regards the dictum: This or that intervention has been proven to work. To assume that what worked somewhere will work in other contexts, and especially in your particular classroom, is nothing more than an assumption. Even if we disposed of a great number of verified educational practices supported by rigorous evidence, the growth of educational science would be endangered, because evidence-based results are not sufficient. There is always a need for the refining of theories that try to answer questions about values in education. What makes a difference, and to whom does it make a difference?

Educational research is not just a matter of the relationship between cause and effect. It is in no way sufficient to accumulate results from well-conducted experiments trying to transfer their findings to different learning contexts. When we have found out what worked, we don't know why it worked, nor do we have sufficient hints as to whether the intervention might be helpful for our particular learners. Researchers are expected not only to furnish accumulated evidence from RCTs, quasi-experiments, or correlation studies, but also to deduce explanatory theories from their findings. Without consistent theories educational research will not advance, or at least will not advance in a way expected of a scientific discipline. Olson puts this claim as follows:

> The reputation of educational research is tarnished less by the lack of replicable results than by the lack of any deeper theory that would explain why the thousands of experiments that make up the literature

of the field appear to have yielded so little. That explanation would take us more deeply into an analysis of the school's place in the institutional structures of a bureaucratic society and the categories and rules, knowledge and procedures, that are required for successfully participating in it. (Olson, 2004, p. 25)

Educational research limited to questions about what works and the more or less successful implementation of findings in classrooms suffers from a lack of theoretical assumptions that may lead to further experimentation in order to generate richer theories.

You may oppose this: Teachers are looking for practical advice, not for theories. What is true on a conscious level has its counterpart in subconscious thinking, so-called tacit knowledge (Polanyi, 1966). Atkinson enumerates a host of these tacit convictions:

> Teachers may deny that their actions are underpinned by any such theoretical infrastructure, and may be unaware of the sources of their professional knowledge, yet it would be hard to find a teacher that did not believe in the value of concrete experience, the power of language, the importance of adult interaction or support, or the recognition of developmental stages in children's learning. It would be hard to find a teacher who did not emphasize the value of revisiting concepts, of encouraging children to adopt a range of strategies to enhance learning, or of presenting problems that challenge children to look at the world in a new light. (Atkinson, 2000, p. 325)

The excessive concentration on what works or what works better limits the focus of educational research. Furthermore, this type of scientific result exercises control over teachers and, in consequence, over their students. Educational research is not carried out in order to dictate to teachers what to do and learners how to interpret this input. In education (as in the human sciences in general), research results should help teachers and students to make informed decisions about what to do in their specific contexts.

The overall aim of educational research is to equip teachers and other education professionals with results that increase their freedom of choice as well as their commitment toward the students. To force teachers more or less directly to implement what worked means to de-professionalize them, causing detrimental effects for the learners.

3.7. HOW TO DEAL WITH RESULTS OF EVIDENCE-BASED RESEARCH

In my view, it is necessary to underscore the limitations of evidence-based research into education, in order to prevent teachers from assuming that proven findings will automatically work in their context without taking into account the specifics of the presented cases. On the other hand, if we don't want to turn back to opinion-based teaching, there is no alternative to evidence-informed or at least evidence-aware teaching and learning. Some advice will be given on how to discern evidence from meaningless experimental results.

Qualitative as well as quantitative studies are not always free of shortcomings. Oakley (2002, p. 283) states that it is less difficult to apply quality screening for experimental research than to separate trustworthy from untrustworthy qualitative studies. The latter can be evaluated looking for items such as persistent observation, understanding data within holistic contexts, and the privileging of subjective meaning. Assessing the quality of quantitative studies, you may look for criteria such as a clearly stated study purpose and an adequate and appropriate final sample, which includes a clear description of the sample and how it is recruited. A third item frequently cited in the literature is careful recording of data, namely an adequate description of how the findings were derived from the data.

There is currently what Oakley calls a "new orthodoxy" that propagates strong experimental research excluding qualitative studies. According to her, this bias is detrimental not only to educational research but also to the practice of teaching and learning:

> The main danger ahead is that large areas of research, traditionally important in education, escape the evidence net either because no one can reach any consensus about how to sort out the reliable from the unreliable, or (which might be worse) because a new orthodoxy sets in according to which qualitative research is simply a world apart – nothing to do with evidence at all. (Oakley, 2002, p. 284)

In order to facilitate access to evidence-based education, at the end of 2003 the U.S. Department of Education published a guide that "seeks to provide educational practitioners with user-friendly tools to distinguish practices supported by rigorous evidence from those that are not." In overview, three steps are suggested:

Step 1. Is the intervention backed by "strong" evidence of effectiveness?

Quality of studies needed to establish "strong" evidence:		Quantity of evidence needed:
Randomized controlled trials that are well-designed and implemented	+	Trials showing effectiveness in two or more typical school settings; including a setting similar to that of your schools/classrooms = "strong" evidence

Step 2. If the intervention is not backed up by "strong evidence," is it backed up by "possible" evidence of effectiveness?

Types of studies that can comprise "possible" evidence:
Randomized controlled trials whose quality/quantity are good but fall short of "strong" evidence and/or
Comparison-group studies in which the intervention and comparison-groups are very closely matched in academic achievement, demographics, and other characteristics.

Types of studies that do not comprise "possible" evidence:
Pre-post studies.
Comparison-group studies in which the intervention and comparison groups are not closely matched.
"Meta-analyses" that include the results of such lower-quality studies.

Step 3. If the answers to both questions above are "no," one may conclude that the intervention is not supported by meaningful evidence.

(U.S. Department of Education, Institute of Education Sciences, National Center for Education Evaluation and Regional Assistance, 2003, p. 5)

Teachers and educational professionals can benefit from reading this official document (about twenty pages long), which is still valid. They will find understandable advice regarding how to sort studies that generated robust advice from those with less strong evidence. The paper is, in my view, also interesting for other reasons. First, it documents a lack of RCTs in the field of teaching and learning. In the executive summary the authors mention only four research fields in which the "research's 'gold standard' for establishing what works" (ibid., p. III) is reached by RCTs:

- One-on-one tutoring by qualified tutors for at-risk readers in grades 1–3 (the average tutored student reads more proficiently than approximately 75 percent of the untutored students in the control group).
- Life-skills training for junior high students (Low-cost, replicable program reduces smoking by 20 percent and serious levels of substance abuse by about 30 percent by the end of high school, compared to the control group).
- Reducing class size in grades K-3 (the average student in small classes scores higher on the Stanford Achievement Test in reading/math than about 60 percent of students in regular-sized classes).
- Instruction for early readers in phonemic awareness and phonics (the average student in these interventions reads more proficiently than approximately 70 percent of students in the control group).

The third point refers to Mosteller et al.'s (1996) study about the effects of class size discussed earlier (see Section 3.4). Furthermore, in an Appendix, the U.S. Department of Education indicates useful websites on which to find a series of research results rated as gold-standard, with strong evidence, and others with possible or no evidence of effectiveness. In general, documents like this can lead to nothing more than an understanding of possibilities (Biesta, 2007, 2010), always provided that a teacher or another education professional has sufficient time and patience to consult the respective websites.

Second, the paper by the U.S. Department of Education explicitly excludes meta-analyses and avoids defining effect size (see Section 3.8). One can only speculate about the reasons for this: Perhaps the authors are of the opinion that teachers might get lost in the numerous studies assembled in a meta-analysis. Another reason may be the fact that meta-analyses abstract very much from teaching and learning contexts, so that the results are not easily interpretable by teachers looking for advice on how to improve their practice. Furthermore, effect sizes allow for a more or less precise comparison between different interventions, but these numerals neither indicate possible reasons for the success of certain interventions nor provide teachers with hints regarding how to benefit from these findings (for further details see Section 3.8 and Chapter 4).

Even today, we are still far from the possibilities that medical professionals dispose of when looking for research evidence. The review list of the Campbell Collaboration (see Section 3.1), a nonprofit organization similar to the Cochrane Collaboration, is not easy to consult (www.campbellcollaboration.org/all_reviews_from_Campbell_Collaboration/index.php; last accessed July 2015). Among the 113 reviews compiled until May 2015, only fifteen refer to education; the rest are dedicated to social welfare or crime and justice. Among the fifteen reviews with regard to education, only a single one (no. 61) deals with classroom teaching: *The Effects of Teachers' Classroom Management Practices on Disruptive, or Aggressive Student Behavior: A Systematic Review* by Oliver et al. (2011, www.campbellcollaboration.org/artman2/uploads/1/Oliver_SREE_Classroom_Mgmt_Presentation.pdf). Other systematic reviews of research on education treat important issues such as school refusal, sexual violence, dropout prevention, bullying, and parental involvement.

Two important proponents of evidence-based education, the educationalist Robert Marzano and the practitioner Geoff Petty (see Chapter 4), do not miss the opportunity to underscore that the teaching strategies publicized in their books are nothing more than options at the disposal of expert teachers:

> Instructional strategies are tools only. Although the strategies presented in this book are certainly good tools, they should not be expected to work equally well in all situations. (Marzano et al., 2001, p. 8)

> We mustn't abandon our intuition or our own evidence; this is the final court of judgement. (Petty, 2009, p. 1)

Dewey exposed the earlier mentioned considerations on the usefulness and hence the use of research in an impressive way. Knowing, not knowledge, as a way of doing can help us to gain better control over our actions. It leads to the ability to intelligently plan and direct our actions. Inquiry and research show us what has been possible, that is what worked, not what works or what will work. As we are always addressing concrete, unique problems, we cannot follow tried-and-tested recipes. Furthermore, we have to take into account that social situations are constantly changing.

Biesta summarizes the main thoughts of Dewey expressed in *The Sources of a Science of Education* (1929) in this way:

> It also means that in reflective problem solving we do not use "old" knowledge to tell us what we should do; we use "old" knowledge to guide us first in our attempts to understand what the problem might be and then in the intelligent selection of possible lines of action. What

> "old" knowledge does, in other words, is help us approach problem solving more intelligently. Yet, the proof of the pudding always lies in the action that follows. This will "verify" both the adequacy of our understanding of the problem and, in one and the same process, the adequacy of the proposed solution. (Biesta, 2007, p. 16)

REVIEW, REFLECT, PRACTICE

1. Read the article by Mosteller presenting the research design and the results of the Tennessee Class Size Project. Try to find out why the paper has achieved great success. Discuss your points of view with other students or with colleagues.

    Mosteller (1995). The tennessee study of class size in the early school grades. *The Future of Children* 5/2, pp. 113–127.

2. Chose one of the listed RCTs and analyze it according to the requirements described in Chapter 3. If you need further help you can consult the document published by the U.S. Department of Education (see Chapter 3.7).

    Bandura and Schunk (1981). Cultivating competence, self-efficacy and intrinsic interest through proximal self-motivation. *Journal of Personality and Social Psychology* 41/3, pp. 586–598.

    Cardelle-Elawar and Corno (1985). A factorial experiment in teachers' written feedback on student homework: Changing teacher behavior a little rather than a lot. *Journal of Educational Psychology* 77, pp. 162–173.

    Carlo et al. (2004). Closing the gap: Addressing the vocabulary needs of English language learners in bilingual and mainstream classrooms. *Reading Research Quarterly* 39/2, pp. 188–215.

    Fuchs et al. (2015). Inclusion versus specialized intervention for very-low-performing students. What does *access* mean in an era of academic challenge? *Exceptional Children* 81/2, pp. 134–157.

    Iversen and Tunmer (1993). Phonological processing skills and the reading recovery program. *Journal of Educational Psychology* 85, pp. 112–125.

3. Write a summary of the chosen RCT, swap it with another student who worked on the same RCT and discuss your results.
4. If time is available, present your results in plenary.

4

Meta-Analyses on Education

Before analyzing some well-known examples of meta-analytic research on education, we should have a closer look at definitions and implications of this overestimated research design. The results of meta-analyses and their aggregation to mega-analyses could be of value for educational practitioners if the research was carried out according to the standards of quality, which means based on experiments or at least quasi-experimental studies. Quite often, however, meta-analyses include primary studies of lower quality. Therefore it is very difficult for teachers to evaluate the findings of meta-analytic studies. In many cases, educators have to use their expertise to decide if the findings of a meta-analysis may have a positive impact on their students. To be able to do so requires basic knowledge of syntheses of research.

4.1. META-ANALYSES AND EFFECT SIZES

If not taken as unquestionable truth, the results of meta-analyses are valuable sources on the path to an improvement of one's educational practices. What is a meta-analysis and in what way can it contribute to render our teaching more effective and the learning of our students more successful?

If evidence-based education is considered as a means to attain better results, why should educational practitioners limit their work to a single study or one Randomized Controlled Trials (RCT)? Wouldn't it be better to consult as many studies on the same subject as possible? Why not take all available research into account?

Long before the elaboration of meta-analyses, systematic reviews of research, that is to say summaries of all existing research regarding an intervention program or a single teaching and learning strategy, were compiled. How does a scholar proceed when engaged in developing a systematic research review? Even though not all reviewers elaborate systematic reviews in the same way, the steps are mainly as follows: The first step consists of trying to find all studies on a subject consulting bibliographies and other means of literature research. Like all the following steps, the literature research places high requirements on the diligence of the reviewer. Having possibly found all studies on a subject, the reviewing scholars have to consult and to group them scrupulously, and to establish criteria for their presentation. A systematic research review thus tries to summarize all available studies on a subject, describing the findings in a narrative form.

Systematic reviews of research are often criticized as being too subjective and reflecting the preferences of the reviewer, who, in many cases, does his own research in the same field. Furthermore, a systematic research review describing results in a narrative way does not allow for the comparison of results. If a teacher wishes to find out if a certain type of graphic organizers attains better results, for example concept mapping in comparison to clustering, the summaries elaborated by two different reviewers or teams are often not comparable. Meta-analyses, a form of presenting research results in numerals, seem to guarantee greater impartiality and to provide results answering the question posed by many teachers: What works better?

Meta-analyses summarize primary studies and describe, based on statistical methods, the average effect size in a field: that is to say, they analyze if there is an effect and how great it is. It was Gene V. Glass, a U.S. statistician, who introduced the term meta-analysis, defining it as "analysis of analyses" (Glass, 1976). Similar to the purpose of systematic research reviews, the scholar compiling a meta-analysis does not conduct his own empirical studies, but engages in a secondary analysis of possibly all primary studies available.

The first systematic evaluation to be considered as a meta-analysis was carried out at the beginning of the twentieth century by the British mathematician Karl Pearson. Pearson summarized studies with relatively small samples in order to attain more exact and more assured results. The elaboration of a meta-analysis commonly follows six steps:

- The starting point is a research question: for example, how effective is homework? As it is impossible to analyze the effects of homework in all school types, grades, and subject matters, the research topic is restricted to particular learning contexts.
- The second step, as with systematic research reviews, consists of finding all studies on a subject consulting bibliographies and other

means of literature research. In our case, dealing with the effects of homework, the reviewer tries to find all quantitative studies in the defined learning context.
- The purpose of the following secondary analysis of all existing studies is to order the studies applying the research criteria, such as validity and reliability. In order to sort out primary studies of less rigor, the earlier discussed grades of evidence (see Section 3.3) play a crucial role.
- The publications chosen by the reviewer for the meta-analysis, at best only RCTs and quasi-experimental studies, are coded and electronically elaborated.
- What follows is a statistical analysis of the data.
- Finally, the results of the statistical analysis have to be thoroughly processed and adequately interpreted with regards to the research question.

It should be clear from the succinct description of these multilevel elaboration processes that the quality of a meta-analysis depends to a large extent on the choice of the primary studies incorporated in the analysis. An extreme example for sorting out invaluable primary research is that of Torgerson and her team; in order to produce trustworthy findings regarding measures to promote adult literacy and numeracy, they examined 4,555 primary studies but sorted out all but twelve, which they integrated in their meta-analysis (Torgerson et al., 2005). According to the scholars, the eliminated research did not display a crucial relationship between cause (the intervention program) and effect (the improvement of the studies' participants' literacy and numeracy).

Although there are numerous difficulties to surmount when compiling a meta-analysis, some researchers aim at carrying out mega-analyses: that is to say, they put together all available meta-analyses in the field of education. A well-known example is John Hattie's study entitled *Visible Learning: A Synthesis of over 800 Meta-analyses Relating to Achievement*, published in 2009 and enlarged in the following years to more than 900 meta-analyses. If and how teachers and other education professionals may benefit from such accumulation of wisdom is amply discussed in Chapter 5.

In order to value the importance of meta-analyses for our own teaching, we should have basic knowledge of measurement. What is an effect size? How is it calculated?

The effect of an educational intervention analyzed in a study is measured by the effect size. The effect size is a standardized measure for the strength of a relationship. It offers information about the size of the influence of the intervention, that is to say, the independent variable (see Figure 4.1).

A basic way to measure the effect consists of a twofold calculation procedure. First, the difference between the means of the experimental group and the control group is calculated, followed by dividing the obtained difference through the standard deviation, mostly taken from the control group. The standard deviation measures the amount of variation of a set of data, the so-called dispersion. Its calculation guarantees a standardized value indispensable for the comparison of the effects found in different studies.

> mean (experimental group) = 15; mean (control group) = 12;
> standard deviation (control group) = 2.5;
> difference between the means of the experimental and the control group = 3
> 3 divided by 2.5 = 1.2 (effect size)

Why is it important to take the standard deviation into account? Why can't we simply compare the two means? Imagine the following situation: You want to compare the results of two tests, the first consisting of twenty and the second of forty tasks. The difference between the means of the first test is 2 points (mean experimental group: 10.9; mean control group: 8.9), whereas the difference between the means of the second test amounts to 3 points (mean experimental group: 24.9; mean control group 21.9) (Wellenreuther, 2014, pp. 30–32). Are we not induced to think that the second

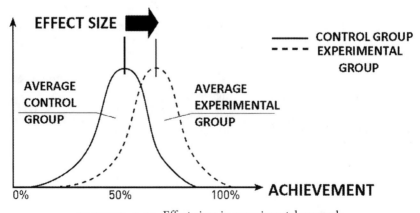

FIGURE 4.1: Effect sizes in experimental research

test produces better results? Using our previous mentioned calculation formula for the two tests, we obtain the following results:

EXAMPLE 1
Difference of the means of the experimental and the control group = 2 divided by the standard deviation 2.73 = 0.73 (effect size).

EXAMPLE 2
Difference of the means of the experimental and the control group = 3 divided by the standard deviation 6.5 = 0.46 (effect size).

Therefore, the comparison of means can lead to false conclusions. When comparing different studies you have to take into account not only the means but also the standard deviation. As previously mentioned, one of the shortcomings of this research design, in my view, is the fact that you have to be an expert in statistics – or, more precisely, in psychometrics – to conduct trustworthy meta-analyses (Hartley, 2012, p. E135). Moreover, it is often difficult for educational practitioners to value the results of meta-analyses.

The main problem of a meta-analysis is the so-called garbage in – garbage out factor. If you integrate garbage, that is to say flawed primary studies, into your meta-analysis, you receive garbage, in other words a meta-analysis of inferior quality. As it is crucial for the users of these studies to build on trustworthy results, the reviewer should at least answer the following questions:

- Does he or she include in her/his meta-analysis only results from RCTs or quasi-experiments?
- Does he or she indicate if and explain why he or she uses other quantitative studies?
- In what way is he or she weighing studies of inferior quality if he or she does not want to sort them out?
- How does the reviewer deal with different sample sizes? Does he or she consider studies with small samples to the same extent as studies with large samples? In what way does he or she weigh different sample sizes?
- Does he or she consider possible differences in the meaning of relevant terms, that is to say, does concept mapping in all studies refer to a similar procedure?

- Does he or she strive to also detect and integrate unpublished studies on the research topic? (The Campbell Collaboration requires a systematic search for unpublished reports).

Possible answers to these questions help educational practitioners to find meta-analyses which can be relied upon, as these studies can contribute to a substantial improvement of teaching and learning practices. More than RCTs concentrated on a single experiment, they indicate important research findings derived from smaller studies and accumulated to an overall view of research efforts. In any case, an evidence-informed or at least evidence-aware practice is better than basing one's teaching on unquestioned traditions, vague opinions, and/or cherished habits (see Chapters 6–11, e.g., of how to benefit from evidence research for your teaching practice).

Cohen, a statistician and psychologist, is one of the pioneers of statistical power and effect size. In his influential publication *Statistical Power Analysis for the Behavioral Sciences*, published in 1969 (second edition 1988), he differentiates between small, medium, and large effects, acknowledging the danger of using these terms out of context.

> Glass et al. (1981, p. 104) are particularly critical of this approach, arguing that the effectiveness of a particular intervention can only be interpreted in relation to other interventions that seek to produce the same effect. They also point out that the practical importance of an effect depends entirely on its relative costs and benefits. In education, if it could be shown that making a small and inexpensive change would raise achievement by an effect size of even as little as 0.1, than this could be a very significant improvement, particularly if the improvement applied uniformly to all students, and even more so if the effect were cumulative over time.
> (Coe, 2002; www.leeds.ac.uk/educol/documents/00002182.htm; last accessed July 2015).

In his paper presented at the Annual Conference of the British Educational Research Association, held at the University of Exeter in September 2002, Robert Coe of Durham University, England, gives a detailed and accessible introduction to *what effect size is and why it is important*. He gives comprehensible and useful answers to the questions: Why do we need effect size? How is it calculated? How can effect sizes be interpreted? Furthermore, Coe explains important details about the measurement and interpretation of effect sizes. His advice on the use of effect sizes is relevant for all teachers and education professionals:

- Effect sizes [...] should be calculated and reported in primary studies as well as in meta-analyses.

- Care must be taken in comparing or aggregating effect sizes based on different outcomes, different operationalisations of the same outcome, different treatments, or levels of the same treatment, or measures derived from different populations.
- The word effect conveys an implication of causality, and the expression 'effect size' should therefore not be used unless this implication is intended and can be justified.

(Coe 2002; www.leeds.ac.uk/educol/documents/00002182.htm; last accessed July 2015).

A **meta-analysis** comprises the aggregation of possibly all (published or unpublished) primary studies dedicated to the same type of educational intervention. In order to allow for a comparison of the results, meta-analyses should only aggregate primary studies based on experiments (RCTs) and quasi-experimental studies.

The findings of a meta-analysis are summarized in a standardized statistical measure. The **effect size** quantifies the size of the difference between two groups, at best between the experimental group and the control group.

4.2. A CRITICAL LOOK AT RESEARCH ON TEACHING EFFECTIVENESS

Analyzing an informative meta-analysis carried out by Seidel and Shavelson (2007) and the meta-analytic research conducted by Marzano and his team (1998, 2001) (see Section 4.4) allows us to come back to the previous mentioned issues in more detail. As this is a resource book for educational practitioners, the main purpose of the following is to heighten your perception of how to deal with the findings of meta-analytic research to the benefit of your students.

In general, a meta-analysis is dedicated to the same educational intervention, for example advance organizers, homework, or reciprocal teaching. It is not unusual, however, to find examples that disprove this assumption and summarize findings from different educational fields. An example is the study by Rohrer and Pashler, two influential educationalists, entitled *Recent Research on Human Learning Challenges Conventional Instructional Strategies*. "The authors review three lines of experimentation – all conducted using educationally relevant materials and time intervals – that call into question important aspects of common instructional practices" (Rohrer & Pashler, 2010, p. 406). The first deals with the learning effects of testing, the second is about temporal variables in distributing study practice over greater time periods, and the third shows that blocked practice (e.g., aaabbbccc) is much less effective than interleaving (e.g., abcbcacab) (ibid., passim).

The meta-analysis of Seidel and Shavelson (2007), "Teaching Effectiveness Research in the Past Decade: The Role of Theory and Research Design in Disentangling Meta-Analysis Results," has a much broader aim that deserves our attention. The results, as important as they are in the field of meta-analytic research, are not concrete enough to be integrated into classroom practice. Why, this being the case, should we have a closer look at a meta-analysis that "summarizes research effectiveness studies of the past decade [1995–2004] and investigates the role of theory and research design in disentangling results" (Seidel & Shavelson, 2007, p. 454)?

- First of all, we learn that effect size is not effect size. The authors (ibid., p. 457) confront two meta-analyses: a study by Fraser, Walberg, Welch, and Hattie (1987) and an analysis carried out by **Scheerens** Scherens and Bosker (1997). Even though the two analyses refer partly to the same educational interventions, the effects of the two studies cannot be compared, because the two research teams did not calculate the effect sizes using the same statistical procedure. So educators always have to be very careful when comparing effect sizes resulting from different studies.
- Seidel and Shavelson found 333 studies matching their initial key words. Sorting out studies that did not report empirical findings, the number of published articles was reduced to 112, but only minimal parts of these 112 studies are based on experimental or quasi-experimental research:

Given the current discussion about the gold standard in American educational research and the call for large-scale randomized field trials, it seemed appropriate to review quasi-experimental and experimental studies separately .[...] The number of experimental studies in the past decade, however, is limited .[...] Thus, investigating the effectiveness of experimental studies in educational research might be the task of a meta-analysis in the next decade but not primarily of the past decade. (Seidel & Shavelson, 2007, p. 464)

- We will come back to this issue in Chapter 5 when discussing the results of John Hattie's mega-analysis. In any case, teachers should be critical when urged to integrate the findings of meta-analyses into their classroom practices.
- The studies that Seidel and Shavelson (ibid., p. 476) included in their meta-analysis showed higher effect sizes for teaching conditions favoring domain-specific learning activities, for example in science, mathematics, or reading. Activities that focus on particular subject matters do not only improve cognitive achievement; they also have a remarkable impact on motivational–affective factors (such as interest or self-concept of ability). There are at least two consequences of this finding: Teachers have to be very careful when transferring interventions working in a special subject matter to another context; and subject-specific teaching and learning interventions can produce greater effects than one-fits-all strategies.

Above all, the meta-analysis on **Teaching Effectiveness Research** conducted by Seidel and Shavelson shows "that the effects of teaching on student learning were diverse and complex but fairly systematic" (ibid., p. 482). To prove their usefulness in classrooms, they have to be scrupulously examined by educators. With this in mind, teacher expertise paired with reflection is an imperative precondition for using research to improve practice.

4.3. THINKING WITHOUT THINKING

Rachel, Martin, and Ismail attend the same undergraduate course in educational psychology. Toward the end of today's lecture the professor gives a short preview of next week's subject. When leaving the course room Martin, who has already got some teaching experience, seems rather annoyed.

> RACHEL: What's up, Martin? You look as if . . .
> MARTIN: I didn't get it. He just mentioned that Donald Schoen makes a difference between reflection-on-action and reflection-in-action. What does that mean?
> ISMAIL: But where is the problem? You can think about what you have done during a lesson. That's nothing new, just the usual evaluation of your teaching.

MARTIN: Yes, sure, but what's reflection-in-action?
RACHEL: Teaching isn't an easy job. During the lessons you have to decide immediately. There are many unexpected problems.
MARTIN: You're telling me! But there is no time to reflect. You must come up with a decision in a second. A teacher does not have an autopilot.
ISMAIL: Didn't you read the book by Gladwell? You can think without thinking, in the blink of an eye. And these decisions are often better than gathering a lot of information.
MARTIN: Yes, I know the book, it is a good read and I had much fun. But Gladwell's assumptions have nothing to do with science.
RACHEL: As I understand it, Gladwell's assumptions are based on scientific findings.
MARTIN: I know, but he selects results from research when it is convenient for him to back up his theories. It is an interesting book, but it has nothing to do with educational science.
ISMAIL: You are right; Gladwell does not talk about teaching and learning. He draws on examples of other professions.
RACHEL: But I see some similarities between reflection-in-action and the thinking without thinking of Gladwell.
MARTIN: How so?
RACHEL: We all make quite informed decisions without thinking very much, don't we?
MARTIN: You mean a gut instinct? That has nothing to do with the informed decisions a teacher has to make when standing before a class.
ISMAIL: Right, but Gladwell does not talk about a feeling. What he means is the intuition of an expert. When you have a long experience you can make good decisions in a second.
RACHEL: Yes, you get this ability to respond intuitively to a situation by experience and training.
MARTIN: I see, but intuition can't substitute for critical thinking. Isn't it better to put together many pieces of information before making a decision?
ISMAIL: Sure, but you don't always have enough time. When necessary, a real expert is able to immediately make sense of a situation and react to it.
RACHEL: And sometimes it is better not to take too much information into account.
ISMAIL: That's it!
MARTIN: You are right that sometimes it is good to look at the context as a whole, but as teachers we should prefer reflection-on-action instead of an intuitive sense of what to do in class.

ISMAIL: Nobody maintains the contrary! But the point of the matter is that during a lesson the teacher often has no time for longer reflections. Didn't you say that a teacher has no autopilot?
RACHEL: I think we are going around in circles. Next week we will learn more about reflection-in-action.
MARTIN: I hope a great researcher like Schoen does not suggest gut reactions.

4.4. A THEORY-BASED META-ANALYSIS OF RESEARCH ON INSTRUCTION

In the preceding chapters I underscored several times the responsibility of teachers and educators in general. They are first and foremost committed to facilitating the learning processes of their students in order to reach the best outcomes for every individual learner. I briefly focused on the partly different interests of teachers and policy makers (see Section 3.3). In my view it is unnecessary to further engage (prospective) teachers in a debate to be held by scholars. It is the challenge of the scientific community to make every effort to apply research designs and methods that guarantee valid and reliable results (at least until they are falsified by newer findings). Educational practitioners, by the same token, have to endeavor to gain the necessary insights into scientific findings and to evaluate them with the aim of improving practice by making an emancipated use of research.

Research-based results and especially evidence-based findings always have to be put to the test in particular teaching and learning contexts. They are tools to be taken into account by engaged and expert teachers. Some of these devices that (as yet) are not underpinned by strong science may reveal valuable means in practice, whereas other highly praised evidence-based results will show themselves as less useful in a specific learning context. For many reasons, it cannot be the task of teachers to replicate scientific research on education. Their efforts should be concentrated on detecting those research findings that work best in their particular classrooms.

Whereas Seidel and Shavelson (2007; see Section 4.2) subject research methods to critical scrutiny, the overall aim of Marzano is to improve the practice of teaching and learning using findings of empirical research.

In 1998 he published a widely noted meta-analysis of research on instruction. Even though he amply discusses his particular approach to research, it remains unclear if his findings are really based on experimental research.

Marzano bases his meta-analysis on a theory of human information-processing comprising four elements: the self-system, the metacognitive system, the cognitive system, and knowledge. Whereas many educationalists and practitioners start with knowledge to be integrated in the cognitive system, so that metacognitive reflection becomes possible and may have an impact on the self, Marzano's approach is top–down. Geoff Petty, one of Britain's leading experts in teaching methods, integrates results of evidence-based research into his teacher guide. On behalf of Marzano, he explains: "He [Marzano] argued that the self-system activates the meta-cognitive system, which activates the cognitive system, which creates learning! (No wonder teaching is so difficult)" (Petty, 2009, p. 73). Marzano's approach is appealing, as we know that the self-system is the main stimulus of learning.

Marzano categorizes teaching strategies and other interventions according to what they activate during the learning processes:

- According to Marzano, the effects on the self of the learner are the most important activator of learning: How do the students measure their possibility to succeed in learning a particular subject? What value do they attribute to the content or skill to be learned?
- These implications for the self-system are followed by the effects on the meta-cognitive system: In what way do learners fix goals for themselves? How do they monitor their learning processes on the way to reaching their goals? How do they deal with (learning) difficulties?
- The outcomes in the form of knowledge and the restructuring of the learner's cognitive system are consequences of the above processes: Which forms of reasoning are caused by the teaching and learning materials? How are mental structures transformed by the study subject in order to attain the stated goals?

Hattie, whose study is based on Marzano's research design and methodology (see Section 4.5), specifies the U.S. educationalist's results about cognitive learning as follows:

> The overall effect was d = 0.65, and this was typical across his four major outcomes: knowledge (d = 0.60), cognitive systems (d = 0.75), meta-cognitive systems (d = 0.55), and self-system (d = 0.74). When the

instructional technique was designed for the student, the effect was higher (d = 0.74) than when the technique was designed for the teacher (d = 0.61). (Hattie, 2009, p. 203)

Marzano summarizes the results of his meta-analysis with regards to teachers:

> The effective teacher is one who has clear instructional goals. These goals are communicated both to students and to parents. Ideally, the instructional goals address elements of the knowledge domains as well as the cognitive, metacognitive, and self-system. Even if the instructional goals focus on the knowledge domains only (as it is frequently the case in public education), the teacher still uses instructional techniques that employ the cognitive system, the metacognitive system, and the self-system, and uses the understanding to make the myriad of instructional decisions that occur in a single lesson. (Marzano, 1998, p. 135)

Which are the concrete strategies and techniques considered as most effective? These high-yield instructional strategies are as follows (Marzano et al., 2001, sections 2–10) (in parentheses: effect sizes; small: 0.20; medium: 0.50; large: 0.80).

1. **Identifying Similarities and Differences** (average effect size 1.61)
   In order to understand complex problems by analyzing them in a more simple way, students should break a concept into its similar and dissimilar characteristics. Teaching and learning aids regarding ways to represent similarities and differences are graphic forms.
2. **Summarizing and Note Taking** (average effect size 1.00)
   These essential skills consist of students finding the important features of a subject and putting them in their own words. In this context it is very useful to provide rules for summary-writing and offer worked examples of effective notes.
3. **Reinforcing Effort and Providing Recognition** (average effect size 0.80)
   As not all students immediately recognize the relationship between effort and achievement, teachers can share stories of people who succeeded by not giving up. Recognition has to be personalized and specified.
4. **Homework and Practice** (average effect size 0.77)
   The students have to be informed about the purpose of assignments. The amount of homework should vary according to the

grade and parent involvement should be minimal. Practice should focus on difficult concepts.

5. **Nonlinguistic Representations** (average effect size 0.75)

   As research shows that knowledge is stored linguistically and visually, that is to say in two forms, visual representations have to be used more widely. They have proven to stimulate and increase brain activity. Besides graphic organizers and a host of images, physical models and physical movement should be used more often.

6. **Cooperative Learning** (average effect size 0.73)

   Organizing students in groups of varying sizes and assignments yields positive effects on learning, when certain premises are observed (see Chapter 10).

7. **Setting Objectives and Providing Feedback** (average effect size 0.61)

   In order to give clear direction to the learning of the students, they should be informed about the overall aims of the teaching unit. Goals have to be sufficiently broad that students can adapt them to their own learning objectives. Feedback has more positive effects when it is kept corrective, timely, and specific.

8. **Generating and Testing Hypotheses** (average effect size 0.61)

   A deductive procedure, that is to say starting from a general rule to make predictions, seems to yield better results. Students may be asked to predict what happens when an aspect of a familiar system, for example transportation, is changed.

9. **Cues, Questions, and Advance Organizers** (average effect size 0.59)

   These last tools are especially effective when presented before a learning experience in an analytical form and focusing on the most important features. Students should be given enough time before answering to teacher questions so that they can deepen their contributions in class.

Compiling his theory-based meta-analysis, Marzano finds out that the nine strategies and techniques have a great positive impact on student learning, but that the effects vary to a large extent according to the student's learning abilities: Using the same strategy, good students reach an effect of $d = 0.91$; students with medium abilities benefit by about $d = 0.70$; and students with learning difficulties only reach an effect size of $d = 0.64$. Therefore, Marzano invites teachers to accompany certain strategies with further learning opportunities for the students in need, so that the effects of an intervention are more or less the same for all learners.

At the end of Marzano's meta-analysis, the researcher indicates the direction of further research:

> Although informative, this meta-analysis falls significantly short of its original goals to provide a comprehensive review of the research on instruction. Even though over 4,000 effect sizes were included in this effort, it is estimated that at least triple this number will be needed to provide highly stable estimates of the effect sizes for each of the various instructional techniques reviewed. Therefore, readers are cautioned that these findings should be considered "indications" of the conclusions that might be drawn from an exhaustive review of the research on instruction. On the other hand, readers should feel confident that these findings represent a sound basis for classroom teachers to begin adapting and experimenting with the instructional techniques described in this report. (Marzano, 1998, pp. 135–136)

Despite this honorable statement, Marzano has published and co-authored about twenty teacher guides since 1998, first in his function as director of the *Mid-Continent Research for Education and Learning* and later on as co-founder and CEO of the MRL (*Marzano Research Laboratory*) in Centennial, Colorado. Directly linked to the above teaching and learning strategies is *Classroom Instruction that Works: Research-based Strategies for Increasing Student Achievement*, published at the beginning of the millennium, a teacher guide that has seen numerous editions (Marzano et al., 2001).

In a review of this book, Lade (2012), an instructional coach at Bridgeport High School, Michigan, explains Marzano's "notable nine," describing them as "nine instructional techniques that have been assigned effect sizes for their supposed correlation with student achievement" (http://bcsinstructionalcoaching.blogspot.de/2012/07/book-summary-classroom-instructional-that.html; last accessed July 2015). Among the numerous publications of the MRL is a guide entitled *Using Common Core Standards to Enhance Classroom Instruction and Assessment* (Marzano et al., 2013), to which we will return later on (see Concluding Remarks).

REVIEW, REFLECT, PRACTICE

1. Consult at least one of the following reviews of research and meta-analyses, respectively. Why do you think that the results can improve teaching and learning practice? Why not? Discuss your reflections with other students or colleagues (especially in the case of the two research reviews on formative assessment both dating from 2011).

Taylor and Rohrer (2010). The effects of interleaved practice. *Applied Cognitive Psychology* 24/6, pp. 837–848.

Wijnia, Loyens, and Derous, (2011). Investigating effects of problem-based versus lecture-based learning environments on student motivation. *Contemporary Educational Psychology* 26/2, pp. 101–113.

Bennett (2011). Formative assessment: A critical review. *Assessment in Education: Principles, Policy and Practice* 18/1, pp. 5–25.

Kingston and Nash (2011). Formative assessment: A meta-analysis and a call for research. *Educational Measurement: Issues and Practice* 30/4, pp. 28–37.

2. According to many educationalists, evidence-based findings of educational research are less reliable than scientific results in medicine. Why? Discuss with other students or with colleagues.
3. What is the difference between research-based and evidence-based education? (see Section 4.1)
4. Do you think that Marzano's "notable nine" are really the most important strategies? Why? Why not?

5

A Synthesis of Over 800 Meta-Analyses Relating to Achievement

By drawing on the examples of the meta-analyses compiled by Seidel and Shavelson (2007) and Marzano (1998), as different as their overall aims may be, we have got a sense of the difficulties connected with carrying out such extensive and complex syntheses. Marzano, who limits his meta-analysis to teaching strategies, neglecting import issues such as classroom management and curriculum design, nevertheless does not neatly separate the high-yield strategies he propagates. It is probable that the primary studies he incorporated into his meta-analysis did not allow for a clearer distinction. For teachers and their learners there is a huge difference between summarizing and note-taking and between homework and practice (see Section 4.4, strategies no. 2 and no. 4). How could someone think of synthesizing all available empirical research on education? In what way and to whom may such condensed findings be useful?

In the preceding chapters it is underscored more than once that this research-based guide to effective teaching and successful learning does not follow a "cookbook" approach. You will not find recipes or even ready-made powdered soups instructing you to "just add water" for two main reasons: First, teaching and learning are complex and multilayered; second, from my point of view, recipes undermine the personality of teachers and students.

That is why you will not find in this chapter (as in the whole book) clear-cut judgments and prescriptions. Hattie's study and the following publications deserve a differentiated and detailed consideration in order to make evident for teachers where to rely on Hattie's suggestions – above all his teaching model – and where to be aware of the limitations of his research findings. On the whole, Hattie's scientific endeavor to synthesize all available research into achievement is a great contribution to the field of education. Nevertheless, there are numerous pitfalls, partly inherent in such a gigantesque enterprise and partly due to Hattie's research interests.

5.1. HATTIE'S STUDY *VISIBLE LEARNING*

As previously mentioned, John Hattie, an educationalist from New Zealand who specialized in statistics and psychometrics, compiled a mega-analysis. His study, entitled *Visible Learning*, synthesized over 800 meta-analyses relating to achievement (Hattie, 2009), and Hattie is still collecting. In his guide *Visible Learning for Teachers*, published three years later, he had already arrived at about 930 meta-analyses, with no end in sight (Hattie, 2012).

Before discussing Hattie's study and his further publications based on his findings of 2009, it is useful to state that Marzano's meta-analysis and Hattie's study are interrelated. An important publication to give insights into this relationship is a compilation of research entitled *Synthesis of Educational Productivity Research*, by Fraser, Walberg, Welch, and Hattie (1987) – a precursor of Hattie's 2009 study. Even though Marzano criticizes the categories of this "synthesis of meta-analyses" (Fraser et al., 1987, p. 187) as too broad and not transferable to practice, he mainly bases his literature research on the synthesis by Fraser et al. On the other hand, Hattie draws to a great extent on the meta-analysis and other publications of Marzano.

John A. C. Hattie started his career as a high school teacher in New Zealand in the 1970s. He earned a PhD in statistics at the University of Toronto, Canada, and lectured as a professor at various universities in the United States and Australia. After his return to New Zealand he spent about ten years as Professor of Educational Research at the University of Auckland and Director of the Visible Learning Labs. Since 2011 Hattie has been Director of the Melbourne Education Research Institute at the University of Melbourne, Australia.

As previously mentioned, Hattie limits his research efforts to student achievement. Synthesizing all available meta-analyses on achievement, he arrives at 138 factors that, according to him, influence the cognitive results of student learning. Criticism already starts at that point: "To be more accurate, he [Hattie] is concerned not with achievement but with achievement that is amenable to quantitative measurement" (Snook et al., 2009, p. 95). Hattie himself acknowledges that his favorite field of research is psychometric analysis. As early as the preface to his 2009 book, he admits that he is not interested in classroom interactions and their specific features, as important as they may be (Hattie, 2009, p. VIII).

In this preface, he underscores the excellent achievement of New Zealand's education system – the country ranks among the world's leading nations (ibid., p. IX). He attributes these positive outcomes to the great engagement of the local teachers. Hattie's statement calls for a correction as, between 2009 and today, student achievement measured in scores changed: Whereas New Zealand was among the leading nations in the PISA test at the beginning of the millennium, its students ranked at an average level in the PISA study of 2013: "In the 2013 rankings, New Zealand slipped from seventh to 13th in reading, from seventh to 18th in science and from 13th to 23rd in maths" (Campbell, 2013).

In the first three chapters of his perennial study, Hattie explains his overall intentions. In chapter 1, *The challenge*, he describes the challenging task connected with the compilation of his mega-analysis (Hattie, 2009, pp. 1–6). This description, however, does not focus on the difficulties with which researchers already have to cope when compiling a meta-analysis. Nor does Hattie mention the problems occurring when synthesizing an enormous number of meta-analyses into a mega-analysis. The purpose of his study is similar to that of Marzano. Existing systematic research reviews and meta-analyses only provide evidence of the factors that somehow influence learning. According to Hattie, these results do not permit teachers to choose between possible alternatives. Only by knowing what works better or what works best can teachers make decisions informed by scientific evidence. Thus, Hattie's big challenge consists of demonstrating which factors have the greatest impact on student achievement.

Chapter 2, *The Nature of the Evidence – A Synthesis of Meta-analyses*, is dedicated to Hattie's research design and the resulting methodology, mostly the calculation of effect sizes (Hattie, 2009, pp. 7–21). In order to be able to evaluate a teaching strategy or another factor that may influence learning, a threshold value is needed. Hattie fixes this "hinge point" (Hattie, 2009, pp. 17–18) at an effect size of $d = 0.40$. Sizes between $d = 0.20$ and $d = 0.40$ indicate a small effect, whereas effect sizes above $d = 0.60$ are to be considered as large. For Hattie, the zone of desired effects starts at $d = 0.41$. Above this hinge point Hattie positions sixty-three factors, whereas seventy-five are to be found below this line. If Hattie had fixed the starting point of the zone of desired affects at $d = 0.50$, as other researchers do, the factors to take into account would have been limited to forty-seven against ninety-one.

Hattie ranks the factors having an impact on student achievement according to the resulting effect sizes (Appendix A; Appendix B contains a list of all meta-analyses). To visualize the effect sizes of the 138 factors (more than 150 in 2012), Hattie uses stylized barometers. Undoubtedly this visualization appeals to the readers, but it induces them to look only at the height of the effect, without reading the brief accompanying texts.

It is indispensable for a teacher who, impressed by the effect size of a factor, wants to try out the respective teaching strategy or another intervention to consult Hattie's explanations of the factor in order to find out in which grades and in which subject matters the larger or smaller effects were found. These accompanying comments give at least some hints about the teaching and learning contexts. In every barometer, Hattie indicates that he considers effects due to maturation from d = 0.00 to d = 0.20, and those caused by an average teacher during a school year from d = 0.21 to d = 040 (see Figure 5.1).

In chapter 3, *The Argument*, Hattie presents his research design in more detail, but nevertheless remains vague with regard to essential issues (Hattie, 2009, pp. 22–38). First, he describes the learning theories his research starts out from (ibid., pp. 26–29). Although Hattie states that his instructional model is based on his quantitative research, he implicitly reverts to qualitative findings (for details see Chapter 6). As is the case for us all, he is not able to exclude the experiences accumulated during his time as a teacher. Hattie bases his research not only on the meta-analyses at his disposition; he includes all his experiences as a teacher and teacher trainer. He filters out relevant and less important factors that may influence results of cognitive learning without any weighing.

In his study he presents 138 factors that he allocates to six fields: (1) influences of the student, (2) those of the home, (3) of the school, (4) of the curriculum, (5) of the teacher, and (6) of the teaching strategies. (The increase to 150 factors in 2012 does not really change the overall picture). Hattie displays his findings in seven chapters, one dedicated to

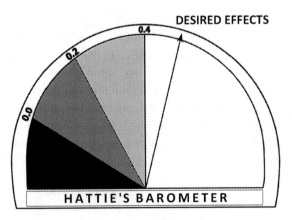

FIGURE 5.1: Barometer

each of the first five fields (chapters 4–8), whereas he deals with the results of teaching strategies in two separate chapters (chapters 9–10). In his conclusion (see chapter 11: *Bringing It All Together*, pp. 237–261), he tries to construct a relationship between the separate factors and to integrate them into a teaching model without scruple about bringing together the averaged effects of very different single factors. Hattie is well aware of comparing apples to oranges – a frequent research pitfall – but tries to resolve the problem by stating that both can be summarized under the broader term "fruit" (Hattie, 2009, passim). In my view as a (former) teacher, oranges are sometimes more convenient than apples, and often other fruit types are the better option.

In sum, we may consider Hattie's research findings the evidence-informed opinions of an expert.

5.2. "KNOW THY IMPACT"

Amelia and Neville both teach science at McKinnon Secondary College in McKinnon, a suburb of Melbourne, Australia. An initiative taken by the principal and members of the staff led to a week of teacher training with a visit from John Hattie. Whereas Amelia read Hattie's study and part of *Visible Learning for Teachers* before the professor gave a talk, Neville, rather annoyed by the hype about Hattie, refused to read anything. Entering the staff room, Amelia sees Neville absorbed in reading a book. Even as she stands before him, he does not notice her.

AMELIA: What's this you're reading? It seems to be a thriller!
NEVILLE: The study!
AMELIA: The study? What study?
NEVILLE: *Visible Learning.*
AMELIA: I can't believe it! Hattie's study ... What about it?
NEVILLE: It is inspiring. It is powerfully written. When I read it, I feel like using it in my lessons at once.
AMELIA: But wasn't it you that was bothered by the hype about our professor?
NEVILLE: Yes, before his talk, but now ...
AMELIA: What now?
NEVILLE: Look at his model of visible teaching and visible learning: "When teachers SEE learning through the eyes of the student – When students SEE themselves as their own teachers."
AMELIA: That's his best known mantra, followed by "know thy impact"! "Teachers as activators," "teachers as change agents," "teachers make a difference," and so on ... I can't hear it anymore.

NEVILLE: Shouldn't our teaching be more student-centered? What is wrong about this?
AMELIA: Nothing is wrong about this. Hattie's suggestions are welcome, but they aren't really backed up by his research.
NEVILLE: How is that?
AMELIA: When you dig a bit deeper you see that the nice barometers with the effect sizes are quite useless for practitioners.
NEVILLE: But didn't he summarize all available studies so that we can be sure of what works better and what works best?
AMELIA: Not at all! Let's have a look at an example ... Here, page 213, cooperative vs. individualistic learning; this factor has a high effect size.
NEVILLE: Yes, it is more or less evident that students learn better in small groups than individually in seat work.
AMELIA: But look here: cooperative learning does not score very high, it is just above the hinge point. What does that mean?
NEVILLE: Reading the accompanying text, I see that it is not clear what Hattie exactly intends by cooperative learning.
AMELIA: That's what I mean ... just tendencies, no practical advice.
NEVILLE: And what about Hattie's teacher guide?
AMELIA: He presents an interesting teaching model that dates back to Madeline Hunter; it was implemented in the past thirty years in thousands of schools in the USA. We all follow it more or less.
NEVILLE: I see; nevertheless, Hattie reminds us of many things we can do to improve our teaching.
AMELIA: That's true; for me it is sort of a reminder.

5.3. SHORTCOMINGS OF *VISIBLE LEARNING*

In order to give the criticism of Hattie's study – that of many scholars, as well as my own – a clearer structure, the following main critique points are introduced by guiding questions (for a comprehensive critique see Higgins & Simpson, 2011).

What have Hattie's study and his further publications got to do with the Holy Grail? In his review of research into self-concept (see Chapter 2.2), Hattie (1992) rejects the claim of basing research only on RCTs, and not on all types of experimental studies. He underscores the necessity of contrasting competing theories in psychology (ibid., p. 8): "Part of the blame lies with the mania for tight experimental design. Meta-analysis studies have demonstrated that the quality of the design has little or no influence on outcomes in some areas (particularly when the effect sizes are not small); yet we continue to seek perfect experiments – psychology's holy grail."

Despite this clear position, nevertheless, printed on the front cover of his study of 2009 is "Reveals teaching's Holy Grail." How did this come about? Mansell, a reviewer of Hattie's study, writes: "It is perhaps education's equivalent to the search for the Holy Grail – [. . .] (*Times Educational Supplement*, November 21, 2008). An interview of Hattie by Evans (*Times Educational Supplement*, September 14, 2012) is entitled "He's not the messiah . . .." Evans speaks with Hattie "about the work some call the 'holy grail.'" The book's marketing strategies might contribute to inducing (rookie) teachers to blindly follow his suggestions instead of making informed decisions.

Which is one of the greatest shortcomings of Hattie's research?

In my view, by limiting his study to one dimension of schooling, that is, academic achievement, Hattie gives policy makers and society as a whole a pretext for neglecting social factors of schooling and achievement. Despite examples that prove the contrary (Snook et al., 2009), Hattie (2009) sustains that schooling cannot influence contextual factors such as poverty.

> This is not a book about what can't be influenced in schools – thus critical discussions about class, poverty, resources in families, health in families, and nutrition are not included – but this is NOT because they are unimportant, indeed they may be more important than many of the influences discussed in this book. It is just that I have not included these topics in my orbit. (ibid., pp. VIII–IX; emphasis by the author)

Is Hattie not aware of the fact that "policy decisions can't be drawn in isolation from the background variables of class, poverty, health in families and nutrition" (Snook et al., 2009, p. 95)?

Which are the most evident biases of Hattie's choice of meta-analyses to be incorporated into his mega-analysis?

Hattie mostly integrates findings of correlation studies and much less those of RCTs, even though there might be notable differences in the definite effect size when "putting garbage in." For example, a study by Anderson (2004; Hartley, 2012) shows that the results differ when considering only RCTs. The negative effects of violent video gaming were much higher when taking only RCTs into account. In the preface to the book, Hattie immediately points out that he integrates all primary research into his study, without putting the design and the methodology of previous studies to the test (Hattie, 2009, p. IX). What counts, according to him, are results "beyond reasonable doubt" (ibid., p. 4). "The aim should be to summarize all possible studies regardless of their design – and then ascertain if quality is a moderator to the final conclusions" (ibid., p. 119). At least there should have been some weighing.

Hattie should have established criteria for the choice of correlation studies to be incorporated into his study. It is obvious that such a catalog would have facilitated the judgment of the readers, but with the enormous amount of meta-analyses, not to mention that of primary studies, it seems impossible to examine them one by one. This consideration is not against useful criteria catalogs, but should make researchers reflect before undertaking the enterprise of a mega-analysis.

In general, Hattie renounces any weighing without giving an explanation. A further example is the fact that he treats small studies with only a few participants in the same way as studies with thousands of people. The effect size of teaching strategies, for example, is based on fourteen meta-analyses with 1,491,369 participants (Hattie, 2009, pp. 200–203), whereas Hattie's average measure of metacognitive strategies results from only two meta-analyses with 5,028 people (ibid., pp. 188–189).

Hattie considers all factors in the same way even when there is no conceptual connection between them, for example diet (rank 123) (ibid., pp. 52–53) and classroom management (rank 42) (ibid., p. 102) or pre-term birth weight (rank 38) (ibid., pp. 51–52) and writing programs (rank 57) (ibid., pp. 141–143) (Higgins & Simpson, 2011). This leads to inappropriate averaging and comparison, as well as to averaging measures of different outcomes.

The chosen meta-analyses mostly focus on surface and deep knowing, much less on conceptual understanding. After a plea for conceptual and constructed understandings, Hattie (2009) has to admit that there is a lack of respective research:

> It is the case that most tests used in the studies in these meta-analyses are particularly effective at measuring surface features, somewhat effective at measuring deep learning, but rarely effective at measuring the construct representations that students build from their classroom experiences. [...] A limitation of many of the results in this book is that they are more related to the surface and deep knowing and less to conceptual understanding. (ibid., p. 249)

Hattie does not justify at all the great differences in effect sizes in his study of 2009 and his earlier research results. In a detailed overview of Hattie's research endeavors over the years, Atherton (2013; www.learningandteaching.info/teaching/what_works.htm; last accessed August 2015) compares the findings of 2009 to prior indications of effect sizes. Petty (2009, passim) bases his practical advice on different outcomes of Hattie's research, comparing them, for example, to those of Marzano.

Another serious pitfall is the interpretation of the content of meta-analyses. Hattie attributes the first place in his ranking to self-reported grades (d = 1.44). He thus assigns great influence to students' self-estimates regarding their chances of success. Hattie's result is based on six meta-analyses comprising 79,433 people. The dominant meta-analysis is the one compiled by Kuncel, Crede, and Thomas (2005) based on 56,265 research participants, which Hattie counts twice because of its multiple focus. Taking a closer look at this meta-analysis, Arnold (2011, p. 220) states: "This paper is about the validity of ex-post self-reported grades (due to imperfect storage and retrieval from memory or intentional deception), not about students' expectations or their predictive power of their own study performance, as Hattie claims." Besides Hattie's misinterpretation, what is the use of knowing that most students correctly predict their success indicated in grades? How can teachers influence this highest-ranked factor?

Last but not least, the mania for high effect sizes leaves out the fact that in some areas a much lower threshold than Hattie's hinge point can be significant (Snook et al., 2009, p. 99). Even strategies or interventions that are much below d = 0.41 can have a great impact on teaching and learning in particular contexts. This is for example the case when their cost is low so that they can be applied to a very great number of students.

5.4. HATTIE'S RESOURCE BOOK *VISIBLE LEARNING FOR TEACHERS*

Visible Learning for Teachers – Maximizing Impact on Learning (Hattie, 2012) cannot be considered a practical guide for (new and experienced) teachers. It is better termed a handbook that presents a valuable teaching model on the basis of Hattie's quantitative research. These findings are (implicitly) combined with suggestions drawing on Hattie's knowledge of qualitative research and his experience as a teacher.

For educational practitioners the book is said to be "still quite heavy going" (Hartley, 2012, p. E136), for the following main reasons:

- The book contains an overwhelming abundance of useful pieces of advice, whereas concrete examples that draw on different subject matters, grades, and goals are rarely to be found. That busy teachers are able to further develop into inspired, expert, and adaptive teachers on the basis of Hattie's suggestions is quite improbable.

- Hattie offers a confusing accumulation of categories, classifications, and fragmentations. A lot of perseverance is needed in order to get to the main features of his teaching model.
- Hattie does not concede any reductions of his model; it has to be taken as a whole. In many places there is a lack of opportunity-to-learn standards, above all different kinds of resources, for such an ample implementation. That is one of the reasons why Hattie offers training for in-service teachers.

Among the customer reviews of *Visible Learning for Teachers*, the following is representative for teachers (August 1, 2013): Under the heading: *Great message, but an inaccessible and academic text. Not for busy teachers*, a teacher sets out her impressions of Hattie's resource book. She wonders why other customers praise Hattie's handbook as precedent-setting and assumes that they did not read it from cover to cover:

> I am a teacher with 5 years of experience and it is my aim to help my pupils not meet but exceed their potential. [...] The book contains lots of theory, some of which is not fully explained (Piagetian models, the SOLO model etc, etc). Hidden amongst the pages and pages of theoretical discussions are some practical discussions. [...]
>
> The blurb on the back of the book suggests that the author offers "concise and user-friendly summaries of the most successful interventions. – IT DOES NOT. The text is dense and highly academic.
>
> The blurb also states that the book offers "practical step-by-step guidance to the successful implementation of visible learning ..." – again – IT IS ANYTHING BUT PRACTICAL. There is a serious lack of practical application and guidance. (www.amazon.co.uk/product-reviews/By elfreda (Sheffield); emphases of the author)

Visible Learning for Teachers (Hattie, 2012) is divided into three parts: In the first three chapters (part I), Hattie summarizes his study of 2009. Right at the outset (chapter 1, *Visible Learning Inside*, pp. 1–6), he explains what evidence-based education is all about. In the following (chapter 2, *The Source of the Ideas*, pp. 9–21), the author develops once more his overall aims when carrying out his mega-analysis. He tries to gain the attention of the readers, underscoring the importance and the impact of the teacher when considering successful learning outcomes (chapter 3, *Teachers: The Major Players in the Education Process*, pp. 22–34). This message is obvious, as everybody knows that there is no learning in schools without teachers. But Hattie does not refer to the teacher as such, but rather to the expert teacher that continues to further develop his professional qualifications. To reach this goal teachers have to continually evaluate their teaching, not only through reflection-in-action, but also by searching for feedback from the students.

In Part II: *The Lessons* (ibid., pp. 35–146), Hattie explains his teaching model in more detail, following a lesson plan from its preparation to its evaluation: chapter 4, *Preparing the Lesson* (ibid., pp. 37–68); chapter 5, *Starting the Lesson* (ibid., pp. 69–91); chapter 6, *The Flow of the Lesson: Learning* (ibid., pp. 92–117), chapter 7, *The Flow of the Lesson: The Place of Feedback* (ibid., pp. 115–137); and chapter 8, *The End of the Lesson* (ibid., pp. 138–146).

The final section (Part III), *Mind Frames*, focuses on the processes of rethinking and reflection indispensable for changes in education: chapter 9, *Mind Frames for Teachers, School Leaders, and Systems* (ibid., pp. 147–170). Of particular interest for teachers are Hattie's *Eight Mind Frames* (ibid., pp. 159–66), which lead to a so-called health check (ibid., p. 169).

Your Personal Health Check for Visible Learning

1. I am actively engaged in, and passionate about teaching and learning.
2. I provide students with multiple opportunities for learning based on surface and deep thinking.
3. I know the learning intentions and success criteria of my lessons, and I share these with students.
4. I am open to learning and actively learn myself.
5. I have a warm and caring classroom climate in which errors are welcome.
6. I seek regular feedback from my students.
7. My students are actively involved in knowing about their learning (i.e., they are assessment-capable).
8. I can identify progression in learning across multiple curricular levels in my student work and activities.
9. I have a wide range of teaching strategies in my day-to-day teaching repertoire.
10. I use evidence of learning to plan the next learning steps with my students.

Hattie's useful list should become the overall guideline for teachers everywhere in the world. Educational practitioners are urged to administer it to themselves, as Hattie suggests, and I would add: not once, but at regular intervals and separately for every class. Furthermore, they should discuss it with colleagues and evaluate the possibilities to come closer to the ten requirements by working together in teacher groups. Hattie's *Personal Health Check* is only in part based on his quantitative findings. It is the catalogue of what he himself calls an inspired, expert, and adaptive teacher. A closer look at his resource book *Visible Learning for Teachers* shows that – besides the introductory chapters and the appendixes – Hattie does not regularly back up the main part of his book with concrete indications of effect sizes drawn from his research.

As previously mentioned several times, the number of the synthesized meta-analyses has grown, from 800 to about 930 in 2012 (see Appendix B, pp. 289–350). As an experienced statistician, Hattie knows that adding further results to a huge amount of findings does not lead to very much change in the averaged means. With the continuous accumulation of newer meta-analyses, Hattie tries to weaken the argument of those critics who discredit his results based to a large extent on older meta-analyses. This criticism is partly justified, but does not consider that meta-analytic research is more or less historical. More important is the fact that most researchers, even though they integrate only newer research findings into their meta-analyses, seem convinced that the future will not be notably different from the past. Educational policy and research into education lack the stability of natural phenomena. We always should remember Dewey's statement that "one's present experience is a function of the interaction between one's past experiences and the present situation" (see Section 2.6).

5.5 AN *INTERNATIONAL GUIDE TO STUDENT ACHIEVEMENT*

In 2013 Hattie edited, together with Eric Anderman from Ohio State University, United States, a reader of approximately 500 pages. The two editors invited world-renowned scholars to give a succinct overview of the main field of their scientific research. After an introduction (section 1), *Understanding Achievement*, written by the editors, the following sections correspond mainly to the six fields of Hattie's study of 2009: section 2, *Influences from the Student*; section 3, *Influences from the Home*; section 4, *Influences from the School*; section 5, *Influences from the Classroom*; section 6, *Influences from the Teacher*; section 7, *Influences from the Curriculum*; and section 8, *Influences from the Teaching Strategies*. The final section 9 opens a view to *Influences from an International Perspective*.

Hattie and Anderman's guide is easy to consult. The editors limited the 150 contributions of the scholars in every field to three pages each. Furthermore, they invited the authors to follow a predetermined structure in order to facilitate the readers' orientation: A brief introduction is followed by a description of the research evidence. Every article is concluded by a summary with recommendations and a short bibliography.

By unifying the contributions in a reader, Hattie shows that a majority of the 138 (150) factors of his study are considered in similar ways and with related results by other scientists who have dedicated their (lifetime) research endeavors to one of Hattie's factors.

Besides the introductory section, only one single contribution of the guide is written by Hattie himself: that is 4.7, "Class Size," one of the influences from the school (Hattie, 2013, pp. 131–133). Hattie was widely attacked and even accused of having manipulated the results of this factor in order to serve policy makers and the system when averaging the effects of learning in small classes of fifteen students with not more than $d = 0.21$ (rank 106 of 138).

Before the study of 2009, Hattie himself scored the effects of a diminution of class size much higher (Petty, 2009, p. 69; Hattie: Table of effect sizes, n.d.). Other researchers could show that class size, that is, a reduction from twenty-five to fifteen students, matters. Hattie does not even mention the results of *The Tennessee Study of Class Size in the Early Grades* presented by Mosteller (1995) (see Section 4.4), even though he synthesizes studies on the effects of reducing class size from 1980 to 2000.

In his article about class size in the *International Guide to Student Achievement*, Hattie states that class size per se does not tell us anything about student achievement. In other words: The reduction of the number of students learning in the same class does not produce the effects desired by parents and a wider public. Better achievement is not caused by the reduction itself, but undoubtedly smaller classes often have a positive impact on student learning. Hattie argues that smaller class sizes have this positive influence on student achievement when teachers are prepared to adapt their strategies and interventions to the smaller number of students. Therefore teachers have to be trained to teach effectively in smaller groups to reach the desired outcomes. "Given the enormous costs and the high levels of advocacy by teachers and parents for lower class size, it is necessary to rephrase the key question from does class size reduction positively influence student achievement toward how can we optimize teaching in small classes" (Hattie, 2013, p. 132).

A great merit of **Hattie's *Visible Learning*** and his further publications (2009, 2012, 2013) is their provocation of a useful discussion of the potential and the pitfalls of quantitative research into education. His teaching model specified in ***Visible Learning for Teachers*** (2012), backed up by research findings from quantitative (and implicitly from qualitative) research, is confirmed by many scholars and practitioners. Particular effect sizes, however, should be considered with great caution for two main reasons: First, Hattie's mega-analysis is based to a large extent on correlation studies, which are less valid and reliable than experiments (RCTs) and quasi-experimental studies. Furthermore, the unweighted aggregation of an enormous amount of studies renders it very difficult for teachers to make practical judgments.

Despite the shortcomings of Hattie's research, **I refer in the following chapters to the effect sizes indicated in his study of 2009. First, because effect sizes of different primary studies and meta-analyses are not comparable**; second, because Hattie's ranking of 138 factors is widely known in the scientific world.

REVIEW, REFLECT, PRACTICE

1. Why is it questionable to use the results of Hattie's mega-analysis in a particular teaching and learning context? Consult for example his findings on homework (Hattie, 2009, pp. 8–10, 17–20, 234–236) and make a list of concrete aspects of homework to be considered when giving an assignment to the students. Compare your list to that of other students or colleagues.
2. Which is the greatest shortcoming of Hattie's study in your opinion? (If necessary reread Section 5.3). Consider the pros and cons from a teacher's point of view.
3. As it is important to know what students think and feel with regard to teaching interventions, transform Hattie's proposal *Your Personal Health Check for Visible Learning* (see Section 5.4) into a questionnaire for learners (perhaps in cooperation with other students or colleagues).
4. Read two of the following chapters published in the *International Guide to Student Achievement* (Hattie & Anderman, 2013):
    - 2.6 'Engagement and opportunity to learn' by Ackerman (ibid., pp. 39–41);
    - 4.3 'Evaluating and improving student–teacher interactions' by Cash and. Hamre (ibid., pp. 119–121);

5.4 'Emotion and achievement in classrooms' by Goetz and Hall (ibid., pp. 192–195);
6.3 'Classroom management and student achievement' by Freiberg (ibid., pp. 228–230);
8.11 'The search for the key for individualized instruction' by Scott (ibid., pp. 385–388);
8.26 'Time on task' by van Gog (ibid., pp. 432–434).

Summarize the two contributions of your choice and explain to another student or to a colleague which aspects are most important for your teaching.

6

Scaffolding Effective Teaching and Successful Learning

Taking Hattie's model of Direct Instruction (DI) in seven major steps as a starting point, a more detailed research-based teaching model in thirty steps is presented and discussed in the following. I draw on various tried-and-trusted examples combing lesson design and instructional design. Many steps of my *Model of Effective Teaching* (MET) are backed up by evidence-based research. It follows the tendencies outlined by Hattie, Marzano, and other scholars. Their results are compared to those of Wellenreuther (2004, 2014), a German scientist, who draws exclusively on experimental research. Excluding correlation studies (and qualitative research), Wellenreuther is in a position to explain the results of preselected RCTs (where available) and quasi-experimental studies in more detail. On the other hand, the exclusive focus on strong experimental research limits the use of his handbook.

On the whole, the MET is not evidence-based but evidence-informed. As my model has to stand the test of practitioners, its purpose is to offer trustworthy guidelines for teachers. What teachers can reach with the help of the MET is comparable to Vygotsky's Zone of Proximal Development, or, rather, Bruner's Scaffolding (see Section 1.4). I offer a scaffold that teachers can use entirely or in part, and which they may put down when they do not need it any more (for details see Chapters 7–11).

Another important goal is connected with this overall aim. In a multi-layered, complex, and changing field such as education, the personality and the responsibility of the teacher are at least as important as averaged means in form of effect sizes. The MET invites teachers to make informed decisions showing them alternatives. Practitioners, however, should not feel limited to scientific results, as these are always falsifiable.

Sometimes inflexibility and authoritarian attitudes of policy makers and school administrators, fixated on so-called evidence-based education, rub off on practitioners, causing harm to many students. Anything goes? Not at all; on the contrary, the MET challenges teachers to review and revise their teaching practices, giving up ineffective traditions and habits. Successful learning of (possibly) all students begins with effective teaching.

6.1. HATTIE'S MODEL OF DIRECT INSTRUCTION (DI)

It was not only the enormous amount of meta-analyses synthesized in Hattie's study that attracted worldwide attention. Surprise and irritation were aroused by the fact that many factors whose effects remained unquestioned over decades did not reach high ranks in Hattie's mega-analysis. *Individualized Instruction* scored only d = 0.23 (rank 100 of 138). On the other hand, strategies or interventions of controversial discussion lead to successful learning, according to Hattie – for example, *Direct Instruction* reached d = 0.59 (rank 26 of 138; in an earlier table of effect sizes reported by Petty, Hattie scores DI d = 0.81; Petty, 2009, p. 65). A great deal of the surprise and irritation is caused by misunderstandings. As we will see later, DI is a comprehensive teaching model that has nothing to do with unquestioned didactical teaching. On the other hand, Hattie defines individualized instruction as "an individualized program for each student" (Hattie, 2009, p. 198), which he compares to programmed instruction. Many practitioners, however, believe in individualized learning as a more or less student-centered approach, giving the learners an opportunity to practice without the direct supervision of the teacher.

With the intention to underscore his model of DI, Hattie contrasts the teacher as activator with the teacher as facilitator (2009, p. 243):

Teacher as activator	d	Teacher as facilitator	d
Reciprocal teaching	0.74	Simulations and gaming	0.32
Feedback	0.72	Inquiry-based teaching	0.31
Teaching students self-verbalization	0.67	Smaller class sizes	0.21
Meta-cognition strategies	0.67	Individualized instruction	0.20
Direct Instruction	0.59	Problem-based learning	0.15
Mastery Learning	0.57	Different teaching for boys and girls	0.12
Goals – challenging	0.56	Web-based learning	0.09
Frequent/effects of testing	0.46	Whole language-reading	0.06
Behavioral organizers	0.41	Inductive teaching	0.06
Average activator	**0.60**	**Average facilitator**	**0.17**

It is not easy to comprehend Hattie's classification: reciprocal teaching, meta-cognitive strategies, and mastery-learning are often part of individualized forms of learning, whereas smaller class sizes and different teaching for boys and girls can be classified under the heading "teacher as activator" without any problems.

Hattie's partly subjective look at the results of his research is further confirmed by his model of DI. He admits that his model might be tentative (Hattie, 2009, p. 4) and refers to Popper:

> The model I will present in Chapter 3 may well be speculative, but it aims to provide high levels of explanation for the many influences on student achievement as well as offer a platform to compare these influences in a meaningful way. And while I must emphasize that these ideas are clearly speculative, there is both solace and promise in the following quotation from Popper:

> Bold ideas, unjustified anticipations, and speculative thought, are our only means for interpreting nature: our only organon, our only instrument, for grasping her. And we must hazard them to win our prize. Those among us who are unwilling to expose their ideas to the hazard of refutation do not take part in the scientific game. (Popper, 1968, p. 280)

What Popper wants to express with the statement just quoted is not only the fact that scientific results are always subject to possible falsification – in other words, that scientific results must be open to correction by more likely findings – but also, implicitly, he reminds us of the fact that the starting point of a scientific theory may be speculative. As previously mentioned (see Section 5.4), Hattie's model is not only based on results of his quantitative research, mostly on correlation studies; without stating it overtly, he also bases his DI model on his experience as a teacher but also on findings of qualitative studies. In my view, there is nothing wrong with this attitude; on the contrary, even though I am among the critics of Hattie's research procedures, I want to emphasize the importance of the teaching model he presents. It is worthy of consideration and discussion. How is this possible?

As we will see, Hattie's DI model draws on a wide range of research findings that other scholars and practitioners gathered during the past decades. While the results of Hattie's mega-analysis are questionable, they do not compromise the teaching model. Therefore, I think it is quite easy to follow Arnold's statement:

> I find the visible learning story a convincing story. I believe most teachers will agree with the book's main message that effective instruction can't

take place without proper feedback from student to teacher on the effectiveness of the instruction. Hattie also convincingly argues that the effectiveness of teaching increases when teachers act as activators instead of as facilitators, a view which I find refreshing in a time when teaching approaches such as problem-based learning have the effect of sidelining the instructor. My problem with the book is, however, that I would have been convinced even without the empirical analysis. (Arnold, 2011, p. 2)

Perhaps the model of teaching and learning that Hattie describes would not have attracted worldwide attention without the barometers indicating the effect sizes. His ranking of factors provides the teaching model with a seal of quality that is only in part due to his research results. Hattie presents the model twice, first in the commentary of his findings on DI (Hattie, 2009, pp. 204–227), and later as the basis of his lesson descriptions in *Visible Learning for Teachers* (2012, pp. 65–66). The model, which, according to Hattie, was first outlined by Adams and Engelmann (1996), involves seven major steps:

1. Before the lesson is prepared, the teacher should have a clear idea of what the *learning intentions* are. What, especially, should the student be able to do, understand, care about as a result of the teaching?
2. The teacher needs to know what *success criteria* of performance are to be expected and when, and what students will be held accountable for from the lesson/activity. The students need to be informed about the standards of performance.
3. There is a need to *build commitment and engagement* in the learning task. In the terminology of DI, this is sometimes called a "hook" to grab the student's attention to the lesson, to share the learning intentions.
4. There are guides to *how the teacher should present the lesson* – including notions such as input, modeling, and checking for understanding. Input refers to providing information needed for students to gain knowledge or skill through lecture, film, tape, video, pictures, and so on. Modeling is where the teacher shows students examples of what is expected as an end product of their work. The critical aspects are explained through labeling, categorizing, and comparing to exemplars of what is desired. Checking for understanding involves monitoring whether students have "got it" before proceeding. It is essential that students practice *doing it right*, so the teacher must know that students understand before they start to practice. If there

is any question that the class has not understood, the concept or skill should be re-taught before practice begins.
5. There is the notion of *guided practice*. This involves an opportunity for each student to demonstrate his or her grasp of new learning by working through an activity or exercise under the teacher's direct supervision. The teacher moves around the room to determine the level of mastery and to provide feedback and individual remediation as needed.
6. There is a *closure* part of the lesson. Closure involves those actions or statements by a teacher that are designed to bring a lesson presentation to an appropriate conclusion: the part wherein students are helped to bring things together in their own minds, to make sense out of what has just been taught. "Any questions? No. OK, let's move on" is not closure. Closure is used to cue students to the fact that they have arrived at an important point in the lesson or the end of a lesson; to help organize student learning; to help form a coherent picture; to consolidate, eliminate confusion and frustration, and so on; and to reinforce the major points to be learned. Thus closure involves reviewing and clarifying the key points of a lesson, tying them together into a coherent whole, and ensuring they will be applied by the student by ensuring they have become part of the student's conceptual network.
7. There is *independent practice*. Once students have mastered the content or skill, it is time to provide for reinforcement practice. It is provided on a repeating schedule so that the learning is not forgotten. It may be homework or group or individual work in class. It is important to note that this practice can provide for decontextualization: Enough different contexts so that the skill or concept may be applied to any relevant situation and not only the context in which it was originally learned. For example, if the lesson is about inference from reading a passage about dinosaurs, the practice should be about inference from reading about another topic such as whales. Advocates of DI argue that the failure to do this seventh step is responsible for most student failure to be able to apply something learned (Hattie, 2009, pp. 205–206).

It is useful to briefly compare Hattie's model with those of his precursors in order to find out to what extent it is backed up by quantitative and qualitative research findings (see e.g., Rosenshine 1979; 1985; Rosenshine & Meister, 1994). Hattie himself mentions the meta-analysis of Adams and Engelmann (1996), the latter being considered the inventor of DI. As early as the 1960s Engelmann and Becker, both professors at the University of Oregon, United States, together developed a teaching and learning model to help disadvantaged students to improve cognitive achievement. Engelmann, who was interested in children with disabilities and at-risk students in pre-schools and the first grades of elementary schools, elaborated a detailed program denominated DISTAR (**D**irect **I**nstruction **S**ystem for **T**eaching **A**rithmetic and **R**eading), which to this day enjoys great popularity in its commercialized form. DISTAR was involved in the greatest U.S. research project in education, *Project Follow Through* (1968–1977). Follow Through was first intended as a service program that originated from President Johnson's War on Poverty campaign of the 1960s. For different reasons, mostly costs, it was soon combined with a research and developmental program. Obviously the cooperation of policy makers and educational practitioners which followed a more or less value-based approach and researchers with strong interests in objective findings was highly conflictual. Other shortcomings resulted from local controversies and general ideological differences.

Regardless, DISTAR became the most successful approach to teaching among the available programs. Adams and Engelmann (1996, p. 72) report an effect size of over 0.75. Nevertheless, DI, in the form of DISTAR, did not become a federal or widely diffused governmental teaching strategy. From the beginning, critics underscored that DISTAR was mainly an intervention to help children in need, and that more gifted students may benefit more from Strategy Instruction (SI), which focuses on effective training in specific techniques.

Hattie is well aware of these and other points of criticism. He emphasizes that DI is not only a teaching model for (disadvantaged) elementary students to improve their basic skills:

> One of the common criticisms is that Direct Instruction works with very low-level or specific skills, and with lower ability and the youngest students. These are not the findings from the meta-analyses. The effects of Direct Instruction are similar for regular (d = 0.99), and special education and lower ability students (d = 0.86), higher for reading (d = 0.89) than mathematics (d = 0.50), similar for the more low-level word-attack (d = 0.64) and also for high level comprehension (d = 0.54), and similar for elementary and high school students (Adams and Engelmann, 1996). (Hattie, 2009, pp. 206–207)

Hattie (2009, p. 207) summarizes the main steps of DI as follows:

> The messages of these meta-analyses on Direct Instruction underline the power of stating the learning intentions and success criteria, and then engaging students in moving toward these. The teacher needs to invite the students to learn, provide much deliberative practice and modeling, and provide appropriate feedback and multiple opportunities to learn. Students need opportunities for independent practice, and then there need to be opportunities to learn the skill or knowledge implicit in the learning intention in contexts other than those directly taught – And, as I would add, to a large extent in cooperation with peers.

6.2. LINKS BETWEEN FACTS AND VALUES

After having attained a Master's degree in Education, Jennifer Windhurst now aims at a PhD in Education. As she is highly interested in educational research, she is attending, among other lectures, a postgraduate course in research design and methodology. Her grandfather, a retired high school teacher of mathematics, is very proud of Jennifer. He always dreamed of carrying out studies in statistics and psychometrics, but, for various reasons, he never had the opportunity to seek an academic career. At the weekends Jennifer often visits her grandfather, as she has noticed that he wants to know as many details as possible about her university courses.

GRANDFATHER: You are looking fine. So the studies aren't too exhaustive, are they?
JENNIFER: It's a lot of work, sure, but most courses are really interesting.
GRANDFATHER: For example?
JENNIFER: This semester I'm attending a more or less practical course in research design and methodology. It's really very fascinating.
GRANDFATHER: How come a good-looking girl like you is fond of research methods?
JENNIFER: (laughs) That's really a good question. My grandpa has taught me mathematics and statistics since my years in kindergarten, so ...
GRANDFATHER: Horrible!
JENNIFER: Not at all, the course is frequented by many attractive male students.
GRANDFATHER: Let's get serious. What is the course about?

JENNIFER: During the last two weeks we tried to analyze a meta-analysis by Adams and Engelmann ...

GRANDFATHER: Oh, Zig Engelmann!

JENNIFER: Why do you call him Zig? If I remember well, he is called Siegfried.

GRANDFATHER: Yes, I know, but in his active times he called himself Zig, perhaps because Siegfried seemed to be too Teutonic. So what did you learn from his meta-analysis?

JENNIFER: I think that his model of DI is very successful, at least for children with learning disabilities. I don't know if it is equally useful for all students.

GRANDFATHER: Yes, in my opinion DISTAR is too teacher-directed; in its rigid form it should be used in limited situations.

JENNIFER: I find it very inflexible, too. It undermines the personality of the teacher.

GRANDFATHER: That's it. As every step is prescribed, DISTAR can be delivered also by unskilled teachers who are willing to learn the main steps by heart.

JENNIFER: But Professor Laughlin told us that this program reached the highest scores in the Project Follow Through.

GRANDFATHER: That's true, but teachers were well trained by Engelmann and his team and the program is well sequenced.

JENNIFER: Yes, and our professor told us that in general, all structured models of Project Follow Through scored higher than unstructured ones. Furthermore, Hattie bases his *Visible Learning for Teachers* to a large extent on Engelmann's model.

GRANDFATHER: I read about it. In any case, DISTAR draws on controlled experiments. At least, this was the intention. For me, DISTAR is too limited. There are other important factors such as self-esteem and affective features to focus on.

JENNIFER: But Hattie reports that his model, which goes back to Engelmann, is successful with students of all ages, and even when aiming at deeper and conceptual learning.

GRANDFATHER: Yes, I read it, but I have some problems with these results. By the way, did you know that DISTAR is derived from a much older teaching program designed by Madeline Hunter?

JENNIFER: No, I've never heard about her, and even our lecturer did not mention her. Who is she?

GRANDFATHER: An educationalist who designed a lesson plan that is quasi-identical to DISTAR and Hattie's model of DI.

JENNIFER: I'll ask Professor Laughlin about her in our next working session.

GRANDFATHER: First, look her up on the internet and you will see that her model, with small modifications, is still much diffused.
JENNIFER: What's her name? I'll write it down.
GRANDFATHER: She is called Madeline Cheek Hunter and, if I remember well, the model is called Lesson Plan Design.
JENNIFER: Why didn't DISTAR gather more momentum?
GRANDFATHER: A main problem with Project Follow Through is a discrepancy between facts and values.
JENNIFER: I don't see what you mean.
GRANDFATHER: Education is always value-based. When you try to do research you have to take into account that facts and values don't exist in isolation.
JENNIFER: If I understand, you mean facts and values somehow act together. Eventually I'll talk to Professor Laughlin about this issue.
GRANDFATHER: Perhaps you first may talk to other students about it.
JENNIFER: That's a good idea.

6.3. PREMISES OF EFFECTIVE TEACHING

The MET presented in the next section (see Section 6.4) describes the single steps of lessons or teaching units intended to enable possibly all students to acquire knowledge, skills, and attitudes. A comprehensive model such as the MET is based on several premises overarching all teaching and learning endeavors. These are learning theories, including newer findings about taxonomies of educational objectives, different types of learners and learning styles. Another overall aspect is motivation, revisited and revised by theories of promoting a favorable mindset through adequate forms of feedback. As many popular teacher guides are outdated, despite having been reedited during the past ten years (see e.g., Borich 1986; 1995; 2010), newer research into the aforementioned aspects of education is briefly presented in the following.

How is learning processed? As long as specific teaching strategies or techniques are not related to learning processes, their effects cannot be analyzed by empirical research. Furthermore, without knowing how learning takes place, effective teaching (and learning) is quite impossible.

Knowledge is only the first step. It is the foundation of further learning processes. That is the reason why unspecific programs such as *Learning to learn* without relating to concrete subject matter content have proved to be more or less useless.

The second step, after having acquired the necessary knowledge, consists in relating it to one's own person; that is, finding out what the particular piece of knowledge or the skill means to you. To make sense of facts or issues, a personal interpretation is indispensable. It does not suffice that the students store a representation of the learning content in their memory. They must build a concept; that is, they have to abstract or generalize from concrete experiences. Many teachers think that this second step leads to knowledge, but that is not sufficient.

In order to dispose of the content or skill, a third step is necessary. Teachers have to help students to relate the new content to existing concepts and to prior learning experiences. This connection is facilitated through different, increasingly challenging learning activities, ideally in cooperation with other students (Bereiter, 2002). How does the transition from surface to deep and conceptual learning take place?

As long as there is no better theory available, we can imagine the processes as follows (Petty, 2009). Thinking in general is pre-lingual; it occurs in a wordless language called mentalese. This language of thought plays a crucial role when it comes to connecting different concepts and transforming them. "The modules of the mind communicate in mentalese too," Petty explains (ibid., p. 9). To make sense of information, its pieces are transformed into mentalese in the working memory (Marzano, 1998). A personal construct is formed, which means a small network of interrelated brain cells. This construct becomes a concept when we connect it with a term of verbal language. Only after these processes is the concept stored in long-term memory.

What can teachers do in order to promote the construction and connection of concepts? First, simple reproduction tasks, for example the repetition of a definition or an explanation given by the teacher or the textbook, further the representation in the short-term memory. What must follow are reasoning tasks that provoke thinking. Simple (closed) reasoning tasks lead to more challenging (open) reasoning tasks. Equally important are reasoning questions, which high achievers in general ask themselves: "Why does it happen this way? What would happen if . . . ? How could this be translated to everyday or to professional life?"

> **Learning processes** start with the acquisition of knowledge or skills, which, sufficient attention presupposed, **in a first step** reach the short-term/working memory. Trying to make sense of the arriving information, learners, **in a second step**, must abstract and generalize from the learning experience.

> They form a limited pre-verbal network of brain cells called a construct. **In a third step**, this construct is transformed into a concept when the learner is able to connect it with a term of verbal language. Teachers can further this **transition from surface to deep and conceptual learning** by reasoning questions and well-graded reasoning tasks.

Why does Bloom's taxonomy of learning objectives call for a revision? With the changes in learning theory, Bloom's taxonomy of the 1950s needed to be revised. Many scholars criticize Bloom's well-known taxonomy for what they feel are incoherent levels. Whereas the first three levels of the cognitive domain, that is, knowledge, comprehension, and application, are considered as forms of knowing, the following three, namely analysis, synthesis, and evaluation, refer to the acquisition of knowledge. Furthermore, whereas knowledge, comprehension, and application develop gradually, analysis, synthesis, and evaluation come into play from the beginning of goal-oriented learning processes.

A revision of Bloom's taxonomy by Anderson and Krathwohl (2001) led to four grades of knowing: first, factual knowledge; second, conceptual knowledge; third, procedural knowledge; and fourth, meta-cognitive knowledge. Even though this classification is part of the basic knowledge of all teachers, it is of limited help for teachers when planning lessons or learning activities.

A useful taxonomy mentioned by Hattie (2009, pp. 26–29) and amply described by Petty (2009, pp. 17–22) is the SOLO Taxonomy elaborated for vocational training by Biggs and Collis (1982). SOLO stands for **S**tructure of the **O**bserved **L**earning **O**utcome and is based on empirical research. The scholars analyzed thousands of student essays on the same subject, classified the differences, and deduced from their analysis a taxonomic model that can be of great use for teachers as well as for learners. Biggs and Collis found out that the structure of elaboration of the essays is decisive for the quality of learning. What does that mean?

According to Biggs and Collis, the transition from surface to deep and conceptual learning can be described in five levels of outcome quality. Contrary to Bloom's taxonomy and its various re-elaborations, they do not base their model on thinking processes, but on products of learning; that is, written work of students. Let us take an example. After a stay abroad or a student exchange, the teacher notices that the partner students' school uniforms caused astonishment on the part of some learners, who are not accustomed to this widespread tradition. So the teacher invites the students to give their view on school uniforms in a written form. Following the SOLO Taxonomy, the results are classified in the following way:

1. **Prestructural level**: A student narrates on which occasions he has encountered students wearing school uniforms. Another student describes the details of the different school uniforms she has seen during her stay abroad. Neither student got the sense of the task, which was meant to express a personal opinion on wearing this particular clothing.
2. **Unistructural level**: Some students base their view on one single aspect of the prescription to wear school uniforms. They express their pros or cons through one single argument.
3. **Multistructural level**: Many students describe more than one aspect, but do not relate pros and cons to one another.
4. **Relational level**: Students whose essays Biggs and Collis qualify as relational, that is interrelated, illustrate important aspects of school uniforms such as group or peer pressure, moneymaking on the part of certain fashion brands, shared identity, and pride at attending a prestigious school. These students also weigh up the pros and cons of different aspects, but their considerations do not reach beyond the learning task.
5. **Extended Abstractum**: The learners at this highest level are near expert. First, they discuss the pros and cons of wearing school uniforms (see level 4). They exceed the precedent multi-structural level, discussing questions such as: Does the constraint to wear a school uniform undermine the expression of one's personality, as clothing is considered a display of individuality? Are there negative effects on school attendance in poorer African countries, where many parents cannot afford expensive school clothing?

As, from level 2 onward, each level builds on the preceding one, it is not very difficult for teachers to create learning activities that lead students from one level to the next. Worked examples may be given to the students so that they can find out by themselves the differences of quality from one level to the next. Not all students may reach levels 4 and 5, and for most learners advancing by the SOLO Taxonomy will not be a linear process. This, however, does not release teachers from their responsibility for the best possible outcomes of all students.

In contrast to taxonomies (Bloom, 1956) based on thinking, the **SOLO Model (**S**tructure of the O**bserved Learning Outcome) of Biggs and Collis (1982) describes the **quality of learning, taking written products of the students as research objects.** The learning outcomes are classified in five graded levels, from unilateral descriptions to expert considerations of various aspects of the subject.

Are there students whose learning is dominated by one of the brain hemispheres? Are there students that learn best when applying their individual learning style? For decades, teachers presented the same content in various ways in order to correspond to the different learner types and the learning styles of their students. According to models of cognitive psychology, some learners seemed to prefer learning bit by bit, in an ordered way and relying on prescriptions and rules. This type of learning was considered to be based mostly on the left hemisphere of the brain. On the other hand, students with a preference for learning with the help of the right hemisphere were considered to prefer an intuitive and holistic approach to the learning content. Results of scientific research proved this contrast to be false, at least when it comes to learning. It seems true that the working mechanisms of the hemispheres differ to a certain extent, but these differences indicate nothing but tendencies and are in no way mutually exclusive.

Coffield and his co-authors (2004a, 2004b) analyzed seventy scientific studies into the working modes of the hemispheres and came to the conclusion that the cognitive learning style of an individual is neither innate nor invariable. The researchers instead found empirical evidence that a learner's cognitive style adapts to the context. What is stated for the working modes of the hemispheres also holds true for learner preferences described as visual, auditory, or kinesthetic. Therefore a whole-brain model is recommended, that is to say, learning opportunities should take as many brain functions as possible into account.

Every individual can and should use all learning styles. Today's challenges in private and professional life confront people with complex learning tasks which necessitate various working modes. Teachers have to invite their students to use those styles which they might neglect. The challenging task for the students, in school as well as in life, consists of applying unusual perspectives and procedures.

Petty (2009, pp. 35–36) offers an interesting example. A teacher is preparing a lesson based on a short story: The students have to put themselves in the position of the different main figures and to discuss in tandem or in teams the most important issues and meanings of the story. The results of the group work are to be presented in plenary. This learning activity can be labeled as based on the right hemisphere of the brain. To encourage students to avoid limiting their learning to one hemisphere, the teacher can pass four different hypotheses or interpretations to his or her learners. The students with the same hypothesis or interpretation work together and evaluate it on the basis of the short story. When presenting their results to the whole class they underpin their results – that is, if the interpretation is in their view in accordance with the text or not – with passages of the short story. In that way the students not only practice a change in perspective, but also learn that there may be more than one interpretation of the same story.

Teachers have to plan different presentations of content and various learning activities to invite students not to rely exclusively on a single style or strategy – for example, right hemispheric or left hemispheric, visual, auditory, or kinesthetic – but **to use as many working modes of the brain as possible.**

Which connections between motivation, feedback and mindset lead to better learning? As previously mentioned (see the beginning of Section 6.3), it is impossible to analyze and improve teaching without a good knowledge of the underlying learning processes of the students. The same is true for motivation, an essential factor of all learning, which Hattie scores with an effect size of d = 0.48 (rank 51 of 138) (Hattie, 2009, pp. 47–49).

Motivation is a so-called intervening variable, which is used to explain the relationship between independent and dependent variables. Motivation plays an essential role not only in school, but in an individual's whole life. Motivation cannot be directly observed. Most of the time we do not know why someone, for example, engages in social work, whereas another person in the same situation does not show any engagement. Therefore, it is very difficult for teachers to find adequate motivational strategies for every single student.

Undoubtedly, classifications such as intrinsic or extrinsic motivations, which dominated in the past decades, do not lead to better instructional designs. At the most, they may give teachers a hint as to why some students engage more in learning than others. Therefore, the following considerations focus attention on those motivational aspects that can be influenced in a positive way by adequate teaching strategies.

Students engage in learning when two conditions are fulfilled. The goals, standards, or objectives must be of value for them. But it is not sufficient that they attribute personal value to the goal: They must be convinced that they can reach it. These two preconditions are summarized in the following formula.

> motivation =
> value of the targeted goal × expectancy of reaching the goal

The value of the goal and the interrelated expectancy of successful learning are not simply added, but multiplied. If a student attends a lesson without confidence that he or she may reach the goals, the motivation is zero even if he or she attributes high value to the goal or objective. By the same token, the motivation equals zero when the student sees no value of the goal even though he or she might have all necessary prerequisites to reach it.

The earlier mentioned formula is a twofold challenge for educational practitioners. First, they have to explain the value of the goals in a student-friendly way. Second, they must further single learners' confidence that they can reach the goal with realistic learning efforts.

1. How can teachers convince their students of the value of the targeted goals?
   - First of all, the goals and objectives chosen on the basis of the curriculum must be meaningful and interesting for the learners and in relation to their life context.
   - As times goes by, teachers should illustrate step-by-step the values of the specific subject matter for learners' lives, even if the students do not identify with those at once.
   - Learning processes have to be ideated in order to correspond to the students' needs for recognition and appreciation, as well as for social belonging (Maslow, 1970).
2. In which ways can teachers further positive expectancies with regard to learning success? This challenge for teachers is much greater than that of convincing students of the targeted goal's value. In this situation we can rely on the scientific findings of Dweck (1999; 2006). According to her we can differ between two groups of learners

(both of 40 percent; the remaining 20 percent are not classifiable. For the following see also Dweck, 2012).
- The first group consists of children and adolescents convinced that intelligence and the aptitude for a subject matter (e.g., mathematics, science, or foreign languages) are innate, and that these cannot be much influenced by learning and effort. That is what Dweck calls a fixed mindset.
- The students of the second group believe that achievement can be improved by learning; that is, these learners think that learning efforts can alter innate dispositions in a positive way. In the terminology of Dweck, this is a growth mindset.

The students of the first group avoid situations in which they may seem less intelligent or in which they have to undergo effort. In general they refuse help because they are convinced that they will not benefit from support and that others may notice their inability. They try to rest in their comfort zone. This attitude leads to increasing knowledge deficits in the respective subject matter(s). Learners with a fixed mindset take this as proof of their (partial) inability. According to Dweck, one of the remedies that mitigate a fixed mindset may be the analysis of biographies of famous and important personalities with learning problems (Dweck, 2012).

The learners with a growth mindset have a positive attitude toward difficulties and mistakes. In their view, these are part of learning processes. If they do not encounter problems with a task, they know that it was too easy for them. Their effort grows with the challenge. Before seeking or accepting help, they try to find a solution to their learning problem on their own.

In general, teachers should inspire the students with confidence that all learners can improve when they make the necessary efforts. Dweck, who replicated her research several times, discourages teachers as well as parents from praising children for their intelligence. This type of praise backfires because it puts children and adolescents in a fixed mindset and induces them to avoid necessary challenges.

> They don't want to risk looking stupid or risk making mistakes. Kids praised for intelligence curtail their learning in order to never make a mistake, in order to preserve the label you gave to them.
>
> [...]
>
> Students praised for the process they engaged in – their effort, their strategies, their focus, their perseverance – these kids take on hard tasks and stick with them, even if they make lots of mistakes. They learn more in the long run. (www.intelltheory.com/dweck.shtml; last accessed August 2015)

> The earlier mentioned considerations regarding **a fixed and a growth mindset** apply to students of all ages and to all subject matters. Nevertheless, teacher strategies that aim at **furthering motivation** have to adapt to the special learning context, and especially to the individual student. Praise of intelligence is counterproductive, whereas praising effort and perseverance improve learning attitudes and achievement.

6.4. MET – A MODEL OF EFFECTIVE TEACHING AND SUCCESSFUL LEARNING

As explained in Section 2.2 (see box), a model is a logical framework intended to represent reality, in this case the course of teaching practice from the planning to the conclusion of a lesson or a teaching unit. Similar to a road map, the MET is created to show particular aspects. Although a model cannot represent reality, it tries to come as close to the truth as possible.

As mentioned several times (see Introduction to Chapter 6), the MET is backed up by experimental research as well as by other quantitative and qualitative findings.

It might seem a contradiction: On the one hand, I opt for an evidence-informed teaching model; on the other, teacher personality and intuition are underscored as indispensable features of effective teaching and successful learning. In my view, what seem incompatible at first sight not only relate to each other, but correspond to the very nature of education. A complex and multilayered activity like teaching should rely not only on results from different types of research, but also on all human resources possible. My emphasis on human qualities does not mean that we should renounce advancements of scientific research. The challenge consists in an informed choice. Democracy does not depend on research methodology; it depends on what we make out of all resources available to the benefit of the individual learner (De Florio-Hansen, 2014a; 2014b).

MET – 30 Steps to Effective Teaching and Successful Learning
Planning the Lesson (see Chapter 7)

1. Choice of curricular goals linked to prior learning; goals, standards, and objectives should be motivating and relate to students' lives.
2. Explicit connection to students' existing knowledge; prior knowing consists of subject matter as well as of world knowledge.

3. Possibly subdivision of the goal(s) in several objectives; in most cases, students need this fragmentation in order to grasp new knowledge and skills.
4. Thorough planning of content presentation and practice; presentation and practice have to fit the special subject matter content as well as the students' needs and interests.
5. Elaboration of alternative forms of content presentation and practice; it is important to plan and elaborate alternative forms to be prepared for students' learning difficulties.

Starting the lesson (see Chapter 7)

6. Explanation of the goals, the learning intentions, and the success criteria; students need to be informed in advance of what respective knowledge and skills they should learn and why, and how they can evaluate the success of their learning processes.
7. Display of the values connected to the particular knowledge and skills; depending on the age of the students, explanations are often less effective than examples.
8. Encouraging students with regard to their possibilities of meeting the goals; student learning outcomes depend to a large extent on their self-confidence.
9. Promotion of students' commitment through motivating hooks or other hints; teachers should dispose of a variety of inspiring examples and short narrations in order to increase students' engagement.

Presenting knowledge and skills (see Chapter 8)

10. Comprehensible explanations or demonstrations of learning content; explanations, modeling, and demonstrations have to be in accordance with students' learning possibilities.
11. Redundant explanations; various formulations of content knowledge and/or skills help students to grasp the learning content and store it in memory.
12. Illuminating, student-centered examples; examples should be easy to understand in order to attract the attention of the students.
13. Exemplification and demonstration of knowledge and skills through visual/audiovisual aids; as visual memory plays an important role in storing knowledge, a display of different means such as pictures, tables, and especially different digital media could possibly be incorporated.

14. Presentation of the steps leading to solution through worked examples; not only in mathematics but in (almost) all subject matters, worked examples show students what to do in order to reach goals and objectives.

Questions and Answers (see Chapter 8)

15. Assertive questioning; during the whole lesson, but especially when presenting new content, teachers have to check through adequate questioning if and what students have understood.
16. Attentive answering of students' questions; students' questions should never be ignored, as they show if and how students have conceived the learning content.
17. Positive attitude toward mistakes; students need to know that mistakes are welcome, as they offer further learning possibilities.
18. Questions regarding the presented knowledge and skills; these questions should be formulated in such a way that all students have an opportunity to take part in the lesson.
19. Repeated presentation of the learning content; if it is found that the students did not comprehend the learning content on the whole or in part, it has to be re-taught.

Guided Practice (see Chapter 9)

20. Graded activities for practice including short self-assessments; under the guidance of the teacher, all students are enabled through practice to improve and evaluate their understanding of the learning content.
21. Further worked examples with explanations of the single steps leading to the solution; in this context the worked examples are part of student practice (see no. 14).
22. Decision on the social setting; by agreement with the students, it is decided whether guided practice takes place in seatwork, in tandem, or in small groups.
23. Formative feedback; it is (most of the time) for the teacher to give feedback to single students in difficulty or asking for help.
24. Short explanations directed to individual students; the teacher should invite all students to seek help when their understanding of the new learning content is found to be insufficient during practice.

Independent Practice (see Chapter 9)

25. Thoroughly planned and elaborated activities that allow for deep learning and transfer; these activities are more complex and demanding, in order to further critical and creative thinking.
26. De-contextualization; the contexts in which the presented knowledge and the skills occur are varied so that students can transfer the learned content to relevant (new) situations.
27. Decision on the social setting; by agreement with the students, it is decided whether independent practice takes place in seatwork/ homework, in tandem, or in small groups (see Chapter 10).
28. Formative feedback; this time it should not predominantly be given by the teacher, but rather by peers (see Chapter 11).
29. Feedback through tests; besides grading, summative feedback possibly could take forms that lead to further learning.

Transition or Conclusion (see Chapter 9)

30. At the end of an important learning phase or at the end of the lesson, the teacher and the students summarize the learning processes so that the students can make sense of the past learning experiences.

Scaffolding teaching and learning processes does not mean prescribing the earlier steps of the MET, but rather **displaying detailed research-based options** that enable teachers to make adequate decisions in order to improve learning in their specific context.

6.5. RESEARCH EVIDENCE AND TEACHER EXPERTISE

Imagine the following situation: You are convinced that one of your greatest challenges is to help students not to limit their learning to superficial knowledge representations, but to reach deeper and conceptual learning. With this intent in your mind and your heart, you are looking for possibilities to initiate and further the conceptual networking of your learners. By chance you have heard about a strategy called "concept mapping" that reaches high effect sizes. A concept map is more elaborate than a mind map. It is an elaborate graphic representation that reaches high effect sizes in different mega-analyses. So you consult Hattie's study, in which concept mapping scores d = 0.57 (rank 33). You skim through his brief explanations:

> Concept mapping involves the development of graphical representations of the conceptual structure of the content to be learnt. [...] As with behavioral objectives and learning hierarchies, concept mapping derives from Ausubel's (1968) claim that concepts can be organized in hierarchical form in the cognitive structure, and it helps learning if concepts related to what is to be learned can be linked to the concept maps a student already has. (Hattie, 2009, p. 168)

Looking for concrete examples, you try to find some hints in Hattie's *Visible Learning for Teachers* (2012). In part II, chapter 5, *Starting the Lesson*, you come to table 5.1, *Effect sizes from various programs*. In this overview, concept mapping scores d = 0.60 (rank 25) (Hattie, 2012, p. 85). You compare the indications in Hattie's study with those of his teacher guide: The number of meta-analyses increased from six to seven, the number of studies from 287 to 325, and the number of effects from 332 to 378, whereas the number of people remained steady at 8,471, as did the standard error 0.0051 (medium). How is that possible? You do not know if this is a simple error on the part of the researcher or if it is due to the secrets of statistics. In any case, there are no examples available that you could somehow adapt to the needs and interests of your students.

I cannot do anything other than advise teachers to be careful when taking the indications of concrete effect sizes into account (as I have already underscored many times). The devil is in the detail! These considerations do not imply at all that you should neglect research findings. But as no busy teacher has the time to go into the details of research, especially those of meta-analyses, research results should be taken as the indication of relevant tendencies, but not as inalterable truth.

Given that it is already difficult to find out the effects of a single teaching or learning strategy, such as concept mapping or advance organizers, you can easily imagine how difficult it is to score a comprehensive teaching program like DI. As previously mentioned, DI reached d = 0.59 (rank 26). Consulting the appendixes of Hattie's two books (2009: Appendix A, 2012: Appendix B; the pages of the appendixes are not numbered), you can see that the results are unvaried. But consulting the rubric variable, that is the precise teaching intervention, you may have doubts as to whether DI is useful for your teaching context.

The four meta-analyses refer to *DI in Special Education* (White, 1988), *DI on Reading* (Adams & Engelmann, 1996), *DI from Comprehensive School Reforms* (Borman et al., 2003), and *Teaching Methods in Algebra* (Haas, 2005).

As early as the first edition of his extensive study *Lehren und Lernen – aber wie? Empirisch-experimentelle Forschungen zum Lehren und Lernen im Unterricht (Teaching and Learning – But In What Way? Experimental Research into Teaching and Learning in the Classroom*, 2004), Wellenreuther states that it is very difficult (if not impossible) to evaluate a multifaceted and comprehensive teaching program like DI as a whole. Nevertheless, he describes the results of Project Follow Through. According to the German educationalist, however, it is possible to evaluate DI in an indirect way. As single features contribute to the overall success of the program, Wellenreuther suggests looking at empirical research, RCTs, or, if these are not available, quasi-empirical studies, into single aspects of DI. It is easy to share his view that the efficacy of the whole program is caused by the aggregation of its single elements, for example structured teaching, teacher clarity, and a propitious learning climate that welcomes errors and does not label students (for details and effect sizes see Chapters 7–11).

In a completely revised new edition of his book (2014), Wellenreuther consequently sorts empirical studies in terms of important single features contributing to the overall success of DI. An informative example is the experimental research of Klahr and Nigam (2004) dealing with the effects of DI in comparison to Discovery Learning. The two scholars analyze how children in elementary schools (at grade 3) acquire experimentation skills through planning and carrying out experiments in science. In their experimental study, Klahr and Nigam show that discovery learning is less effective than teacher-guided instruction.

The title of this section of the chapter, *Research Evidence and Teacher Expertise*, is not intended as a division into two contrasting parts. The expertise of the teacher, as of any educational practitioner, is an obligatory characteristic of educators, as expertise and competence are indispensable features of all professions. How do popular teacher websites describe the qualities of a great teacher?

A great teacher

- is very engaging and holds the attention of students in all discussions;
- establishes clear objectives for each lesson and works to meet those specific objectives during each class;

- has effective discipline skills and can promote positive behaviors and change in the classroom;
- has good classroom management skills and can ensure good student behavior, effective study and work habits, and an overall sense of respect in the classroom;
- maintains open communication with parents and keeps them informed regarding what is going on in the classroom as far as curriculum, discipline, and other issues. They make themselves available for phone calls, meetings, and email;
- has high expectations of their students and encourages everyone to always work at their best level;
- has thorough knowledge of the school's curriculum and other standards they must uphold in the classroom. They ensure their teaching meets those standards;
- has incredible knowledge of the subject matter they are teaching. They are prepared to answer questions and keep the material interesting for the students;
- is passionate about teaching and working with children. They are excited about influencing students' lives and understand the impact they have;
- develops a strong rapport with students and establishes trusting relationships.
(http://teaching.monster.com/careers/articles/9144-top-10-qualities-of-a-great-teacher?page=10; last accessed August 2015)

Amanda Ripley, a renowned U.S. journalist who often analyzes educational issues, presents the initiative *Teach for America* (TFA) in an article entitled "What Makes a Great Teacher?" (Ripley, 2010). She focuses on the required relentless mindset of the TFA teachers, which comprises reflectiveness, perseverance, and grit (ibid., pp. 15–16):

> First, great teachers tended to set big goals for their students. [. . .] Great teachers [. . .] constantly reevaluate what they are doing.

> Superstar teachers had four other tendencies in common: they avidly recruited students and their families into the process; they maintained focus, ensuring that everything they did contributed to student learning; they planned exhaustively and purposefully – for the next day or the year ahead – by working backward from the desired outcome; and they worked relentlessly, refusing to surrender to the combined menaces of poverty, bureaucracy, and budgetary shortfalls. (ibid., p. 9)

When focusing on the single steps of the MET in the next chapters (see Chapters 7–11), we will come back to these issues in more detail. Missing in the necessary discussion of research- and/or evidence-based education until now, in my view, are concrete examples of how to transform the suggestions of scientific findings into concrete teaching and learning activities. Teachers need concrete actions that show what a research result means for a lesson plan so that they can decide if the intervention is worthwhile for them, and above all for their students.

REVIEW, REFLECT, PRACTICE

1. Compare Madeline Cheek Hunter's Lesson Plan Design to Hattie's Model of DI. Which differences are there between the two models? (Enter one of the following terms in a search engine: Madeline Hunter Lesson Plan Format, Madeline Hunter's Effective Teaching Model or Madeline Hunter Method).
2. Explain the three steps of the learning theory dating back to Bereiter (2002) in your own words. How do transitions take place? Compare your findings to those of other students or colleagues.
3. Together with other students or colleagues, elaborate another example for the SOLO Taxonomy. Try it out with other students or in your classroom. You have two options: Invite students to give their view of a controversial issue or prepare an essay at level three of the SOLO Model as a worked example and ask students to comment on it.
4. Consulting Hattie's list of the 138 (over 150) factors that have an impact on student achievement (Hattie, 2009, pp. 297–300), try to relate effect sizes to the teacher qualities described in the blog and by Amanda Ripley. Work in tandem or in teams with other students or colleagues. Try to find out which characteristics are not in accordance with Hattie's findings.
5. In your view, what makes a great teacher? Choose five features of the blog list and Ripley's indications and explain to another student or a colleague why those, in your view, are more important than others. Try to scale them, putting the most important at the top of your list.

7

Planning and Starting the Lesson

Finally we get to practice, some of you might be thinking. In some ways you are right, because in the following chapters we will find out in what ways we can concretize the single steps of the Model of Effective Teaching (MET) for your teaching. As my model does not apply to a particular school system but should be open to teachers all over the world aiming at improving their classroom practice, the following examples do not refer to a special curriculum. But I am confident that my examples can be adopted and adapted to many teaching and learning contexts. Above all, they are presented to show what it means to be a teacher. Furthermore, no proposal can be transferred one-to-one. Even if you want to apply a new teaching strategy proposed by a colleague who works in a comparable context, you have to look for adaptation. Every intervention program and every teaching strategy or technique call for changes in order to reach the individual learners. Or do you use your textbooks like programmed instruction?

Before starting with explanations and examples of how to plan and start a lesson or a teaching unit, we will do what you are expected to do with your learners. How can you as a teacher relate to the knowledge you – hopefully – have acquired during the previous Chapters 1–6? We will do so consulting the *Sutton Report* of October 2014. I have chosen the research results of Rob Coe and colleagues of Durham University, U.K., in order to show you that reviewing is more effective when it does not consist of simple repetition, but offers food for further thought.

In general you are right when you expect more concrete considerations, but, nevertheless, they are based on theory, or, better, on various theoretical foundations. Thoughtful practice is always grounded in theory. Think of the following example. You want your students to summarize an experiment you have conducted in class in one of the most recent lessons. You hesitate to invite your learners to summarize it in written form because you have doubts that they well remember all important details. You reflect on what to do: Should you carry out the experiment again? What about revising the important features in the form of Interactive Whole-class Teaching, giving all students an opportunity to recall the experiment? What if you summarize it yourself? Or is a worked example in the form of a written summary more appropriate? Whatever decision you arrive at, it is based not on one but on various theories, for example theories about the limits of short-term memory, theories about learning from oral or written models, and assumptions of spaced versus massed practice (Hattie, 2009, pp. 185–186, d = 0.71, rank 12).

Planning a lesson or a teaching unit implies considerable work on the part of the teacher. You have to go through every detail as far as you can to anticipate the extent to which your teaching will promote the appropriate learning processes for your students (see MET, steps 1–5). Presupposing that even well-planned teaching does not lead to adequate learning of all your students, you have to be prepared to compensate misinterpretations with teaching and learning alternatives at hand.

Before we discuss possible beginnings of a lesson, you will read about a little boy's experience with Miguel, his teacher of Spanish, who planned a lesson start that captured the attention of most of his students.

For me, starting the lesson (see MET, steps 6–9) is an enterprise comparable to sailing around the world without the assistance of others. Before the start of your journey you have prepared everything well and gone through every detail and eventuality. But your preparations do not guarantee that situations you did not imagine will not arise. The expertise of a teacher does not consist only of his ability to plan a lesson or a comprehensive teaching unit and put it into practice; at least as important as these basic tools of the teaching profession are knowledge and flexibility regarding how to surmount unexpected difficulties. In educational practice, unforeseen problems arise quite often. It is useful to analyze them later on in an evaluation, or rather in a reflection-on-action. In the teaching situation, however, you are asked to act immediately, with great flexibility and intuition.

7.1. A THOUGHTFUL REVIEW OF EFFECTIVE TEACHING

The Sutton Trust is a foundation set up in 1997, dedicated to improving social mobility through education (www.suttontrust.com/newsarchive/many-popular-teaching-practices-are-ineffective-warns-new-sutton-trust-report/; last accessed August 2015). The Director of Policy and Development at the Sutton Trust introduces the research-based report of 2014 in the following way:

> *What Makes Great Teaching*, by Professor Rob Coe and colleagues at Durham University, warns that many common practices can be harmful to learning and have no grounding in research. Examples include using praise lavishly, allowing learners to discover key ideas by themselves, grouping attitudes by ability and presenting information to students based on their "preferred learning" style. On the other hand, some other teaching approaches are supported by good evidence of their effectiveness. Many of these are obvious and widely practiced, but others are at odds with common assumptions. (ibid.)

The Report lists six common components, the first two of which show strong evidence of impact on student outcomes, whereas the following two (no. 3 and no. 4) display moderate evidence of impact and the final two (no. 5 and no. 6) only some evidence of impact on student achievement. So, which are the most important?

In their executive summary, Coe and colleagues underscore as most effective:

1. (Pedagogical) content knowledge

> The most effective teachers have deep knowledge of the subjects they teach, and when teachers' knowledge falls below a certain level it is a significant impediment to students' learning. As well as understanding of the material being taught, teachers must also understand the ways students think about the content, be able to evaluate the thinking behind students' own methods, and identify students' common misconceptions. (Coe et al., 2014, p. 2)

Is an expert's content knowledge to be considered *pedagogical content knowledge?* We know that people who are very competent in their profession quite often cannot explain (part of) their expertise to a layperson in an understandable way. In fact, Coe et al. include in this very important requirement of a teacher a detailed view of how students at different ages and with differing abilities conceive of the content of the respective subject matter.

It is astonishing that the research led Hattie to score teacher subject matter knowledge as low as $d = 0.09$ (rank 125 of 138 factors). This finding is based on two meta-analyses comprising ninety-two primary studies, but Hattie does not indicate the number of people that participated in the studies (Hattie, 2009, pp. 113–115). With reference to Shulman (1987), Hattie admits that the claim for teachers' good subject matter content knowledge is plausible, but that he did not find sufficient research to underscore the importance. Once again: Effect sizes should be considered with caution.

Pedagogical content knowledge is followed by:

> 2. Quality of instruction
>
> Includes elements such as effective questioning and use of assessment by teachers. Specific practices, like reviewing previous learning, providing model responses for students, giving adequate time for practice to embed skills securely and progressively introducing new learning (scaffolding) are also elements of high quality instruction. (Coe et al., 2014, pp. 2–3)

It is commonplace that well-planned and thoroughly prepared instruction is a decisive factor for improving students' learning outcomes. In Hattie's study (2009, pp. 115–118), the quality of teaching scores $d = 0.44$ and occupies rank 56 (of 138). Here, too, the number of participants is not available, but all of them are college or university students rating their teachers. Also in this case, as in many others, indications of effect sizes are relative.

According to Coe and colleagues, classroom climate and classroom management have only moderate impact. Teacher beliefs, mostly their theories and conceptual models of teaching and learning, as well as professional behaviors, for example participation in professional development and communicating with parents, show only some evidence of impact on student outcomes (see Coe et al., 2014, p. 3). According to my experience as a teacher, classroom management intended in a productive way is very influential (see Section 8.1). Moreover, the impact of a particular intervention program or strategy depends to a large extent on the empathy of the teacher, which means the point up to which he or she is able to anticipate the students' desired reactions to the planned activities.

7.2. PLANNING THE LESSON

Do you remember the five steps of lesson planning? Here they are again:

1. Choice of curricular goals linked to prior learning; goals, standards, and objectives should be motivating and relate to students' lives.
2. Explicit connection to students' existing knowledge; prior knowing consists of subject matter as well as of world knowledge.
3. Possibly subdivision of the goal(s) in several objectives; in most cases, students need this fragmentation in order to grasp new knowledge and skills.

4. Thorough planning of content presentation and practice; presentation and practice have to fit the special subject matter content as well as the students' needs and interests.
5. Elaboration of alternative forms of content presentation and practice; it is important to plan and elaborate alternative forms to be prepared for students' learning difficulties.

How should we choose goals, standards and objectives in accordance with the needs and interests of the students? When going through ready-made lesson plans, textbook units, or cookbook recipes, one of my greatest problems is the fact that the authors in general underscore those objectives that will be reached by carrying out their more or less detailed suggestions. It goes without saying that teachers have to implement the educational goals and standards fixed by the state. Quite often, however, statements such as *learner-centered* or *corresponding to real life* in the introductions that accompany the lists of standards are nothing more than rhetorical exercises without concrete reference to individual learners (see Concluding Remarks).

When planning a teaching intervention, the most important question often remains unasked: In what ways does the chosen learning content or skill refer to the needs and interests of the students? Is the goal challenging enough to contribute to the development of targeted knowledge and skills? Moreover, what is a challenging goal? By which means can teachers find out and decide on goals that are a challenge for every individual student? Goals are a sort of bridge between the past – that is, what the student already knows and can do – and the future – which means the knowledge and skills the learner will acquire with the help of the teacher or expert peers.

More than once, Hattie (2009) makes clear that challenging goals should not be confused with "do-your-best" goals. Goals have to be chosen with the intention of offering an identifiable progress for the single student. The goals should not only be in accordance with the curriculum. Furthermore, it is the well-tuned challenge that is decisive for success:

> A major reason difficult goals are more effective is that they lead to a clearer notion of success and direct the student's attention to relevant behaviors or outcomes, whereas "doing your best" can fit a very wide range of goals. It is not the specificity of the goals but the difficulty that is crucial to success. (Hattie, 2009, p. 164)

According to Hattie, challenging goals score $d = 0.56$ (rank 34). As the difficulty of mastering the goal is a crucial factor, how can we fix an adequate degree of challenge? As a rule of thumb, Hattie proposes "at least 90 percent known to unknown items in the task" (ibid., p. 166). In my experience, 70 percent known to 30 percent unknown is more convenient, but the ratio depends on the age of the students and their ability. Furthermore, we have to see the difference between surface and deep learning, and we should not forget that it is the teacher who facilitates the acquisition of knowledge and skills.

When choosing sufficiently challenging goals for the students, we should not limit them to knowledge and skills, but consider attitudes too.

Is the selected goal challenging enough to influence the students' attitudes? This last aspect, even though the most crucial and the most difficult to attain, plays only a subordinate role – if any – in the majority of prescriptions and suggestions. Attitudes toward learning, toward one's self, toward society, and toward the world are at least as important as knowledge and skills if we want to contribute to the personal development of any single student. This is an ambitious goal, sure – but that does not release teachers from any responsibility.

It is not the student that has to be adapted to the objectives, but the other way round. Goals, standards, and objectives have to be selected in order to help students to learn something for themselves, that is to say for an improvement of their personal lives, for their participation in the society they live in, and for the cultural surroundings of which they want to be part. Do the chosen objectives promote student attitudes toward others, toward society, and/or toward cultural life contexts? What can we do to adapt the goals, standards, and objectives prescribed by the state and integrated into textbooks or other teaching materials so that we can possibly reach all our students?

This is not an invitation to boycott the state standards; on the contrary. But they should not dominate your choices in a way that undermines your personality and those of your students. Teachers have to strive for the best possible results for their learners. We can express this challenge in evidence-informed terms. Teacher expectations that all students can improve and make gains in their learning are decisive to whatever a teacher might plan. Teachers as well as all educational practitioners should have the greatest aspirations with regard to the learning outcomes of their students. Not labeling students is crucial for success in learning as well as in life. In Hattie's list of 138 factors influencing achievement, *labeling students* reaches rank 21; the effect size is indicated as $d = 0.61$ (Hattie, 2009, pp. 124–125). Regarding teacher expectations, Hattie states:

Based on this evidence, teachers must stop overemphasizing ability and start emphasizing progress (steep learning curves are the right of all students regardless of where they start), stop seeking evidence to confirm prior expectations but seek evidence to surprise themselves, find ways to raise the achievement of all. Stop creating schools that attempt to look in prior achievement and experiences, and be evidence informed about the talents and growth of *all* students by welcoming diversity and being accountable for all regardless of the teachers' or schools' expectations. (Hattie, 2009, p. 124; author's emphasis)

Example: Talking about Preferences and Hobbies

This learning activity can be part of different subject matters. Let us consider the following learning context: As agreed, with your learners you will read the novel *Breath* by Tim Winton, a contemporary Australian writer (born in 1960). Winton's novel published in 2008 (Sydney: Picador) describes how windsurfing, the hobby of the protagonist and his friend, increasingly takes the form of a vital challenge when the two boys come into contact with Sando, a veteran big-wave surfer with a mysterious past (for a summary and reviews see www.bookbrowse.com/reviews/index.cfm/book_number/2140/breath).

Before starting to read Winton's book, you invite your students to reflect on and talk about their own preferences or hobbies. What seems a simple task at first turns out to be a demanding learning activity when you take your particular students into account. I propose you invite them to prepare at home a drawing of their hobby/hobbies or their preferred leisure activities. As it may not be easy to draw, for example, a computer game, the students might cut pictures out of magazines and brochures, which they assemble into collages.

Already at this point teacher clarity is of utmost importance (teacher clarity scores d = 0.75, occupying rank 8; Hattie, 2009, pp. 125–126). There will be surprises if you do not indicate precisely what the students are intended to represent in their drawings or collages. In accordance with the students, it has to be specified if they are expected to represent a preferred leisure activity or their hobby even if they do not pass the greatest amount of their free time with it. Or should the learners represent more than one of their hobbies, so as to show their widespread interests? This assignment is intended also as a hint to what will be the content of the next lessons; that is, Winton's windsurfing protagonists.

If enough time is available, the teacher might collect the drawings and graphic representations of all students with the aim to put them together on a poster to hang up in the classroom. This activity allows the teacher to gain deeper insights into the private lives of the students. He or she will not only get to know what the learners do in their leisure time, but also find out who does not have any hobbies, perhaps because of a lack of money: in this way the teacher is able to avoid embarrassing situations for some of the students. Furthermore, the teacher is already informed about hobbies that might draw mockery from peers and can prepare adequate reactions.

What can the learners do with the drawings of their leisure activities or with the poster put up in the classroom? There are several possibilities: for example, the students can guess what activity is represented or which classmates pass time with certain hobbies and – if you wish to do it before reading Winton's novel – can discuss the joys and dangers of particular leisure-time activities (De Florio-Hansen, 2014b).

In the first place, curriculum content and teaching objectives have to be chosen **in due consideration of students' needs and interests**. They have to be **challenging** and relate to students' lives. They should not be limited to **knowledge and skills**, but should also focus on the steady development of **attitudes**. Learning tasks and activities are designed to improve the learning outcomes of all students and **not only to correspond to prescribed goals and standards**.

How do we relate to learners' prior knowledge, skills and attitudes? The answer to this question is closely connected to the choice of challenging goals. In order to find out what is a real challenge for the learners, the teacher should have concrete ideas of what the students already know. The above question is at least threefold: First, how can a teacher find out what every single student already knows regarding content, skills, and attitudes in the particular subject matter? Second, and more demanding, what world knowledge did the learners accumulate in their families and their life contexts? Third, in what ways can teachers relate to the prior school and world experiences of individual students?

Most teachers follow external state and/or internal school curricula. Therefore it is not too difficult to answer the first question. Teachers know more or less exactly which pieces of knowledge and which skills the students have acquired by following the curriculum. Indications may also be drawn from textbooks and sequenced teaching materials.

Nevertheless, teachers cannot really be sure which aspects of knowledge, skills, and attitudes of previous learning are stored in students' long-term memory and, more importantly, which of these can be accessed without reviewing. In order to assert what their students are able to recall from previous didactic experiences, most teachers use some form of oral or written survey, or similar activities, such as the following selected examples for asserting arithmetic knowledge toward the end of elementary school:

1. I can write and read great numbers,
    for example: nine million six hundred thousand three hundred eighty
    ....
2. I can explain that 3,211 is more than 3,121.
    ....
3. I can do mental math:
    $4 \times 12 + 44 : 20 \times 15 : 9 =$ ....
4. I know mathematical language:
    division means ....
    addition means ....
    product means ....
    multiplication means ....

The students may indicate if they can do the single tasks well, less well, or not at all so that they need help.

Subject matter learning outcomes do not refer only to subject-related knowledge and skills. They comprise relations between subject matters, too – for example, between science and math or science and geography, between the mother tongue and a second language, or between different foreign languages, as well as between literature and art. A useful strategy to uncover students' attitudes initiated through previous learning is sentence completion, for example:

In my view lifestyle migration is ....,
because ....

Even if students have ample knowledge of different aspects of the respective subject matter, they may not create the desirable links between their knowledge. In most cases it is for the teacher to help them, through explicit indications or adequate activities, to assemble their existing concepts and schemata. According to Petty, the teacher can invite students to create the necessary connections between what they have already acquired and the new content through some type of assertive questioning (Petty, 2009, p. 206; effect size 0.91). In reflecting on the answers to these questions, most learners arrive at the bringing together of acquired knowledge, skills, and attitudes in order to be prepared for learning new content.

Sometimes a learner may know more about subject matter content than the rest of the class, for example as a result of a family member's profession. Teachers can invite these students to present part of the content or – a better option – to help their peers in tandem or in teams to overcome learning difficulties. N.B.: If an expert student is willing to tutor some peers, he or she must be prepared, not to say trained, to be of real help to the others (see Chapter 10).

While it is not easy to relate to all important features of previous subject matter knowledge, it is even more difficult to get an idea of the world knowledge that students of a certain age bring to the school and into the classroom. There are two different aspects of this. Developmental psychology presents models of the knowledge and skills children have acquired at a certain age. In this sense the concepts of Piaget, Vygotsky, and Bruner (see Chapter 1) are still relevant. Following Piagetian programs of cognitive development scores very high, at d = 1.28, rank 2, according to Hattie (2009):

> Thus, knowing the ways in which they think, and how this thinking may be constrained by their stages of development may be most important to how teachers choose materials and tasks, how the concept of difficulty and challenge can be realized in different tasks, and the importance of developing successive and simultaneous thinking. (Hattie, 2009, p. 43)

Unfortunately these results are based on one single meta-analysis comprising fifty-one primary studies.

Whereas it is possible to become informed regarding what most children know and can do through maturation, it is more difficult to have access to the knowledge, skills, and attitudes they have acquired in the particular contexts in which they live, including virtual worlds and social networks. Teachers should make all possible efforts to get to know their students. In what ways can teachers and other educational practitioners gain insights into the lives of their learners?

- They may profit from extracurricular activities, sports events, excursions, or exchange programs to look for more or less private contact with individual students.
- They can hold a regular consultation hour for their students.
- They should develop good knowledge of digital media and social networks.

- A good means to gain insights are children's and youth magazines.
- Graham Nuthall's *The Hidden Lives of Learners* (2007) reveals a great deal about students' thoughts and feelings (see Nuthall, chapters 9 and 10).

The following summary of lesson planning includes the answer to the third question: In what ways can teachers relate to the prior school and world experiences of individual students?

Effective Lesson Planning Means:

- giving priority to students' needs and interests;
- involving the learners with lesson planning;
- adapting prescribed goals, standards, and objectives to the respective learning context in order to further motivation and contact with students' lives;
- getting to know the hidden lives of the learners;
- integrating separate aspects of knowledge and skills into a meaningful whole;
- choosing adequate parts of textbooks and other teaching and learning materials in view of the particular objectives;
- thoroughly planning details of the lesson or unit, namely starting, presenting new content, phases of guided and independent practice, and evaluation through feedback;
- being self-critical: to be a well-liked teacher is desirable but not the leading goal of teaching; effective teaching aims at the successful learning of all students.

7.3. THE REALM OF THE SMARTEST

Emily is in the eleventh grade of high school; her little brother Nick attends a private elementary school. Their parents, both engineers at a great construction company that operates in Latin America, have chosen the private elementary school for Nick because it offers Spanish as a foreign language from grade two. The very popular teacher of Spanish is a young man from Spain whose second language is English.

Despite the great difference in age, Emily has a good relationship with her little brother. Nick is an uncomplicated, cheerful child. There is only one thing that she cannot stand: Nick wants to share most details of his Spanish lessons with his sister, even when she has friends over.

Several times Emily has told him not to disturb them, but without great success. Today she is with Sophia, a new girlfriend, when Nick suddenly comes in:

EMILY: Oh, Nick...
NICK: I must tell you something. You can't imagine what happened in our Spanish lesson today.
EMILY: We can talk about it later on. You see I have a new friend over. Sophia, that's my brother Nick.
SOPHIA: Hi, Nick.
NICK: Hi, Sophia. Pleased to meet you.
EMILY: As you can see, he is well educated, above all when he wants something.
SOPHIA: But why not let him tell what is so important for him. He seems to burst with joy.
EMILY: If it doesn't bother you.
SOPHIA: Not at all! I have got no siblings. I find it quite amusing that a Spanish lesson can cause such interest. If our Spanish classes were like that...
EMILY: You are right. So what happened?
NICK: We made a fantasy trip with closed eyes; we were on a beach and Miguel wrote some Spanish words in the sand with a little branch. We went further and further along the beach. There was also music playing.
SOPHIA: What music? A band on the beach?
NICK: No, no, it was sort of slow music, that Miguel probably chose to keep us quiet. From time to time he carved another word into the sand, always in the plural.
EMILY: Perhaps irregular plural forms...
NICK: I didn't realize it during our fantasy trip, but you are right, the forms were different from those we had learned before.
SOPHIA: And what happened next?
NICK: At a certain point the teacher told us to open our eyes and tell him which words we remembered. I immediately named two and was allowed to come to the door to the realm of the smartest.
SOPHIA: The realm of the smartest? What does that mean?
NICK: Miguel always has great ideas when we start a lesson. This time he had made a sort of door out of card that can be opened. If you give the right answer, he opens the door.
It is the door to the realm of the smartest.
EMILY: If I understand well, those who give the right answer can enter the realm.
NICK: That would be too easy. On the other side of the door Miguel has placed flashcards, but we cannot see the questions. Then you choose a

card and if your answer is right you are allowed to go into the realm of the smartest. This time I didn't get in, but next time ...
SOPHIA: Perhaps Emily can help you.
NICK: Sister, what do you say?
EMILY: Yes, we'll do some exercises.
NICK: Cool, so I may not only be among the smartest but sooner or later I will join the Club of Hispophonics, as it is called.
SOPHIA: Perhaps you mean the Club of Hispanophones?
NICK: Yes, that is what Miguel said. What is it called?
EMILY: His-pa-no-phones. We will repeat it later on again so that you can impress the others tomorrow.
NICK: It's not so much the others but Miguel. He's really a good teacher.
SOPHIA: Yes, you are right. You are really lucky.

7.4. STARTING THE LESSON

Here once again are the steps for a good start to the lesson:

6. Explanation of the goals, the learning intentions, and the success criteria; students need to be informed in advance of what respective knowledge and skills they should learn and why, and how they can evaluate the success of their learning processes.
7. Display of the values connected to the particular knowledge and skills; depending on the age of the students, explanations are often less effective than examples.
8. Encouraging students with regard to their possibilities of meeting the goals; student learning outcomes depend to a large extent on their self-confidence.
9. Promotion of students' commitment through motivating hooks or other hints; teachers should dispose of a variety of inspiring examples and short narrations in order to increase students' engagement.

How can teachers introduce the goals and learning intentions so that their students can see the value of the respective knowledge, skills, and attitudes? Teachers have to find valuable answers to student questions such as: Why do I have to learn this? What does that mean in the world in which I live? The respective descriptions and examples are the starting point of the lesson.

How can students be informed about the learning intentions? A good means with which to inform the students about the learning content and the structure of the lesson are advance organizers, which Marzano, on the whole, scores at an effect size of 0.48. But the researcher makes important distinctions. Surface learning reaches 0.56, whereas the effect size of using advance organizers in the context of deep learning arrives at 0.78. Information on the targeted goals is more effective when the students add their own pieces to the advance organizer. In this case the advance organizer contributes to the learning outcome by an effect size of 1.2 (Marzano, 1998, Marzano et al., 2001).

How do the learners recognize that they have met the goals, or at least that they are a good way toward doing so? The students should know step by step during the flow of the lesson the degree to which they have reached the objectives. In this context it is crucial that the teacher takes the limits of the working memory into account. Perhaps you know or remember the formula *seven chunks plus minus two* (Miller, 1956), which as a rule of thumb is still valuable. A more detailed view offers the *Cognitive Load Theory* elaborated by J. Sweller (1988) (see Chapter 8).

Success criteria are often illustrated in the form of "Can-do" descriptions. These should not be vague, but as concrete as possible. "At the end of the lesson we will do this or that" is much better than formulations such as "you should be able to do this and that." Adequate portfolios further students' self-assessment as well as their self-confidence.

In my experience, a very decisive factor in starting the lesson and introducing the goals to be aimed at is the hook. In the following you will find a series of hooks that can be used alone, for example as a riddle, or in combination with one another according to the teaching and learning objectives (for the following see De Florio-Hansen, 2014b).

Example: A Choice of Hooks

Talking about one of the most amazing cities in the United States
A famous school of architecture
In 1871, a great fire broke out, destroying an area about 4 miles long and one mile wide – a large section of the city at the time. Fortunately, much of the city, including railroads and slaughterhouses, remained intact. The citizens took the opportunity to replace the previous wooden buildings with modern constructions of steel and stone. During the rebuilding period, the world's first skyscraper was erected in 1885, using a steel-skeleton construction.

To become president of the United States
In Frank Sinatra's song *New York, New York* it says:

If I can make it there
You know, I'm gonna make it anywhere ...

In a song about this city it may say:

> If you can make it there
> You know, you can become president of the United States …

A modern-day Robin Hood

From 1920 to 1930 approximately, an infamous American gangster of Italian origin led a crime syndicate in the city, dedicated to criminal activities such as smuggling illegal alcoholic beverages during Prohibition. Although they knew about his illegitimate occupation, many citizens saw him as a modern-day Robin Hood, because he used part of the money he made from his activities to sponsor charity projects.

Postal service

In the city we are looking for, there is a tower which, for a long time, was the highest building in the world. It lost its first rank, but still has its own zip code nowadays.

Beaches in the business district

Do you know another city where you can reach a beach in five minutes by foot from your school or your work place? There are twenty-four public beaches along 26 miles of the waterfront.

The Blind Men and the Elephant

In a guide (Viskochil, 1984) which shows 122 historic views from the collection of the city's Historical Society, you can find the reproduction of the famous poem The Blind Men and the Elephant by John Godfrey Saxe (1816–1887), based on an Indian parable. It starts like this;

> It was six men of Indostan
> To learning much inclined
> Who went to see the elephant
> (though all of them were blind),
> That each by observation
> Might satisfy his mind.

When thinking about inspiring formulations of a hook or another introductory form of goals, standards, and objectives, the six principles of Chip and Dan Heath are very useful. The Heath brothers carried out extensive research to find out what makes ideas stick. Chip Heath is a professor of organizational behavior in the Graduate School of Business at Stanford

University; Dan Heath is a senior fellow at Duke University's Center for the Advancement of Social Entrepreneurship.

They published their findings in a book entitled *Made to Stick* (Heath & Heath, 2007). As the principles refer to every form of exposition of content, they transferred their results from the domain of business to the field of education under the title *Teaching that Sticks* (2010). As the following principles are a helpful basis for teacher talk in general, we will come back to them during the following chapters.

Principle 1: Simplicity

To convey an idea in a simple form means to focus on the main point of the learning content and to communicate it in as simple and catchy a fashion as possible, relating it to the existing knowledge and concepts of the leaners. Examples, comparisons, and analogies contribute to simplicity.

The Heath Brothers compare the work of a teacher to that of a journalist: "Journalists use a model of writing called the 'inverted pyramid', which demands that the most important news be put in the first paragraph and then, with each successive paragraph, the news value declines" (Heath & Heath, 2010, p. 2). So you are forced to prioritize and to find the core message. When you have ranked the features of new learning content, you can go down to the bottom of your list and cancel the less important points. That is also a good exercise for students, who often find it very difficult to separate important from unimportant issues.

Principle 2: Unexpectedness

You unfold the new learning content like the plot of a mystery, arousing the curiosity of your students. Your story should contain a gap of knowledge that your students are eager to close. You can also invite the learners to make a prediction, called "concept testing" (Heath & Heath, 2010, p. 4).

According to the Heath brothers (and many other scientists), "curiosity arises when we feel a gap in our knowledge" (ibid.):

> Movies cause us to ask, *What will happen?* Mystery novels cause us to ask, *Who did it?* Sports contests cause us to ask, *Who will win?* Crossword puzzles cause us to ask, *What is a 6-letter word for psychiatrist?* [...]

> One important implication of the "gap theory" is that we need to open gaps before we close them. Our tendency is to tell students the facts. First, though, they must realize they need them. (ibid.)

Principle 3: Concreteness

To help students enter information in their short-term memory and store it later on in their long-term memory, the new content has to be described in form of actions and sensual experiences. At the start of the lesson, abstractions and specialized terms should be avoided. Abstract truths must be expressed in concrete language.

Example: Making Punctuation Visible by Using Macaroni

Chip and Dan Heath reproduce in detail a learning experience of an eighth-grade teacher that is worth reproduction. It shows that concreteness depends to a large degree on some extraordinary idea:

> The students were given cards with sentences printed on them that were missing punctuation like quotation marks, periods, exclamation points, commas, apostrophes. The students were divided into groups of two and three and were given baggies that contained elbow macaroni, small macaroni shells, and ritoni [sic; rotoni: pasta in short pieces with a helical shape; Oxford Dictionary]. The students were asked to place the pieces of macaroni in the correct place in the sentence. For example, they were given the sentence:
>
> Jackie shouted Gwen come back here
>
> The students had to use the elbow macaroni as commas and quotation marks, the ritoni [rotoni] and small macaroni shell together as an exclamation point, and the small macaroni shell as a period. I knew that a lot of my students were confused about whether the comma went inside or outside the quotation marks, so this gave my visual learners and really all of my students a chance to "see" the correct way to punctuate quotations. Once they were finished, they knew the sentence would read: Jackie shouted, "Gwen, come back here!" (Heath & Heath, 2010, p. 5)

Principle 4: Credibility

Credibility depends mainly on students being given the opportunity to test the information that the teacher wants to transmit. Furthermore, it consists of examples that make statistical results tangible so that the learners can relate them to something they can easily imagine.

When you have to use statistics in class, a helpful strategy is to focus on relationships, not on numbers. A good example is the probability of winning the lottery, which is about 1 in many millions. What if we ground the probability in a relationship? "You are more likely to be struck by lightning than to win the lottery" (Heath & Heath, 2010, p. 7).

Principle 5: Emotion

Many steps of a teaching and learning model such as the MET can be enriched by visual, audiovisual, and other aids that evoke the emotions of the students. Why not start the lesson with an extract from a movie or a song that relates to the following content, skill, or attitudes? Why not show at the beginning of a new teaching unit an enigmatic picture whose sense the students will discover during the flow of the lesson?

Example: A Lot of Prejudice

When introducing a teaching unit about intercultural communication, I wanted the students to recognize from the beginning at least two important preconditions of interculturality. First, we can make sense of cultural conventions only if we can relate what we see and hear to something known. Second, if based only on our suppositions, we have to be very careful before coming to a judgment.

I chose a documentary film about a nomadic tribe at an annual meeting in the Sahara. The selected extract from the documentary shows a series of young men in white garments moving back and forth toward a group of women who observe them attentively. The wide-open eyes of the men were surrounded with black; their open mouths offered a view of very white teeth. The scene was set to *Ave Maria*.

My students' guesses ranged from a theatre rehearsal to a secret society. They were amazed when we watched some other scenes of the documentary, hearing a speaker's commentary: It was sort of a beauty contest in the Sahara. The most beautiful men of the tribe exhibit themselves to be chosen by women – unmarried or married – to pass the following night with one of the winners. The learners discovered that they were full of preconceptions about the sexual lives of African women. Furthermore, we discovered that beauty depends on cultural conventions: The young nomad elected as winner of the beauty contest was not the one my students would have elected.

Principle 6: Stories

It goes without saying that most phases of a lesson or a teaching unit benefit from narrations. A story – it does not need to be a masterpiece – is in general more effective than the best explanations, because it touches parts of the brain that make the ideas behind the story stick. The narrative elements cause a sort of simulation: When the students hear, for example, the story about a historical character, many of them imagine themselves in the place of this great personality. So why not start the lesson with a story, provided it is short and significant?

Chip and Dan Heath explain the effect of stories (Heath & Heath, 2010, p. 10): "Mental simulation is not as good as actually doing something – but the next best thing. And, to circle back to the world of sticky ideas, what we're suggesting is that the right kind of story is, effectively, a simulation. Stories are like flight simulators for the brain."

Many scholars, for example Hattie and the Heath brothers, point out that educational practitioners or business executives display a behavior that can be described as the *Curse of Knowledge*. If a teacher or another expert has come to know many professional details, it is very difficult for them to put themselves in the position of a person that does not (yet) have that knowledge or expertise. Referring to Piaget's model of cognitive development (see Section 1.3), learning is very often more successful when we base it on concrete operations, even though the learners are already able to operate on a formal level.

> When starting the lesson, transparency of goals, learning intentions, and success criteria is crucial. **Teaching is more effective and learning more successful when students participate in planning and starting the lesson.** The form in which teachers convey what they have to say is very important. **Simplicity, unexpectedness, concreteness, credibility, emotions, and stories** are among the best tools at the disposal of teachers and – why not? – of students.

REVIEW, REFLECT, PRACTICE

1. Do you agree with Coe's findings that pedagogical content knowledge and quality of instruction are the most important issues of effective teaching? Why? Why not?
2. What are the main features of lesson planning? Compare your list to that of other students or colleagues and discuss your results.
3. What do you think of the reaction of the second teacher in the example *Teachers Can Make a Difference*? What would you have done in a similar situation?
4. Invent a hook for the introduction of a new learning content on the basis of one of the six principles of the Heath brothers. You can even combine more than one principle, for example emotions and stories. If possible, try your hook out in your classroom and discuss the learners' reactions with them.

8

Presenting Knowledge and Skills – Assertive Questioning

The presentation phase is the core unit of Direct Instruction or Interactive Whole-class Teaching. It is the most decisive phase of the Model of Effective Teaching (MET), too. As aforementioned, DI and similar teaching models are not to be confused with didactic teaching, which consists of one-way teacher-guided transmission of knowledge learned through repetition or rote learning.

Any scrupulously planned lesson or teaching unit will reach your learners only in part (or not at all) if you do not eliminate disruptive behavior or distractions as far as possible. At the outset of your teaching in a particular class, you should clarify the rules and routines of classroom and learning behavior with your students. Do you remember the advice of Esmé Raji Codell (see Section 1.5) to be consistent? "It means you do what you say and you say what you mean," telling the students: "This is the way we do things around here," sticking to articulated rules, procedures, and consequences without walking right into the trap of "inflexibility" (2009, p. 244).

Liem and Martin invite teachers to carefully "sequence lessons that comprise appropriately scripted/well-thought through instructions" (Liem & Martin, 2013, p. 368). Whereas Hattie's research into DI is limited to measurable achievement of college and university students, Liem and Martin's overview of research evidence is more differentiated and detailed. On the one hand, they describe empirical studies demonstrating "the effectiveness of various DI programs relative to other programs" (ibid., p. 366). On the other, they illustrate the varying results of DI in different subject matters and their dependence on student ability.

Their research report is not limited to cognitive achievement. Liem and Martin underscore the positive affective outcomes of DI, which are often negated by its critics. Furthermore, DI is in accordance with constructivist approaches, as it promotes the construction of knowledge and skills through well-sequenced systematic steps during the presentation phase and the following guided and independent practice (ibid., p. 368).

What is evident for DI programs on the whole is also demonstrated for single components of DI through empirical, mostly experimental, research findings. "Ongoing debates (see e.g., Kirschner, Sweller and Clark, 2006; Mayer, 2004; Tobias and Duff, 2009) have contrasted the achievement yield of DI and its various procedural components with that of minimally guided instructional approaches, including discovery learning, problem based learning, and enquiry-based learning" (ibid., p. 367).

In the context of *Cognitive Load Theory* (CLT), Sweller, its initiator, conducted – together with other educationalists – an experimental study entitled *The Effect of Written Text on Comprehension of Spoken English as a Foreign Language* (Diao et al., 2007). The authors make an interesting distinction between *biologically primary knowledge*, which is acquired by the child without external interventions even though the development can be supported by others, for example walking and speaking, and *biologically secondary knowledge* – that is, cultural knowledge – which is acquired through organized learning processes based on the *borrowing principle*. It is not the *randomness as a genesis principle* by which a learner acquires biologically secondary knowledge. Considering the amount of knowledge that humanity accumulated during centuries of randomized learning is impossible. Moreover, it would lead to an overload of short-term/working memory, which teaching models try to avoid.

For this reason, Sweller and his team advocate borrowing from the long-term memory of others. This is provided best through instruction. They add: "Techniques for facilitating knowledge acquisition through the borrowing principle are central for cognitive load" (Diao et al., 2007, p. 238). In my view, scientific truth sometimes has something to do with common sense. Why should learners not benefit from the expert knowledge of their teachers?

When stating that the presentation of knowledge and skills is the most important phase of instruction, this does not mean at all that it is the longest phase. Interactive presentation is crucial because it is the foundation of all further learning processes. Advocates of individualized learning – whatever they summarize under this label – do not take into account that the presentation of knowledge and skills is not only based on sequenced instructional items, but also interrupted by short assertive questions by the teacher and – hopefully – by the students (see Section 8.4) in order to ensure that all or at least most learners have got it.

Imagine the following: A teacher prepares a worksheet to transmit new content so that students can work alone or in small groups with the aim of acquiring new knowledge or skills. It is an illusion to think that such a procedure is to be considered as individualized. Students' individuality is much more restricted, because the teacher has to anticipate all erroneous paths the students might take. This limits them to rote learning and hinders the promotion of attitudes. Interactive Whole-class Teaching, on the contrary, provides more freedom of thinking for the learners than programmed transmission of content (besides the higher workload of teachers who try to create "individualized learning" worksheets). Nevertheless, in the MET (as in many similar teaching models), individualization is an important feature, especially beyond the presentation phase.

8.1. CLASSROOM MANAGEMENT AND CLASSROOM CLIMATE

The ApaeK (*Archiv für pädagogische Kasuistik*; www.apaek.de; last accessed July 2015), an initiative of the department of education at the University of Frankfurt, Germany, is a collection of more than seven hundred transcripts of entire lessons from all grades and subject matters. These transcripts – some of them commented upon by the lecturers – were elaborated by teacher students who, during practical stages at schools, observed the lesson they afterwards transcribed in order to allow for case studies of the department. It is not difficult to find lessons with more than insufficient classroom management. Teachers, evidently unable or unwilling to put an end to disruptive behavior, struggle through lessons with nearly no learning outcomes. How is that possible?

Classroom management is a decisive factor not only at the start of the lesson, when the learning goals are communicated and students are oriented to learn (Liem & Martin, 2013, p. 366), but also during all following steps of a model like the MET. Classroom management comprises two closely interrelated premises of effective teaching and successful learning; that is, on the one hand, the conduct of the teacher in the classroom, as well as, on the other, the learning atmosphere that results from teacher behavior.

Jerome Freiberg, professor at the College of Education, University of Texas, defines classroom management, underscoring its importance:

> Classroom management is the gatekeeper of learning and is framed by social, cultural, instructional, and organizational contexts. It provides teachers and students with the opportunity to participate and build a positive framework of interpersonal and academic interactions. (Freiberg, 2013, p. 228)

He draws on a great amount of research to show the eminent influence of classroom management and learning climate on student achievement, for example on the meta-analyses of Wang, Haertel, and Walberg (1993) and of Cornelius-White (2007). Another important source is the historical overview of research on classroom management conducted by Brophy (2006). There is such an abundance of research because "school discipline" is often "the primary educational concern for parents and the public" (Freiberg, 2013, p. 228).

Example: Teachers Can Make a Difference

That teachers can make a difference through their classroom management in shown the following example reported by the ApaeK, which provides not only lesson transcripts but also other documents, such as teacher students' personal statements. The following is an outline of an episode which the teacher student qualifies as a "valuable pedagogical event."

In a phase of independent practice in third grade, a boy uses his seat as rocking chair, runs through the classroom, throws himself to the floor, laughs, and shouts. He is disturbing not only the other kids but mostly the young teacher, who uses the sign agreed upon when she wants the students to be quiet and pay attention: She puts her finger on her mouth and raises her arm above her shoulder. The children all recognize that the teacher wants them to calm down, except the boy, who continues with his disruptive behavior. The teacher gets angry. Some of the classmates intervene, because the boy seems not to notice how much his behavior disturbs the teacher. He blushes and shows signs of a guilty conscience. The teacher student who observed and reported the scene estimated that the interruption of the lesson's flow took more than five minutes.

Another teacher starts the lesson with the same class with a short moving unit, from which the boy profits, making a lot of uncontrolled movements, laughing, and shouting. As the whole class is moving, the teacher allows this. At an agreed sign the students all sit down and take out their textbooks, except the little boy, who continues to fidget and to make noise. Immediately the teacher admonishes him to sit down. She speaks very loudly but does not show any sign of anger. The boy is frightened and recognizes that he did something wrong. He keeps more or less quiet during the whole lesson and participates in the learning activities, quite motivated.

The teacher student draws the following conclusion from this experience. The example shows that some students have to be admonished where they are, that is in class, and told that their behavior is disturbing others. Instead of losing much time and taking the student's behavior to heart, it seems better to admonish him and to clarify one's position.

Everyone – and all the more teachers and other education professionals – can imagine that classroom management and a propitious learning climate depend on a great amount of factors. Furthermore, the features of effective classroom management and a beneficial classroom climate are closely entwined. The following overview concentrates on the most important factors of classroom management and classroom climate. At the end of Section 7.4, a conclusive quote brings the main aspects together.

What are the most influential features of classroom management? What can teachers do to guarantee the basis of effective teaching and successful learning? Ample research on this matter mainly considers two aspects (Wellenreuther, 2014, pp. 303–305): prospective classroom management and active–reactive classroom management.

"Prospective" in this context means that teachers make clear statements about rules and routines from the beginning of their teaching activity in a class (see Section 7.4). It is not sufficient to explain them and write them down. Their concrete meaning and adherence to them has to be stressed to the learners again and again. Effective classroom management in this sense depends not only on agreements with the students; the principles of conduct also have to be transmitted to the parents, and, last but not least, discussed with colleagues that teach in the same class. School-wide rules and routines are a rational basis for the smooth flow of teaching and learning.

Prospective classroom management refers to social behavior such as work attitude, concentration, attention, and motivation. Teachers and students are held accountable for compliance with the agreed classroom behavior conventions. Prospective classroom management is completed by methodological factors, which structure knowledge and help students to create links between the concepts they have formed and stored in the brain, as well as prior learning experiences. The factors of prospective classroom management in the above sense have been amply researched and described by Evertson et al. (2004).

Active–reactive classroom management goes back to the studies of Kounin (1970), who wanted to overcome behavioral models of teacher conduct based on sanctions and external remuneration. Active–reactive classroom management refers to current events in the classroom that arise during the lesson. The social aspects of active–reactive classroom management in general are combined with adaptive teaching strategies such as task differentiation and scaffolding.

Both approaches, prospective and active–reactive classroom management, are complementary. There is no successful learning when the teacher does not conceive of classroom management in advance and is not eager to introduce rules and routines from his first time with the respective learning group. But this is not enough. The multiple events that come up during the flow of lessons call for a detailed repertoire of teacher strategies and techniques.

In this context, "teacher with-it-ness" – the term was introduced by Kounin (1970) – is crucial (Hattie, 2009, p. 102, d = 1.42). With-it-ness refers to the omnipresence of the teacher, who is able to foresee possible disruptive behavior or a lack of attentiveness caused by distractions. Teachers are held to prevent them not by having recourse to sanctions, but in an emotionally objective way (as with the second teacher in the previous example). With-it-ness is linked to many other behavioral aspects of the teacher: For example, teachers should always circulate in class and not remain entrenched behind their desks. They should do this in such a way that students are not able to predict when the teacher will come to them. Furthermore, all students should be prepared to be called upon even if they do not put their hand up. This "cold call" keeps students' attention alive and is an important source for the teacher to discover the point up to which individual students have understood the learning content or the task, and if there are misconceptions or misinterpretations to be corrected by re-teaching.

Another very important component of classroom management is so-called "smoothness." Every teacher has experienced the turmoil caused by the transition from one activity to another. This attrition not only costs time, but also diminishes the concentration and engagement of the learners. Smoothness means planning the single steps of a lesson so that the transitions are not abrupt, and, more importantly, so that the students are informed about the single steps in advance. They should understand why a phase of guided practice is followed by independent practice. Transparency is a premise of effective teaching during all steps of a teaching model.

What can teachers do to create a supportive learning atmosphere for all their students? Important features of classroom climate are welcoming errors and providing a safe and caring learning environment (Hattie, 2009, p. 33). This benefits from the earlier mentioned strategies and techniques and is further promoted by so-called "momentum," which means the drive of an engaged teacher. Teachers should be able to activate, not to say inspire, students to engage in learning. Reciprocal respect, good teacher–student relationships (Hattie, 2009, pp. 118–119, d = 0.72), and high teacher expectations (Hattie, 2009, pp. 121–124, d = 0.43, rank 58) that all students can improve and reach the goals are also prerequisites for a favorable learning climate. But the classroom atmosphere does not only depend on the interactions between teachers and students. The influence of peers (Hattie, 2009, pp. 104–105, d = 0.53, rank 41) and the cohesion between the students (ibid., classroom cohesion d = 0.53, rank 39) should not be underestimated (for more detail see Chapter 10).

When **with-it-ness, smoothness, and momentum** come together, further teacher characteristics will be developed:

> To create a climate for moulding their students into **a cohesive and supportive learning community**, teachers need to display personal attributes that will make them effective models and socializers: a cheerful disposition, friendliness, emotional maturity, sincerity, and care about students as individuals as well as learners. The teacher displays concern and affection for students, is attentive to their needs and emotions, and socializes them to display these same characteristics in their interactions with one another. (Brophy, 2000, p. 8)

8.2. PRESENTING KNOWLEDGE AND SKILLS

The presentation phase comprises five major steps:

10. Comprehensible explanations or demonstrations of learning content; explanations, modeling, and demonstrations have to be in accordance with students' learning possibilities.
11. Redundant explanations; various formulations of content knowledge and/or skills help students to grasp the learning content and store it in memory.
12. Illuminating, student-centered examples; examples should be easy to understand in order to attract the attention of the students.
13. Exemplification and demonstration of knowledge and skills through visual/audiovisual aids; as visual memory plays an important role in storing knowledge, a display of different means such as pictures,

tables, and especially different digital media could possibly be incorporated.
14. Presentation of the steps leading to solution through worked examples; not only in mathematics but in (almost) all subject matters, worked examples show students what to do in order to reach goals and objectives.

What is a good explanation? Explanations should be clear and well-structured. They should take students' age and their prior knowledge into account. They are supposed to correspond to the interests of the learners.

Explanations can be enriched by short narratives inspired by one or more of the principles of the Heath Brothers. If you want to introduce the (biological) adaptation to different forms of life, for example of birds to terrestrial life conditions, depending on the age of the students, you could start with a short version of the Maori legend *How the Kiwi Lost his Wings* (see e.g., http://hoopermuseum.earthsci.carleton.ca/flightless/losewing.htm; last accessed July 2015).

Intelligent guesses are another method of attracting learners' attention. Mathematical equations are introduced and exemplified by a student-friendly invitation to hypothesize about the answer to the following question: Imagine that you have tightened a rope around the circumference of the earth. Now you add 40 inches of rope. Would it be possible for a fly to pass under the rope? After comparing students' different guesses, it furthers their attention and their motivation to hear the answer: Not only a fly but also a small dog or cat could pass under the rope without any effort.

What does modeling mean? Learning through modeling consists of observing an expert, in our case the teacher, demonstrating a skill. It is also called observational learning or learning through imitation. Modeling is not limited to the demonstration of a skill; intellectual strategies and techniques can also be presented and learned through modeling, for example mathematical operations, how to write a summary, or how to analyze the metaphorical language of a poem.

Modeling is often based on worked examples which score very high in the research reviews of many scientists (e.g., Hattie, 2009, pp. 172–173: d = 0.57, rank 30). "A *worked example* is a step-by-step demonstration of how to perform a task or how to solve a problem" (Clark, Nguyen, & Sweller, 2006, p. 190; authors' emphasis). It is the teacher or an expert student who supports the initial acquisition of cognitive skills by presenting the single steps leading to the final solution of a more or less complex problem (Renkl, 2005). Worked examples display mental models of experts so that the learners benefit highly from this teaching strategy.

A newer experimental study into worked examples was carried out by Kyun et al. (2013). It consists of three separate experiments which offer further insights into the possibility of using worked examples in the teaching of English as a second language and, in my view, of English Language Arts in general. Learning materials used in the worked examples of the study are integrated in an appendix (ibid., pp. 405–408).

My following example of a presentation phase is designed for students at the end of junior high school and beyond. It aims at raising awareness of cultural differences and the ways of dealing with them. It by no means shows all the ways of presenting the MET's new learning content. I have chosen this example for the following reasons:

- It illustrates that teacher-directed instruction, in the sense of Interactive Whole-class Teaching, has nothing to do with didactic teaching, often confounded with DI.
- It shows how the steps of the learning process can be sequenced in order to lead students to an understanding of the new learning content.
- It avoids cognitive overload by scaffolding its content.
- It demonstrates how learning processes may evolve by starting with superficial knowledge and continuing toward deeper and conceptual learning.

Example: Toward a Better Understanding of Cultural Differences

The following questions and clues from the teacher indicate – where necessary – the direction. They can be substituted by other explanation strategies. In any case, questions and hints should be clear and succinct. Even though there has to be sufficient waiting time for the learners to react, the teacher should proceed with the successive completion of the model without losing too much time on peripheral considerations.

1. Hook or teaser

In this example, the teacher does not immediately indicate the subject and goals of the lesson/the teaching unit. Instead, he or she draws the following form on the blackboard or exhibits it on the whiteboard. He or she asks the students:

What could it be?

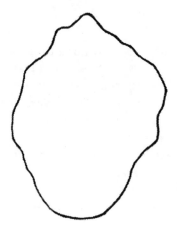

2. Explanation

The teacher draws the following line. Now the question is:

What is it? (Scaffolding: Think of the *Titanic*.)

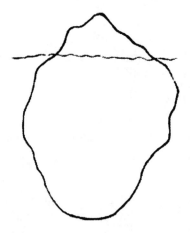

3. Relating to prior knowledge

The teacher writes "iceberg" as part of the header above the drawing. The students are asked:

What do you know about icebergs?

On the basis of the answers, he or she labels the two parts as visible and invisible.

Presenting Knowledge and Skills – Assertive Questioning 147

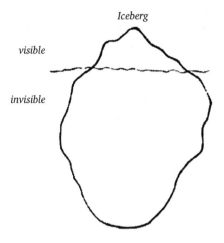

4. Introduction of the topic

The teacher illustrates the topic of the lesson:

The iceberg is often used as a model for aspects that are visible and for others that are invisible and hidden.

(Scaffolding: You all know the expression *It is just the tip of the iceberg* in the figurative or metaphorical sense.)

The teacher adds the word "hidden" and completes the heading:

The Iceberg Model: visible and invisible aspects of culture

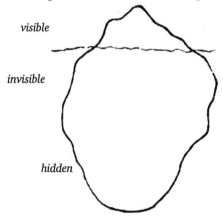

The teacher explains the goals, learning intentions, and success criteria.

5. Goals, learning intentions, and success criteria

Goals: The students have (attained) a differentiated view of the most important conventions of their own cultures and those of others, so that they are able to communicate and to react politely and without prejudice in intercultural encounters.

Learning intentions: The students use various linguistic modes and behavioral attitudes that are indispensable in intercultural encounters (e.g., accepting – refusing, agreeing – disagreeing).

Success criteria: In (simulated) critical incidents, the learners react adequately, without renouncing their own cultural positions.

(The example aims at a general comparison of cultural aspects, with an iceberg proceeding to a description of the main features of culture. Subsequently, every student should create his own Iceberg Model of visible, invisible, and hidden aspects of culture, as discussed in section 6.)

6. Further development of the model

Teacher question:

Which aspects of culture are visible?

(Scaffolding: When you are abroad, e.g., in the city of a foreign country, which aspects of culture can you see in the streets?)

Examples: food, styles of dress

Which aspects of culture are really invisible?

(Scaffolding: Think of cultural dimensions that are not connected with doing something like making music or painting, but refer to thinking and feeling.)

Examples: concept of justice, nature of friendship

The model is completed by the respective aspects.

The Iceberg-Model: visible and invisible aspects of culture

7. Deepening the model

The learners receive a worksheet (see Figure 7.4) showing an iceberg, entitled **My culture and me**. It says:

Write down three dimensions in each of the two sections which are particularly important for you. (Scaffolding: possible aspects are dance, styles of communication, concept of present and past, music, relationships to animals, flags, gestures, religious rituals, religious beliefs, festivals, and sports. The scaffolding can also consist of a worked example which the learners discuss and relate to their own cultural positions.)

Explain the preferences of X/your preferences and discuss them with other students.

8. Asserting comprehension

Explain why the Iceberg Model is useful for representing different aspects of culture.

At the beginning of his chapter about *Methods to Present New Material*, Petty (2009, p. 207) summarizes the main points of the presentation phase:

> **New material is presented** and explained to students by teacher, text, video, etc. Abstract ideas are illustrated with concrete examples.
>
> **Practical and intellectual skills are demonstrated**, for example how to use a tool, formula, or thinking skills. This stresses both process and product. Methods are shown on the board. Students study "exemplars" (good work).
>
> During this, there is interactive dialogue so that you and your learners get feedback in "real time," to gauge understanding and correct errors and omissions in learning.

8.3. THE IMPACT OF AN EXPERT PEER

Daniel is very interested in flying objects and flight in general. His father, who has studied physics and engineering, works for a leading aircraft manufacturer. From early childhood Daniel, who now is in sixth grade, learned very much about flying from his dad, and together they have constructed a collection of beautiful kites, which Daniel flew first with his dad and later alone or with friends. When Daniel hears toward the end of the day's science lesson that the next teaching unit will be about flying, he is eager to contact Mr. Brown, his science teacher, to make a proposal.

MR. BROWN: Hello, Daniel, do you have a question?
DANIEL: Not really, but I would propose something.
MR. BROWN: So out with it!
DANIEL: I have beautiful kites; I can bring some of them to school.
MR. BROWN: So kite-flying in the schoolyard?
DANIEL: No, no, not at all. I want to explain why a kite flies.
MR. BROWN: If I have got it right, you will teach.
DANIEL: Yes, somehow.
MR. BROWN: Have you already got an idea what exactly you will do?
DANIEL: Not exactly, but at the beginning I could show them my kites and talk about who invented the kite and that in Asian countries there are festivals and contests.
MR. BROWN: Have you heard about the book *The Kite Runner*?
DANIEL: Yes, my mother has sometimes read to me from it, but I'm more interested in the technical aspects.
MR. BROWN: Oh, I see. But festivals and competitions . . .
DANIEL: That is just to start with. They will be more interested when they see my kites and can touch them.
MR. BROWN: And then?
DANIEL: Then I will explain why an object flies: hot air from below, cool air from above.
MR. BROWN: You are a real expert!
DANIEL: No, no, my father says that these are just the basics.
MR. BROWN: So your father is the expert.
DANIEL: Oh, yes, he is an engineer and works for an aircraft factory.
MR. BROWN: Now I understand better. He has taught you many things about flying and flying objects.
DANIEL: Oh, yes, he is a really good teacher; he showed me what it means and why an object flies. He constructed a lot of kites and other flying objects together with me and we flew them.
MR. BROWN: That is really fine. So you will explain to the class why objects can fly.
DANIEL: Naturally, you will correct me and complete the whole thing.
MR. BROWN: We will see. You seem to know a lot.
DANIEL: I think I know just the basics.
MR. BROWN: So, tell me when you are ready and we will start with the flight unit.
DANIEL: That is not all, Mr. Brown.
MR. BROWN: What do you mean "that is not all"?
DANIEL: I would also do some experiments.

MR. BROWN: For example?

DANIEL: I can bring our hairdryer and some small balls and I can show them that they fly, but differently.

MR. BROWN: Great! What else?

DANIEL: If it's possible, I want everyone to make a small parachute. We can find out what to do so that an egg in a little chest does not break when the parachutes fall from the window of our classroom.

MR. BROWN: Yes, I have read about this experiment but never tried it out in class. I thought it was too time-consuming.

DANIEL: That depends. When you know in advance how great the parachute has to be and what material to take, most eggs come down without breaking.

MR. BROWN: They can do it in small groups of three or four, so it will be easier.

DANIEL: No, excuse me; everybody should construct his own one. That's more interesting.

MR. BROWN: Yes, it's more motivating. But you can't do all this in one lesson.

DANIEL: Sure, I thought, I will start with the kites and the basics, then you will teach, and later on I can do the experiments.

MR. BROWN: That's a good idea. So we will do sort of team-teaching.

DANIEL: What does that mean, team-teaching?

MR. BROWN: Normally it is when two teachers of different subject matters teach together, for example the science teacher with the teacher of math in one course.

DANIEL: I see ...

MR. BROWN: We will be a good team, I think.

DANIEL: My mother always says: Wait and see!

8.4. ASSERTIVE QUESTIONING AND INTERACTIVE DIALOGUE

During most phases of the MET, questions and answers play a significant role. In Hattie's study (2009, pp. 182–183), questioning scores d = 0.46 (rank 53). Perhaps you think here of teacher questions and student answers. That is only one part of assertive questioning in Interactive Whole-class Teaching. It is at least equally relevant for the developing learning processes and, thus, the final outcomes that students ask questions answered by the teacher or classmates. One of the greatest challenges for the teacher is to create a classroom climate and to support class cohesion so that all students feel free to ask the questions which come to them during different phases of the learning process.

To see in more detail how to get there, here are again the related steps of the MET.

Questions and Answers

15. Assertive questioning; during the whole lesson, but especially when presenting new content, teachers have to check through adequate questioning if and what students have understood.
16. Attentive answering of students' questions; students' questions should never be ignored, as they show if and how students have conceived the learning content.
17. Positive attitude toward mistakes; students need to know that mistakes are welcome, as they offer further learning possibilities.
18. Questions regarding the presented knowledge and skills; these questions should be formulated in such a way that all students have an opportunity to take part in the lesson.
19. Repeated presentation of the learning content; if it is found that the students did not comprehend the learning content in whole or in part, it has to be re-taught.

Why is assertive questioning so important? What are adequate teacher questions to assert students' understanding? Even a well-prepared and thoroughly thought-through presentation of new content or skills will not reach all students. In any case, it will reach the students in very different ways. When we talk about aiming at the individual learner in classes of twenty students or more, we always have to decide upon the lesser evil. Teachers do their best when they try to find out the Zone of Proximal Development of the majority of their learners (see Section 1.4). As the ZPD may vary from task to task, even the learning processes of the same student vary from learning content to learning content. In my view, every learner has to get the chance that teaching fits perfectly his or her mind and heart, sometimes more, sometimes less. On the other hand, every student has to engage in learning and to make the best out of the *offer* presented by the teacher or by a peer.

Teachers remedy shortcomings by drawing on *mediated scaffolding* intended as a support for the whole class. Undoubtedly, mediated scaffolding is one of the best possibilities to give the learner an opportunity to grasp the most important parts of new learning content, be it knowledge, skills, or even attitudes.

Nevertheless, teachers cannot know for sure what an individual student will take from the offer. The way in which a construct emerges that will later on be transformed into a concept and stored in the long-term memory of the learner is not at all observable by the teacher. Therefore assertive questioning is to be considered an integrated part of the presentation phase, as well as of all the following steps of the MET. Assertive questions are to be asked for at least three reasons:

1. During the presentation phase, short questions that refer directly to (parts of) the content help the teacher to assess to what extent single students have come to understand the main points of the new learning content. This checking for understanding takes place during the presentation itself as part of the interactive dialogue in which the MET is embedded. In accordance with the age and grade of the students, questions should only be just above the level of the students, so that every learner has an opportunity to display his or her understanding.

    Coming back to the example of the Iceberg Model (see Section 8.2), short assertive questions during the presentation phase may include:

    How much of the volume of an iceberg is above water? (see Section 8.2, 3. Relating to prior knowledge). The answer does not need to be exactly "one-tenth," but it should be clear that the main part is invisible under the surface.

    Why are cultural dimensions connected with doing considered visible? (see Section 8.2, 6. Further development of the model). A possible answer might be because doing something in general leads to a product, music, a painting, an automobile, etc.

2. At the end of the presentation phase assertive questions can be more complex, for example: *Explain why the Iceberg Model is useful for representing different aspects of culture?* (see Section 8.2, 8. Asserting comprehension). If it becomes evident from student answers that some of them did not fully understand the Iceberg Model or cannot explain its sense in their own words, teachers have to find the exact point from which to start their re-teaching. I propose to use the term *learning loop* for this re-teaching. Always providing that teachers have thoroughly planned and thoughtfully started the lesson, there is nothing wrong with learning loops. Some students will come to understand; the majority will reach a deeper understanding than before.

3. Assertive questions not only refer to a brief checking for understanding during the presentation phase or at its end to be sure that all

students understood the main aspects of the learning content. They can also take an organizational character, like: Who needs more time? Quite often such questions reveal something to the teacher about the learning processes of single students. It is the same with supplementary questions such as: Why do you think that it is/happens that way? Supplementary questions are very important for less gifted learners because, in contrast to their more gifted peers, they do not ask such questions by themselves.

Teacher questions should be clear and concise; they should be friendly and fair; and they should in no way be embarrassing or even humiliating for the students. In particular, the short questions inserted in the presentation or the demonstration itself should not be repeated several times or reformulated so that the learners can, sooner or later, guess the right answer. That does not mean that there should not be sufficient waiting time so that less gifted learners also have an opportunity to show their progress.

Interactive whole-class teaching comprises interactive dialogue, which is not easy to develop when teachers insist too much on the scheme question–answer, question–answer, and so on. There is a danger of arriving at the old interaction scheme initiative (teacher)–reply (student)–evaluation (teacher), which does not allow for more natural communication in the classroom. In the course of time, an assertive question from the teacher followed by the answer of a student should lead to an assertive question from a student answered by the teacher, or, better, by another student, so that the learners increasingly participate in the dialogue.

How should teachers react to (assertive) questions of the students?

The final considerations about the relevance of interactive dialogue show that student should use clear and concise, friendly and fair forms of questioning, too. Therefore, many teachers practice assertive questioning with their learners from time to time. Assertive questioning does not consist of student statements such as: "I didn't get it." To make it easier for the teacher and the classmates to support a struggling peer assertive questions have to refer to (part of) the content, for example: Why is the material of flight objects important?

As many student questions are a form of feedback for the teacher, no question should be delayed: "Not yet, you may ask your question later on" is a reaction with which teachers surely hinder the development of an interactive dialogue. Students, even those who have questions that teachers may consider as irrelevant, have a right to be listened to and to get an answer. What should a teacher do, when students ask questions to waste time? In that situation, teachers have to think about their relationship with the class or with single learners. Teacher–student relationships arrive at high scores of effect sizes (e.g., Hattie, 2009, pp. 118–119: d = 0.72, rank 11). Student questions are a significant form of feedback for the teacher (for more details about feedback see Chapter 11).

In general, many students hesitate to ask assertive questions because they fear either the reaction of the teacher or that of their peers. This relates to the *culture of errors*, which means that errors and mistakes should not only be tolerated but welcomed. In my view, the main problem for teachers is to convince the learners that there is a classroom culture in which errors are welcome. How can students' fear of admitting their misunderstandings or their misconceptions be diminished? What can teachers do so that all learners feel free to make the necessary mistakes that characterize all learning processes?

Teachers can discuss with their students why somebody who makes no mistakes does not achieve any progress. They may invent stories or use biographies in which someone has learnt a lot from his or her mistakes. Why not hang up in class a poster featuring the quote from Samuel Smiles (1812–1904): "He who never made a mistake, never made a discovery?"

In an interactive classroom dialogue, **questions and answers** are

> **clear and concise,**
> **open and positive,**
> **respectful and fair**

in order to guarantee that as many students as possible benefit from the presentation, modeling, or demonstration of (new) knowledge and skills.

REVIEW, REFLECT, PRACTICE

1. Together with another student on your course or a colleague, choose a subject for learners of fifth or ninth grade and make a systematic lesson plan based on steps 10 to 14 of the MET. Try to find worked examples, too.
2. Choose a teaching unit in a textbook on your subject matter and try to find out to what degree it corresponds with the earlier mentioned steps of the MET. Discuss your results with other students or colleagues.

3. Read and summarize the following chapter: Sweller (2006). How the human cognitive system deals with complexity. In J. Elen and R. E. Clark (Eds.), *Handling Complexity in Learning Environments: Theory and Research* (pp. 13–25). Amsterdam: Elsevier.

    Which consequences do you draw from Sweller's article for your teaching?
4. Why is assertive questioning very important in the context of Interactive Whole-class Teaching? Give at least two reasons and, if possible, discuss them with your learners.
5. Invent or find a story about the importance of errors and mistakes. Search the Internet for quotes and aphorisms dealing with errors and select one or two which may be relevant for your learners.

9

Guided and Independent Practice

After the presentation phase, knowledge, skills, and attitudes are, at most, stored in short-term/working memory. In other words: fragments of the new learning content – hopefully the most relevant – have reached the students' minds. They will fade if presentation, modeling, or demonstration is not followed as soon as possible by practice.

Before we deal with the next steps of the Model of Effective Teaching (MET) that regard guided and independent practice, a summary of the preceding phases of planning and starting the lesson, as well as presenting the new learning content, is given in order to better relate the following types of practice to the goals, standards, and objectives of the lesson or the teaching unit.

Practice of presented knowledge and skills – also called the "apply" phase – does not only relate to different aspects of the targeted goals. There are various types of practice, such as exercises, tasks, and more encompassing learning activities with regard to the involvement of the teacher and, most importantly, of the learners. The differentiation between guided and independent practice is only a rough distinction which comprises much overlapping. Therefore, it is crucial to know what form of practice and which task types to choose for different learning intentions.

Guided and independent practice, as with all steps of the MET, have to be thoroughly planned on the basis of students' needs and interests. Some examples will show what has to be taken into account in order to reach as many students as possible and to help them pass from surface to deeper and conceptual learning.

9.1. SUMMARY OF THE PRECEDING STEPS OF THE MET

During the orientation phase, which means the beginning of the lesson, the teacher has informed the students about the goals, the learning intentions, and the success criteria (Hattie, 2009, pp. 163–167, challenging goals d = 0.56, rank 34). This orientation happens best in an interactive dialogue. As early as the start of the lesson, the students may be asking questions about what, why, and how. As it can be a long process to encourage them to enter in this form of dialogue with the teacher and their peers, every student question should be welcomed and answered (Hattie, 2009, pp. 182–183, questioning d = 0.46, rank 53). The learners may arrive more easily at these assertive questions when they are trained during the orientation phase to show their understanding, summarizing why it is useful for them to learn the new content and how they can assess their individual learning processes on the basis of the success criteria.

With the help of the teacher, the students have activated prior (didactic) knowledge. They are invited to verbalize significant pieces of information of the respective subject matter they already know. Even if the learners repeat more or less what the teacher has told them during the start of the lesson, these verbalizations prepare them for what follows.

In order to avoid abrupt transitions, the orientation phase should pass smoothly into presentation of the new learning content. The presentation, modelling, or demonstration has led to a construct that is still incomplete. Perhaps it is based on misunderstandings or misconceptions and superficially stored. The construct is not yet integrated into the learner's network of previously acquired concepts. It is not yet functional, so that the students are not able to apply the knowledge or skill to real problems.

9.2. TYPES OF PRACTICE

All forms of practice aim at the activation and motivation of the students. Petty illustrates the basic aspects of guided and independent practice as follows:

> Students work on tasks that require them to apply the learning, so that they familiarize themselves with it, and so come to understand it.
>
> Knowledge is usually a means to an end. It is the ability to use it that gives it value. So tasks should be vocationally and/or academically realistic and relevant. Tasks build vocational and academic skills which are *transferable*. Knowledge can date, and isn't transferable.
>
> Working on tasks gives the learner, their peers [sic] and the teacher feedback on the learner's understanding and skills, enabling these to be improved. (Petty, 2009, p. 234)

Activities of practice can be roughly divided into three types: exercises, tasks, and learning activities. In the context of teaching and learning, an exercise qualifies as a restricted part of a goal, for example spelling. In general, exercises have only one correct solution, whereas tasks lead to broader knowledge and thinking. Different answers or solutions are possible or even necessary. A learning activity may consist of exercises and tasks which, put together, aim at activating critical thinking or the application of knowledge and skills in a particular project.

Petty does not explicitly refer to attitudes. In my view, practice, as well as starting the lesson and presenting knowledge and skills, has to go further than tasks that "should be vocationally and/or academically realistic and relevant." Different types of practice should promote attitudes, too, even if the latter are not directly applicable to the solution of a vocational or academic problem. Responsible citizenship in a democratic society is more than problem-solving. Aspects of meaningful positive thinking and behavior should be integrated whenever possible. Learning practice should not renounce aspects that go beyond utilitarian goal setting.

With the appearance of educational standards, the danger of "teaching to the test" has become more imminent. What does that mean for practice? Teaching and learning through practice is often limited to the requirements of tests. Students often no longer learn what they would be able to learn, but are instead restricted or restrict themselves to answering what is asked in the next test or the final testing at the end of the school year (see Chapter 12). Besides teaching to the test, another shortcoming limits practice in the classroom. There is an unjustified differentiation between tasks for learning and tasks for testing.

- First, all tasks should be meaningful and motivating, not only those destined for classroom practice. Quite often tasks used for testing lack aspects of real life. Their construction is dominated by the possibility of clear scoring. Therefore they are mostly limited to the results of surface learning.
- Second, all tasks have to contribute to an improvement of learning; not learning to become test-wise, but contributing to attain the targeted goals and learning intentions.

Whoever constructs the tasks used to control the degree to which students meet the goals should primarily think of the students, and not of correctors and policy makers. In a recent meta-analysis, two renowned educationalists, Rohrer and Pashler, viewed and analyzed newer experimental studies that try to discover if and how tests improve learning. The scholars show that test tasks not only further learning, but also improve the storage and retrieval of the respective content in memory. On the basis of a study carried out by Kang et al. (2007), which is representative of most other research into this question, Rohrer and Pashler point out:

> that an initial test requiring respondents to choose the correct answer from a list of alternatives (i.e., a multiple-choice question) did not produce as much benefits as a test requiring recall (i.e., a short-answer question). Moreover, these authors found that explicit retrieval, as required by a recall task rather than a recognition task, strengthened knowledge better than a multiple-choice test even when the final test itself involves multiple choice – and thus the effect is not attributable to a simple principle that practicing a given type of test best enhances performance on the same type of test. (Rohrer & Pashler, 2010, p. 406).

Example: A Test of Reading Literacy: The Miser and His Gold

The following example is part of PISA (Program for International Student Assessment). PISA reading literacy is based on a pragmatic concept. Questions such as "why should students read certain texts in class" and "what does reading mean to the learners" can be answered in differing ways. In an OECD document we find the following definition of reading literacy:

> In the PISA study, reading literacy is understood as follows: Reading literacy is understanding, using, and reflecting on written texts, in order to achieve one's goals, to develop one's knowledge and potential, and to participate in society.
>
> PISA examines to what extent adolescents are able to understand and integrate texts they are confronted with in their everyday lives. (www.pisa.tum.de/en/domains/reading-literacy/; last accessed February 2015)

A closer look at an exemplification of this definition offers further insights into the concept of reading literacy in a test. The example (OECD 2010, Vol. 1) deals with a version of a fable by Aesop and is entitled *The Miser and his Gold*. It is adapted for the PISA test (for a newer translation of the original see Laura Gibbs, http://mythfolklore.net/aesopica/perry/225.htm; last accessed August 2015).

The Miser And His Gold

A fable by Aesop

A miser sold all that he had and bought a lump of gold, which he buried in a hole in the ground by the side of an old wall. He went to look at it daily. One of his workmen observed the miser's frequent visits to the spot and decided to watch his movements. The workman soon discovered the secret of the hidden treasure, and, digging down, came to the lump of gold, and stole it. The miser, on his next visit, found the hole empty and began to tear his hair and to make loud lamentations. A neighbor, seeing him overcome with grief and learning the cause, said, "Pray do not grieve so; but go and take a stone, and place it in the hole, and fancy that the gold is still lying there. It will do you quite the same service; for when the gold was there, you had it not, as you did not make the slightest use of it."

Use the fable "The Miser and his Gold" to answer the questions that follow.

Miser – Question 1

Read the sentences below and number them according to the sequence of events in the text.

- The miser decided to turn all his money into a lump of gold.
- A man stole the miser's gold.
- The miser dug a hole and hid his treasure in it.
- The miser's neighbour told him to replace the gold with a stone.

Scoring

Full Credit: all four correct: 1, 3, 2, 4 in that order.

COMMENT. Fables are a popular and respected text type in many cultures and are a favourite text type in reading assessments for similar reasons: they are short, self-contained, morally instructive, and have stood the test of time. while perhaps not the most common reading material for young adults in oecd countries, they are nevertheless likely to be familiar from childhood, and the pithy, often acerbic observations of a fable can pleasantly surprise even a blasé 15-year-old. miser is typical of its genre: it captures and satirizes a particular human weakness in a neat economical story, executed in a single paragraph.

Since narrations are defined as referring to properties of objects in time, typically answering "When" questions, it is appropriate to include a task based on a narrative text for a series of statements about the story to be put into the correct sequence. With such a short text, and with statements that are closely matched with the terms of the story, this is an easy task, around the middle of level 1a. On the other hand, the language of the text is rather formal and has some old-fashioned locutions. (Translators were asked to reproduce the fable-like style of the source versions.) This characteristic of the text is likely to have added to the difficulty of the question.

Miser – Question 2

How did the miser get a lump of gold?

Scoring

Full Credit: States that he sold everything he had. May paraphrase or quote directly from the text.

He sold all he had.

He sold all his stuff.

He bought it (*implicit connection to selling everything he had*).

COMMENT. This is one of the easiest tasks in pisa reading, with a difficulty in the middle of level 1b. the reader is required to access and retrieve a piece of explicitly stated information in the opening sentence of a very short text. to gain full credit, the response can either quote directly from the text – "he sold all he had" – or provide a paraphrase such as "he sold all his stuff." the formal language of the text, which is likely to have added difficulty in other tasks in the unit, is unlikely to have much impact here because the required information is located at the very beginning of the text. although this is an extremely easy question in pisa's frame of reference, it still requires a small degree of inference, beyond the absolutely literal: the reader must infer that there is a causal connection between the first proposition (that the miser sold all he had) and the second (that he bought gold).

Miser – Question 3

Here is part of a conversation between two people who read "The Miser and his gold."

> SPEAKER 1: The neighbour was nasty: He could have recommended replacing the gold with something better than a stone.
> SPEAKER 2: No, he couldn't. The stone was important in the story.
>
> What could speaker 2 say to support his point of view?

Scoring

Full Credit: Recognises that the message of the story depends on the gold being replaced by something useless or worthless.

It needed to be replaced by something worthless to make the point.

The stone is important in the story, because the whole point is he might as well have buried a stone for all the gold did him.

If you replaced it with something better than a stone, it would miss the point because the thing buried needs to be something really useless.

A stone is useless, but for the miser, so was the gold!

Something better would be something he could use – he didn't use the gold, that's what the guy was pointing out.

Because stones can be found anywhere. The gold and the stone are the same to the miser (*"can be found anywhere" implies that the stone is of no special value*).

COMMENT. The task takes the form of setting up a dialogue between two imaginary readers, to represent two conflicting interpretations of the story. in fact, only the second speaker's position is consistent with the overall implication of the text, so that in providing a supporting explanation, readers demonstrate that they have understood the "punch line" – the moral import – of the fable. the relative difficulty of the task, near the top of level 3, is likely to be influenced by the fact that readers need to do a good deal of work to generate a full credit response. first they must make sense of the neighbour's speech in the story, which is expressed in a formal register. (as noted, translators were asked to reproduce the fable-like style.) secondly, the relationship between the question stem and the required information is not obvious: there is little or no support in the stem ("what could speaker 2 say to support his point of view?") to guide the reader in interpreting the task, though the reference to the stone and the neighbor by the speakers should point the reader to the end of the fable.

As shown in examples of responses, to gain full credit, students could express, in a variety of ways, the key idea that wealth has no value unless it is used. Vague gestures at meaning "The stone had a symbolic value," are not given credit.

(OECD 2010: PISA 2009 Results: What students know and can do – Volume 1, pp. 104–106; less relevant details of scoring are omitted.)

The earlier mentioned tasks are probably quite different from those that most ELA or other mother tongue teachers would practice with students of fifteen years of age (see Review, Reflect, Practice at the end of this chapter).

> **Practice** – exercises, tasks, and broader learning activities – has to be **meaningful and motivating** for the students. **First and foremost**, tasks have to **improve the learning outcomes** of possibly all students. This is especially relevant when tasks are used for testing.

9.3 PLANNING GUIDED PRACTICE

Neuroscientists underscore the importance of practice in general, and of guided practice in particular. Learning results depend, according to Roth (2011), one third on intelligence, another third on motivation, and the last third on practice. Therefore, he calls for practice, practice, practice. In his popular book *How the Brain Learns* (2011, p. 282), Sousa gives a description of guided practice: "During this time, the student is applying the new learning in the presence of the teacher who provides immediate and specific feedback on the accuracy of the learner's practice. Later, the teacher checks any corrections that the student made as a result of feedback."

The MET provides five steps related to guided practice.

Guided Practice

20. Graded activities for practice including short self-assessments; under the guidance of the teacher, all students are enabled through practice to improve and evaluate their understanding of the learning content.
21. Further worked examples with explanations of the single steps leading to the solution; in this context the worked examples are part of student practice (see no. 14).

22. Decision on the social setting; by agreement with the students it is decided whether guided practice takes place in seatwork, in tandem, or in small groups.
23. Formative feedback; it is (most of the time) for the teacher to give feedback to single students in difficulties or asking for help.
24. Short explanations directed to individual students; the teacher should invite all students to seek help when their understanding of the new learning content is found to be insufficient during practice.

What types of guided practice should teachers provide to the students after the presentation phase? This is the main question in the first part of practice. As with teaching, nothing is ever simple; there are multiple answers to this question when it comes to guided practice, depending on the learning content, the age and the ability of the students, the subject matter, and whether surface or deep and conceptual learning are intended. Moreover, teachers have to consider which affective and social objectives are related to the presented, modeled, or demonstrated knowledge or skills.

Example: Describing the Iceberg Model of Culture

In order to show what role worked examples can play in the phase of practice, I have chosen the following task.
  Worked example: Describing the Iceberg Model of Culture
  Culture is often seen as an iceberg. Only a small part is visible, for example dressing styles or food. Most cultural dimensions, such as thinking and feeling, are below the surface. You can find out something about them when you come into contact with members of the other culture – for example, their concept of punctuality or their rules of etiquette. Some cultural aspects remain invisible or hidden to outsiders – for example, the nature of friendship or religious beliefs.
  Task: Read the text and underline/highlight at least five words or expressions related to culture. Copy the text leaving blanks of the same length for every "cultural" word or expression you omit. Work in tandem or in teams of up to three. Exchange your copied texts. Fill in the gaps in the text of your partner or another group member. Compare your results (De Florio-Hansen, 2014b, p. 119).
  Guided practice is mainly determined by two characteristics of expert teachers: empathy and with-it-ness. Empathy in this context means to

know the students so well that the practice activities will be as adequate as possible. As mediated scaffolding that refers to the whole class is inherently insufficient to some extent, the with-it-ness of the teacher allows him or her to find out through continuous observation and assertive questions at what point individual students cope with difficulties. Formative feedback is one of the best remedies to inconsistencies.

Example: Know Thy Students

The following example is based on a lesson transcript in the context of TIMSS (**T**rends in **I**nternational **M**athematics and **S**cience **S**tudy). It refers to mathematics in grade 8 and deals with the calculation of value-added tax (VAT) in the context of entertainment electronics. During the precedent lessons the teacher has presented, mostly by modeling and worked examples, the calculation of percentage.

In the lesson summarized here, the students practice calculating VAT under the guidance of the teacher. The different tasks are not only well graded, with easier tasks at the beginning, moving to quite difficult calculations toward the end of the lesson; furthermore, the teacher avoids any loss of time: He has prepared a work sheet containing the easier examples. The more difficult tasks are written on the inner part of the blackboard, which is closed at the beginning of the lesson. The teacher is well aware that many students will need help, if not at the beginning then when it comes to the more demanding tasks. He is well prepared for this guided practice.

Introduction

The lesson starts with a little competition. The students are invited to solve as many tasks as possible out of sixteen exposed on an overhead transparency, for example:

1. _ % of 98 = 61.74
2. 15 % of 92 =
   ...
15. _ % of 74 = 6.66
16. 28 % of 87 =

The students are allowed to use their calculators. They have four minutes of time. The best student is able to solve twelve of the sixteen problems. When comparing the results the teacher is careful with praise.

Guided Practice I: Interactive Whole-class Dialogue

After this short warm-up, in the following main part of the lesson, the students have to solve tasks regarding the calculation of VAT. The following tasks are formulated in text form. The teacher opens the left-hand side of the blackboard, where the learners find written task one:

Peter wants to buy a recorder. On the internet he finds a good offer on the device he is looking for: Its price is ... without VAT.

In an interactive whole-class dialogue the students – with the help of the teacher – have to find out not only what the task consists of, but also what single steps to take to arrive at the solution, that is the exact calculation of the VAT. It is not the task in itself that is worth longer consideration, but also the help of the teacher, which consists mostly of questions that lead the students through reflection to the right answers and, more importantly, to ask questions by themselves. The students seem to be accustomed to this straightforward interactive dialogue without feeling limited in their need for information. At the end of this phase the teacher writes the result on the left-hand side of the blackboard.

Guided Practice II: Seat Work

The following tasks lead from a comparison of the price of an electronic device without VAT found on the internet to the offer of the same device including VAT in an electronics market. To my knowledge, the tasks are more or less the same in many countries all over the world. It is much more useful to analyze the forms of help the teacher displays during the different phases of guided practice.

From the beginning of the seat work he walks around the classroom, knowing quite well who may need help with the various parts of the tasks – for example, if the student does not understand what the task is about, that is, what has be to calculated. Other students struggle with the calculation of the base value; still others cannot find out which prices to compare. What is amazing to see is the with-it-ness of the teacher. It is not the with-it-ness of being present and waiting for student questions, but the experience and intuition of a teacher to know which student may need which type of help.

The teacher is continuously whispering with different students. During these short conversations with the students, the teacher does not ask commonplace questions like "how are you getting along" or "all clear?" He seems to have precise questions for the students, anticipating the problems of individual learners very well. His experience, due to his attentiveness, tells him who tends to make calculation errors and who has more general problems with the comprehension of a task. The students are accustomed to the with-it-ness and the empathy of their teacher. They are not timid and ask their individual questions openly.

Guided Practice III: Re-teaching

While walking around, giving advice, answering student questions, and having a look at the solutions the better students have already found, the teacher finds out which students need some form of re-teaching because they still lack a general understanding of percentage calculation. The teacher is well prepared for this phase. He offers supplementary problems which the more gifted learners have to solve while he re-teaches essential parts of the lesson to a group of less gifted students. He invites these learners to come with their chairs to the teacher's desk and form a circle, partly addressing them by name, partly in a more general form: Whoever is having problems should come to the desk. (That some students hesitate to expose themselves is mostly due to the situation: The presence of a number of observers and the fact that the lesson is videotaped.)

Considering the classroom climate, we can state that the teacher is not only able to offer individualized guidance and help; he has obtained the confidence of the majority of his students so that they feel free to join the circle formed around his desk. The re-teaching, too, consists mainly of questions. The students who give the right answer to the questions return to their places and continue on their own. Before continuing with the re-teaching, the teacher underscores the fact that the calculation of percentage is something completely new, in order to avoid the possibility that the remaining students with greater learning problems might feel ashamed. In my view, the most amazing thing about this example of guided practice is the fact that the teacher does all this without wasting words and time.

Guided Practice IV: Seat Work

After the last students have returned to their places, all learners continue solving the tasks in seat work. The teacher walks around again now, paying more attention to the students who, from the beginning, have worked on their own. Furthermore, these students have the possibility to control their results, which the teacher has written on the covered side of the blackboard. During this phase of guided practice, the differences between the students become evident. Some of them are already working on supplementary tasks, whereas others are still occupied with the two basic problems of percentage calculation. Again, the teacher involves individual learners in short conversations. As was the case during the previous part of the lesson, even now there is no disruptive behavior at all. The teacher does not have to remind any student to behave.

Guided Practice V: Interactive Whole-class Dialogue

After a short comparison of the main results, the teacher interrupts the seat work in order to bring together the work of the whole class. He now relates the calculation of VAT to real-life situations. He wants the students to get a feeling for the amount of VAT. While this tax seems small when considering cheap objects, he invites them to think of the acquisition of expensive goods. A student immediately mentions cars. With the help of a work sheet prepared in advance by the teacher, the learners now calculate the amount of the tax when an auto dealer buys thirty cars from an automobile manufacturer. After having compared and considered the results, the lesson ends with wishes for wonderful holidays.

(Source: Tiedtke, Michael: Unterrichtstranskript einer Mathematikstunde in einer Volksschule zum Thema Prozentrechnung (8. Klasse). Textaufgaben zur Berechnung der Mehrwertsteuer. PDF-Dokument (1 Datei), 15 Seiten, 2005, URL: https://archiv.apaek.uni-frankfurt.de/23, last accessed August 2015)

This example shows well that guided practice does not only consist of graded tasks, but also contains varying phases regarding teaching and learning of the whole class, small groups, and individual students.

To Be Effective, Guided Practice Has To

- relate to the special features of the learning content;
- take the students' needs and interests into account;
- differentiate between exercises, tasks, and broader learning activities;
- be well-graded;
- vary the arrangement: seat work, work in small groups, or interactive dialogue in plenary;
- be supported by questions and answers of teachers and learners;
- provide feedback to the teacher and the students.

9.4 EVEN GOOD THINGS CAN BE IMPROVED

After the lesson about percentage calculation, two students have a short talk about it in the hallway. Charlotte, who is among the students with learning problems, talks with Naruto, the only one who was able to solve twelve of sixteen problems in four minutes in the introductory phase of the guided practice.

> CHARLOTTE: Finally holidays!
> NARUTO: I understand you well, no more maths for several weeks.
> CHARLOTTE: No, no, after all, I like maths even though I don't do well.
> NARUTO: I never would have thought that. So, where is the real problem?
> CHARLOTTE: I would prefer to write more down in my notebook.
> NARUTO: He writes too many tasks only on the blackboard without giving us a handout, you mean?
> CHARLOTTE: Yes, I think I would benefit from revising the exercises and tasks we have done in class.
> NARUTO: Perhaps you are right. I have heard sometimes that reviewing tasks can lead to better learning. Why don't you talk to the teacher about it? You can make a proposal. I'm sure he understands.
> CHARLOTTE: I don't want him and the others to waste time. Take for example Ben and yourself. You are almost ready when I have got the problem and begin to calculate.
> NARUTO: That doesn't have to mean anything! Every student is different.
> CHARLOTTE: You are really well educated. Thanks.
> NARUTO: When I think about it, work sheets or handouts with the tasks wouldn't be wrong. So I could write down every time how many problems I solved.
> CHARLOTTE: But you know that you are doing fine!
> NARUTO: With a sort of personal grading I would perhaps do better.
> CHARLOTTE: You mean, you would be more motivated?
> NARUTO: Yes, that's it.
> CHARLOTTE: Perhaps we can ask the teacher together if we can get work sheets.
> NARUTO: That's a good idea. After the holidays we will ask him. My cousin always says: Even good things can be improved!

9.5 INDEPENDENT PRACTICE

The earlier suggestions for guided practice are valuable for independent practice, too. This consists of five main steps.

Independent Practice

25. Thoroughly planned and elaborated activities that allow for deep learning and transfer; these activities are more complex and demanding, in order to further critical and creative thinking.
26. De-contextualization; the contexts in which the presented knowledge and the skills occur are varied so that students can transfer the learned content to relevant (new) situations.
27. Decision on the social setting; by agreement with the students, it is decided whether independent practice takes place in seat work/homework, in tandem, or in small groups (see Chapter 10).
28. Formative feedback; this time it should not predominantly be given by the teacher, but rather by peers (see Chapter 11).
29. Feedback through tests; besides grading, summative feedback possibly could take forms that lead to further learning.

Independent practice and the conclusion of the lesson or teaching unit, as described in the remainder of this chapter, do not mean that practicing the respective content comes to an end. The necessary overlearning, which means reviewing and revising acquired knowledge, skills, and attitudes, takes place in spaced practice, which scores d = 0.71 and occupies rank 12 (Hattie, 2009, pp. 185–186, spaced vs. massed practice). We will further examine and exemplify overlearning in the context of cooperative and project-based learning in Chapter 10.

Guided practice can be compared with landing on an island where a helpful guide shows you around so that you get accustomed to the main features of the landscape. Independent practice starts when you have reached a certain level of familiarity with the new surroundings. During independent practice, schemata stored in the long-term memory are transferred into the working memory in order to compare the new, insufficient, and unstable constructs with the already acquired concepts and schemata. Adequate learning activities during independent practice help the students to transform constructs into concepts and transfer them into long-term memory. These learning processes lead to a transformation of existing concepts and schemata so that the new concepts can be stored in the network of the brain.

The role of the teacher during both forms of practice is characterized by his or her with-it-ness. But there may (not must) be differences: Many teachers reduce their direct availability during independent practice in order to give the learners an opportunity to try out how far they can get without the continuous support of the teacher. During independent practice the students rely mostly on themselves or on their peers. Many educationalists see an important difference between guided and independent practice in the more prominent role of small-group work in the second phase of practice.

Deepening the learning processes during independent practice should at least prepare the transfer of new concepts or schemata to other situations than those in which the new content first occurred. What does transfer mean in the context of newer empirical and experimental research? In its ultimate form, transfer means the application of acquired knowledge, skills, and attitudes to real life. How can teachers prepare their learners to apply content learned in class to situations outside school – that is, their present (and possibly future) life contexts?

Older scientific studies have shown that a transfer from outside school to the classroom does not occur. Street children are often able to do mental calculations quite well, but cannot transfer this ability to the classroom when given the opportunity to attend school. Constructivist-oriented educationalists and practitioners leapt to the conclusion that knowledge and skills acquired in a school context cannot be transferred to real-life situations. Therefore they sustain so-called situated learning.

Anderson, Reder, and Simon (1996) prove that the most important postulates of situated learning are wrong:

- An action does not have to be anchored in the concrete situation in which it normally occurs. If the students are guided to work out the most relevant abstract features, they are able to transfer the learning experiences to other contexts.
- A transfer of knowledge can even take place between tasks, provided that the teacher helps the students to recognize the possible transfer. These processes of recognition are furthered through multiple examples underscoring their common characteristics.
- Abstract practice has to be completed by concrete examples. Without combining abstract and concrete practice, a transfer of learned material is improbable. Concrete practice is less successful than the combination of both forms.
- Anderson and colleagues are even able to disprove the claim that classroom learning has always to be embedded in complex social contexts. A counter-example is an orchestra musician who practices

alone before being integrated into the whole orchestra. It is through adequate incentives that communities of practice cause the transfer of skills.

9.6 ALL'S WELL THAT ENDS WELL

Transition or Conclusion

30. At the end of an important learning phase or at the end of the lesson, the teacher and the students summarize the learning processes so that the students can make sense of the past learning experiences.

In most cases, the thirtieth step of the MET concludes the lesson or the teaching unit. Often, however, this sort of summary also takes place between two separate phases. Transitions from one learning activity to the next might call for an arrangement of the past experiences in order to make sense out of the next steps.

Together with the teacher, the students reflect on their progress. They state individually and as a learning group at what point of the learning ladder they have arrived, and what remains to do to reach the top. This summarizing step helps them to put together disparate elements and to attribute sense to the new content and the connected learning processes. Supported by the teacher, the students integrate the reorganized and completed concepts and schemata in a wider context.

This review gives the students the possibility to better organize their learning in the future. This concluding step reinforces the main points of the past learning experience in order to diminish confusion and irritation. Learning is always connected with great effort, even for gifted students. Concentration, persistence, and engagement are reinforced during the whole learning process (Hattie, 2009, p. 49, concentration/engagement d = 0.48, rank 49). Transitions and conclusions, however, offer a particular opportunity to draw strength from the past learning. It lightens the burden if the teacher is able to work out the main features and prepare the ground so that the students can form a more or less coherent whole. Expert and adaptive teachers should be able to make learning not only a useful cognitive but also an emotionally attractive experience.

An anonymous (2013, p. 6) author summarizes **the most important teaching and learning strategies for lifelong learning at work and at home.**

- Materials presented in verbal, visual, and multimedia form provide richer representations than a single medium.
- Outlining, integrating, and synthesizing information produces better learning than rereading materials.
- Stories tend to be better remembered than facts and abstract principles.
- Most students need training in how to self-regulate their learning.
- Spaced schedules of studying produce better long-term retention than a single session.
- An understanding of an abstract concept improves with multiple and varied examples.
- Making errors is often a necessity for learning to occur.

REVIEW, REFLECT, PRACTICE

1. What is the main difference between exercises, tasks, and learning activities? Look in textbooks featuring your subject matter and try to find examples for the three forms of practice.
2. What does teaching to the test mean? Why is it often unproductive when you aim at higher order learning? Read the article on https://en.wikipedia.org/wiki/Teaching_to_the_test and note the three ideas that seem most important to you. Discuss your position with other students or with colleagues.
3. Explain Petty's statement that academic skills are transferable whereas knowledge is not transferable (see Section 9.2). Do you agree with Petty? Why? Why not?
4. What are the main differences between guided and independent practice? Find examples in your subject matter to show what guided and what independent practice can consist of.
5. Have a look at textbooks featuring your subject matter. Do the authors make a difference between guided and independent practice? Find examples and discuss them with other students or with colleagues learning the same subject matter.
6. Thinking of the end of a lesson or teaching unit, is it true that all's well that ends well?

10

Cooperative and Project-based Learning

With step 30, the transition or conclusion of the first learning cycle, the new concepts are related to other concepts and schemata already stored in the brain. In the flow of the lesson, the students have gone through important learning phases: they have been informed about the goals, the learning intentions and the success criteria; the teacher has presented, modeled, or demonstrated the new learning content in interactive dialogue furthered by assertive questioning; the students have deepened their learning processes through guided and independent practice, interacting with the teacher and their peers. Last but not least, misconceptions or lack of understanding have been objects of learning loops.

10.1. COOPERATIVE VS. COLLABORATIVE LEARNING

The end of the first cycle has to be followed by further activities in order to create automaticity. Educationalists and experienced teachers know that knowledge, skills, and attitudes have to be overlearned at least four times during the days and weeks after the end of the first learning cycle. As previously mentioned, massed practice is much less effective than spaced forms distributed over time. This deliberate practice is characterized by variation of context and situations, multiple experiences, and continuous feedback (see Chapter 11). Overlearning in the sense of deliberate practice differs from the previous forms of practice.

> Deliberate practice is *different* from just practice. Deliberate practice involves concentration and someone monitoring and providing feedback during the practice. Furthermore, the activity being practiced is usually a challenge for the student and it helps if the student is aware of the goal of the practice and has a clear idea of what success looks like.

> A major role of schools is to teach students to *value* deliberate practice and learn that this type of practice leads to competence. (Anonymous, 2013, p. 7; author's emphases)

Quite often teachers use cooperative or collaborative learning to further deliberate practice. Scientists as well as practitioners differentiate between cooperative and collaborative learning even though many characteristics of both strategies of small-group learning are alike. Cooperative learning is a team approach that aims simultaneously at academic and social skills. The success of the group depends on every member being accountable for the positive outcome of the group as a whole. Social learning is an explicit objective of cooperative learning. In order to help students to deepen basic knowledge, skills, and attitudes, this form of team learning is widely structured by the teacher.

Collaborative learning, on the other hand, is more focused on an artefact or a product. More than cooperative learning, it follows a constructivist approach. The students team up in order to explore a problem or create a project. The results of cooperative learning activities, even though meaningful and motivating, are more closed than those of cooperative learning, which can have more than one outcome (Rockwood, 1995a, 1995b).

As both forms overlap and are used interchangeably, in the following the term "cooperative learning" refers to different forms of deliberate practice (Johnson, Johnson, & Holubec, 1994, 2008). Both academic and social objectives are crucial for lifelong learning. Besides deepening knowledge and skills, cooperative learning, in my view, leads to increased self-esteem and better communication skills, and helps to create an atmosphere of reciprocal support and responsibility. That is not to say that collaboration should be neglected. It will be discussed and exemplified in the form of project- or problem-based learning (PBL) (see Section 10.7).

> The conclusive step of the first learning cycle is followed by **deliberate spaced practice. Cooperative learning and problem-/project-based approaches** aim at further deepening the new learning content. They offer the learners multiple and motivating opportunities to promote automaticity of knowledge and skills, and to promote the desired attitudes.

10.2. THE MESSAGE OF JOHN DEWEY

Before looking at details to work out if and how cooperative and PBL activities can promote academic and social learning, it is useful to consider the role of

John Dewey (1859–1952) in this context (see Section 2.6). The U.S. philosopher and educationalist is seen as the initiator of developing democratic learning in communities. As early as the beginning of the twentieth century, Dewey pointed out the close relationship between democracy and education.

Most of us refer, not only in school but also in private and work contexts, to the motto *learning by doing*, by which Dewey underscores the importance of experience for all learning (Dewey, 1938). Cooperative and project-based learning are closely entwined with this concept of education. Not only advocates of progressive education but also scientists that follow quantitative methodologies refer to Dewey's concept of experience-based action. At least as noteworthy as this concept is Dewey's claim for democratic forms of education.

More than two decades prior, Dewey exposes in one of his main works that democracy is above all a form of living together based on shared values and the wish to improve society (Dewey, 1900, 1916). According to him, through adequate schooling and education, it is possible to transform the structures of capitalism into a social humanism, with every member of society being able to conduct a meaningful, not alienated, life. In order to put his ideas into practice, together with his wife Alice Dewey, he founded the *laboratory school* in Chicago.

In an early publication, *The School and Society* – his first writing on education – Dewey describes society as a group of people holding together for many reasons.

> A society is a number of people held together because they are working along common lines, in a common spirit, and with reference to common aims. The common needs and aims demand a growing interchange of thought and growing unity of sympathetic feeling. The radical reason that the present school cannot organize itself as a natural social unit is because just this element of common and productive activity is absent. Upon the playground, in game and sport, social organization takes place spontaneously and inevitably. There is something to do, some activity to be carried on, requiring natural divisions of labor, selection of leaders and followers, mutual cooperation and emulation. In the schoolroom the motive and the cement of social organization are alike wanting. Upon the ethical side, the tragic weakness of the present school is that it endeavors to prepare future members of the social order in a medium in which the conditions of the social spirit are eminently wanting. (Dewey, 1900, 1916, pp. 14–15)

The length of this quote is not only due to Dewey's eminent role in the philosophy of education. It is also due to the fact that many educationalists and practitioners alike refer to his thoughts without considering the particular context. The quote offers sufficient support for cooperative learning and PBL. Nevertheless, Dewey's implicit claims give rise to questions:

- How can Dewey be sure that communities are based on different, but nevertheless shared, interests? Does this position not contrast with our contemporary constructivist view that people create their own realities based on their exclusive experiences?
- Does Dewey's ideal of a community not pertain to criminal organizations such as gangs or mafia-like groups, too?
- How is Dewey sure that it is possible to surmount rivalry and concurrency in such a way that everybody is able to participate in social development and economic growth in order to lead a fulfilled life?

Despite these critical questions, Dewey's main ideas are still relevant, but they date back to a time in which experiences that determine today's life were lacking. Heterogeneity, a characteristic feature of our global societies and consequently our schools, includes diversity. Moreover, economic prosperity, as we can experience on numerous occasions, does not lead automatically to a fulfilled life. Nevertheless, Dewey's thoughts exert still a great influence on experiental (experience-based) as well as cooperative learning.

10.3. BASICS OF LEARNING IN SMALL GROUPS

In many cases small-group work is not sufficiently structured and supported by the teacher. For example:

- Small-group work takes place in every phase of the lesson, even if the students do not have the necessary knowledge or skills to practice independently. In the conviction that students should learn on their own from time to time, teachers prepare work sheets without considering if the learners have the necessary basic knowledge or skills.
- Quite often the tasks for cooperative learning do not sufficiently consider the single steps that have to be taken by the students. When preparing work sheets or other group assignments, teachers do not apply backward design, which would show them in which way the learners may proceed.
- In many cases the instructions do not indicate at all, or in a clear fashion, what students should do and how they should do it. Furthermore, students are not informed about the goals, the learning intentions, and the success criteria.

- What is worse is the fact that students often do not know in which way they should cooperate or collaborate. An instruction such as: "Everybody has to solve the given problem, but you may work together and help each other" is by no means sufficient. As we will see in Chapter 11, helping each other so that peers can benefit from this feedback must be practiced several times and supervised by the teacher.
- Before a phase of small-group work it occurs that the students have not been informed on what to do if they struggle. May they seek help from other groups or from the teacher? Statements like "We don't get along" should be transformed into concrete questions. Even this part of cooperative or collaborative learning has to be amply trained.

Working in small groups on the basis of trial and error has nothing to do with learning by doing. To reach the full potential of small-group work, students have to be informed and prepared so that they know what to do, with whom, and why they are doing it.

Effective small-group work, especially cooperative learning, is based on clear, reasonable instructions with regard to

- the goals, learning intentions, and success criteria, as well as the connections to prior subject matter content and world knowledge;
- the composition of the small groups: Should the learners work in tandem or in small groups of up to four students? Which supplementary role, such as moderator or speaker, should single group members take? About what and in which way should they communicate? May there be cooperation beyond the own group with other groups?
- the aspects of content by which every member contributes to the common result;
- the form of presenting the results of group work and the evaluation of the single contributions to the group results;
- the feedback given by students to the teacher as a form of accountability.

10.4. NEWER RESEARCH INTO COOPERATIVE LEARNING

During the past decades Johnson and Johnson, leading experts in the field, came to the conclusion that cooperative learning is the most effective form of small-group work. They focus on different objectives of cooperation, not limiting their research endeavors to cognitive achievement. In this sense they go far beyond Hattie (2009, 2012), who bases his synthesis to a great extent on Johnson and Johnson, but excludes their findings dealing with affective and social outcomes as they are not in the focus of his research.

The great effects of well-conceived cooperative learning, thus, do not only refer to knowledge and skills. In their extensive research over the years, Johnson and Johnson summarized a great amount of primary studies and meta-analyses (Johnson & Johnson, 1989). Furthermore, they conducted their own empirical, mostly experimental, research (Johnson et al., 1981). Analysis and interpretation of a great amount of scientific data led them to the conclusion that cooperative learning is a highly effective form of small-group work under the condition that the tasks are adequately conceived (see Section 10.5).

Johnson and Johnson (2013, p. 372) circumscribe the overall aim of cooperative learning as follows: "Within cooperative situations, individuals seek outcomes that are beneficial to themselves and beneficial to all other group members." Neither competitive nor individualistic learning are as successful as the cooperation of well-trained students working together to attain meaningful results.

The two U.S. educationalists are indebted to Social Interdependence Theory, which is comparable to Dewey's claim for democratic education reducing or eliminating rivalry and competition among group members (Johnson & Johnson, 2005). This theory of social interdependence was introduced mainly by Deutsch (1949, 1962), who draws a distinction between two forms of interdependence within groups that share common objectives. The positive form of interdependence is characterized by cooperation, whereas competition is the prevalent feature of its negative counterpart. With regards to learning in the classroom, Johnson and Johnson describe competition in the sense of negative interdependence as a behavior by which students try to attain better results for themselves at the expenses of other group members (Johnson & Johnson, 2013, pp. 372–374).

Positive interdependence is reached when the students understand that they can reach their own objectives only if the other group members also attain the targeted goals. Under this condition, (most) learners are disposed to support their peers, because their own outcomes and success depend on the results of the whole group (see Section 10.5). Self-interest has to be transformed into joint or mutual interest. This leads to a change in attitudes toward less selfishness, an overall goal of education. These positive outcomes have to be supported by adequate tasks and activities allowing for real cooperation. In my view, it is a great challenge for teachers to develop tasks that contemporaneously focus on academic and socio-affective outcomes and invite students to cooperate.

Besides the positive and negative consequences of social interdependence, Johnson and Johnson (ibid.) introduce a further aspect into the discussion: Learning situations without any form of interdependence. This happens when students get the impression that they can reach their objectives on their own without cooperation or competition. This form of small-group work is called individualistic learning, which means that the students apparently work in small groups, but do not relate to each other. Johnson and Johnson show that the lack of any interdependence does not lead to better outcomes than competition. Individualistic learning is successful neither regarding cognitive achievement nor for furthering any other goals.

Related to the research findings of Johnson and Johnson, Hattie compares the main forms of small-group learning, calculating the effect sizes for different combinations (Hattie, 2009, pp. 212–214):

- cooperative learning versus heterogeneous classes: $d = 0.41$
- cooperative learning versus individualistic learning: $d = 0.59$
- cooperative learning versus competitive learning: $d = 0.54$
- competitive versus individualistic learning: $d = 0.24$

These findings, as with most results of Hattie's study, do not say anything about the age of the students; the forms of cooperative, competitive, and individualistic learning; and if and how the students were trained for cooperation. As we have seen before, the effect sizes of various researchers often differ widely with regard to the main strategy or technique. As previously mentioned (see Section 4.3), this depends in part on statistical procedures. In part, the differences are due to the research interests of the scholar. Marzano et al. (2001) score cooperative learning with an effect size of 0.73, measuring the learning outcome on the foundation of criteria other than Hattie's; he limits his study to cognitive achievement. Furthermore, Marzano bases his results partly on meta-analyses carried out by himself and his team.

In the course of their research, Johnson and Johnson presented a series of overviews of the effects of cooperative learning on different aspects (Cooperative Learning Institute: www.co-operation.org), indicating the effects on subject matter content and social learning. Furthermore, they underscore the increase of self-esteem and self-regulation caused by cooperative learning. They summarize the effects of cooperative work in small groups as follows: "Cooperative learning has powerful effects on academic achievement. It is directly based on social interdependence theory, there are hundreds of research studies validating its effectiveness, and there are clear operational procedures for educators to use" (Johnson & Johnson, 2013, p. 372).

Do you believe that competition is sometimes refreshing? You are quite right. Even though most educationalists, such as Johnson and Johnson, Marzano, Hattie, and Wellenreuther, are in favor of cooperative learning, competition and individualization should not be completely excluded (De Florio-Hansen, 2014a, p. 127). Johnson and Johnson enumerate seven premises under which competitive or individualistic learning may be advantageous. This is the case when they occur in a cooperative context in order to avoid monotony: "... for fun changes of pace and to provide some variety in instructional situations" (Johnson & Johnson, 2013, p. 374).

> The message is clear: **Cooperation is necessary for learning in different educational fields; competitive and individualistic learning are just for fun and variety.**

10.5. MAJOR FORMS OF COOPERATIVE LEARNING

Before presenting some well-documented forms of cooperative learning, we will have a brief look at general guidelines referring to "clear operational procedures for educators to use" mentioned by Johnson and Johnson (2013, p. 372). These are the all-round premises for successful cooperative learning that the two scholars deducted from empirical research.

- All learners know that no single group member can reach goals without the others. There is positive group cohesion.
- Every group member feels responsible to contribute as much as possible to the common results.
- The group members support each other through adequate interaction and exchange of resources regarding academic and socio-affective objectives.
- The learners are trained in productive behavior by the teacher so that they are able to apply interpersonal and small-group skills.
- The students use meta-cognitive strategies in order to discuss the results of their cooperation from time to time. They try to find out to what extent they attained the targeted objectives, which group

behavior was more or less successful, and how they might improve their cooperative learning.
- At the end or at the beginning and end, short tests have to take place with the aim of self-assessment. Furthermore, these tests will reveal which group members need more help from their peers (or from the teacher).

We will concentrate on five forms of cooperative learning which enrich lessons in most subject matters (De Florio-Hansen, 2014b, pp. 134–141; Wellenreuther, 2014, chapter 9). The following cooperation strategies are considered to be highly effective:

1. TGT (Teams-Games Tournament)
2. STAD (Student Teams-Achievement Divisions)
3. TAI (Team Assisted Individualization)
4. Jigsaw Method

Whereas the first three forms of cooperative learning, that is TGT, STAD, and TAI, contribute to deepening knowledge and skills already acquired, the Jigsaw Method is used to discover new content. Even though the gains of academic content learning are not very high, this method scores very high on social effects in classes with extremely heterogeneous student populations.

5. RT (Reciprocal Teaching)

In contrast to the above forms of cooperative learning, this highly successful strategy does not apply to every content and skill. Reciprocal Teaching aims at improvement of reading comprehension. It takes time and engagement on the part of the learners and the teacher until the students are able to exploit the full potential of Reciprocal Teaching, but the effort is worthwhile.

I. TGT (Teams-Games Tournament)

The following three forms of cooperative learning were introduced and elaborated by Slavin, a U.S. educationalist, who has dedicated his research since the 1980s to the analysis of existing forms of cooperative learning and the development of new strategies of student cooperation. With his *Success for All Model*, Slavin (see e.g., 1995) contributed to positive developments in the American school system.

TGT is based on cooperation and competition at the same time. After the presentation of new content through the teacher in interaction with the students and various forms of practice, the new knowledge is deepened and further integrated into the mental network in heterogeneous groups of four students.

The results obtained during this group work are assessed in a competition among students of comparable ability. They compete with the members of other groups which attained similar results. As every student is now in contest with learners of comparable ability and the results of the new formations are equally scored, every student contributes in the same way to the success of his former group of four members. The best group may receive a team certificate. Short formative assessments that normally take place at the end of every cooperative learning session may be omitted in the case of TGT.

Example: Take It Easier

Students can be prepared for TGT by use of an easier version. With the help of the teacher – if necessary – students of similar ability and at comparable stages of learning form groups of four members in order to work with flashcards. The first student takes a flashcard from the covered pack in the middle of the table, turns it around, and reads out the task written on the card. The other (three) learners write down their individual answer. After a control, every student who has found the correct solution is credited a point. The learners with similar scores can compete in a second round.

In order to avoid too much work for the teacher, and to offer further learning opportunities to the students, they design the flashcards by themselves. At home, every student designs four cards referring to the recently acquired knowledge or skills. These four tasks invented by each student go from easy to demanding and from difficult to very challenging. For the tournament, the teacher chooses the exact number of flashcards.

As previously mentioned, the questions or tasks should refer to content learned before. The following tasks apply to a great deal of content in different subject matters:

- The learners judge if a sentence is right with regard to vocabulary choice and grammaticality. The sentences on the cards may be correct or incorrect.
- The students evaluate if the content of a sentence or a short text paragraph is correct or incorrect. The variance may refer to the content of different text types including literary texts.

- Similar to the game "Taboo," the learners paraphrase a word or an expression indicated on the card in a comprehensible manner. Vice versa, the students have to find the right word or expression from a paraphrase written on the flashcard.

II. STAD (Student Teams-Achievement Divisions)

The teacher distributes to teams of two students two different worksheets relating to knowledge, skills, or attitudes recently presented, modeled, or demonstrated by the teacher in Interactive Whole-class Teaching and reinforced through guided and independent practice. The first tandem partner reads out his or her tasks and tries to come to a solution with the help of the other student. In the following, this second tandem partner works on his or her worksheet in the same way, this time supported by tandem partner one. If the two partners don't get along, they can ask for help from another tandem. Last but not least, the teacher is also available for support. At the end, the two students take a short individual test. The success of the tandems is based on the addition of the two test results.

According to Slavin, the STAD can also be taken by groups of four learners. In this case, every group should be composed of one proficient learner, two of the middle field, and one lower-level student. Every student supports the others, so that all attain better results and reach a higher score in the final individual test.

III. TAI (Team Assisted Individualization)

The name of this form of cooperative learning might give rise to misunderstandings. TAI has nothing to do with individualistic learning. Slavin points out that TAI as well as TGT and STAD are very effective aspects of Direct Instruction. Originally TAI was conceptualized for mathematics, but it can be used with great success also in other subject matters. The best results with TAI are obtained in grades 5–7.

After the transition or conclusion (see MET, step 30), every individual student completes a worksheet which contains motivating examples. Corresponding to the age of the learners, these examples consist of narrations about animals, short fantasy stories, or comics with empty bubbles. The solutions are controlled with the help of a handout prepared by the teacher and placed in a central place in the classroom. As soon as single students arrive at a quota of 80 percent correct solutions, they are admitted to a Check-Out Test. If they do not pass this test, the other group members (or as a *ultima ratio* the teacher) are available for help until all learners take the final test with success.

TAI is often used in preparation of official tests. The cooperation with peers and the scaffolding offered by the teacher contribute to the great success of this form of cooperative learning.

IV. Jigsaw Method

This form of cooperative learning can be compared to a puzzle, because the group members contribute with different parts of the new content to the final result. This makes every group member equally important and contributes to diminishing racial conflicts (Petty, 2009, p. 145). In most cases, the students team up with three peers. Considering different learning stages and student ability, the teacher divides the new content, for example a textbook unit, into four aspects or segments of differing levels. Every group of four receives four different worksheets or handouts. It is up to the teacher to attribute the respective worksheet to the student of the corresponding level. Only learners that have long experience with the Jigsaw Method are able to choose the proper worksheet corresponding to their level or to distribute the sheets without losing precious learning time.

Every student has to become an expert on his or her part of the new learning content. In their jigsaw group, the members start working individually in order to find out as much as possible about the aspect attributed to them. They gather further expertise getting together with the members of other jigsaw groups assigned to the same segment. They team up contemporarily, seeking further information. When their research is finished – that is, when, in their view, they have got all the necessary details – they return to their jigsaw groups and inform the others about their findings.

This information from the other group members is the main challenge of the Jigsaw Method. Only after specific training under the supervision of the teacher are students able to choose the significant pieces of information and summarize them in a way that leads to completion of the puzzle for the other peers. Assertive questions from the group members further this comprehensive understanding. Each piece of information has to fit so that all group members get the whole picture in the end. This form of cooperative learning is usually brought to an end by a final test. All group members have to display their comprehension of all segments in this individual test. The test scores are counted twice: for the individual student and together for the group as a whole.

As previously mentioned, most researchers do not see much gain in cognitive achievement. According to Wellenreuther (2013), the effort and work of the teacher in dividing the new content into different segments and preparing the respective worksheets does not correspond to an improvement of academic achievement in comparison with heterogeneous classes. In my experience, cognitive outcome in Jigsaw groups is high under the following conditions: Well-trained students learn to explore an aspect on their own, they practice to separate important from unimportant issues, and they rehearse how to present their results in a comprehensible manner.

As other scholars, Wellenreuther (ibid.) nevertheless favors the Jigsaw Method because of the aforementioned socio-affective outcomes. Petty (2009, p. 145) indicates the effect size of the Jigsaw puzzle to be as high as 0.75. Many scientists as well as practitioners are convinced that this form of cooperative learning contributes to the reduction of racial conflicts. How is this possible? In classrooms that are characterized by great heterogeneity, students of the same ethnic group stick together. The interaction among peers of different ethnicities is very limited. Quite often there is an implicit or even overt rank order of ethnic groups (De Florio-Hansen, 2011).

The Jigsaw Method not only attributes equal importance to every learner; as it is for the teacher to assign the segments to the students, these cannot influence with whom they work together in the expert groups. Once the ice is broken there is no longer resistance to working together across ethnicities. Petty points out:

> Such thoughts are often criticized as "social engineering", or as patronizing, or even racist, but I am unrepentant. It is not disrespectful of a student, or of an ethnic group, to want to include them, and to want them both to understand others and to be understood by others. It is not patronizing or racist to want everyone in our society to flourish.
>
> I believe we must have it all, multiculturalism *and* a less divided society. The identity that comes from difference *and* a shared set of values worked out in real-world encounters with each other. Classrooms may be the very best places to do this. (Petty, 2009, p. 144; author's emphases)

V. RT (Reciprocal Teaching)

Reciprocal teaching is, at the same time, an easy and challenging form of cooperative learning that promotes reading comprehension. It can be applied to texts of all subject matters and with students from the age of seven years on. Reciprocal teaching goes back to Palincsar, who presented this powerful strategy as early as 1982 in her doctoral thesis at the University of Illinois, Urbana-Champaign, USA. Two years later, together with a colleague, Palincsar published an article about her new strategy in a specialized review (Palincsar & Brown, 1984) not only explaining her research design, but also describing in detail the four steps of Reciprocal Teaching. In the meantime, Reciprocal Teaching has become known worldwide as highly effective.

During the past decades, Palincsar and her team carried out many experimental studies in order to analyze and interpret the outcomes of Reciprocal Teaching in different subject matters, with differing objectives, and with students of different ages (Palincsar, 2003). Independently from her research, other educationalists conducted meta-analyses that confirm the positive results of this strategy of cooperative learning. Palincsar herself refers to the study of two renowned U.S. scholars:

> Rosenshine and Meister (1994) completed a meta-analysis of 16 studies of RT, conducted with students from age 7 to adulthood, in which RT was compared with: traditional basal reading instruction, explicit instruction in reading comprehension, and reading and answering questions. They determined that when standardized measures were used to assess comprehension, the median effect size, favoring RT, was .32. When experimenter-developed comprehension tests were used, the median effect size was .88. (Palincsar, 2013, p. 369).

Hattie (2009, p. 204) indicates for RT an effect size of d = 0.74 (rank 9), whereas Petty (2009, p. 154), based on Marzano's research, states a higher effect of 0.86.

What makes RT so effective? Which are the aims of the four steps? Why does the combination of the four differing strategies lead to better reading comprehension than other methods? Usually the students work together in groups of four with a text or an excerpt of text chosen by the teacher. The task should be challenging, but within the reach of the students.

RT starts with silent reading of the text by every individual student, followed by four steps or strategies.

Strategy 1: Questioning

The *teacher* – that is, at the beginning, the teacher him- or herself; later on, the role is taken by a student – answers questions about the text. When the learners are trained in RT, this questioning displays a progression. At the beginning, the students ask easy questions about the content. The three remaining group members evaluate the answers of their teacher. If necessary he or she helps the learners to correct their answer and/or explains the correct solution. When students have experience with RT, the questions become increasingly complex and demanding.

Strategy 2: Summarizing

Another group member summarizes the text. The remaining three students evaluate the summary in interactive communication. If necessary, they state some parts more precisely or correct them.

Strategy 3: Clarifying

The third member of the group is responsible for explaining difficult text passages or for answering questions that need further explanation. Also, this time it is for the whole group to evaluate the clarification. (If no clarification is necessary, the text was probably not challenging enough for the learners.)

Strategy 4: Predicting

It is the task of the fourth group member to predict what will happen or what is dealt with in the next paragraph or in the rest of the text. The remaining three students complete this prediction by proposing their own hypotheses. Also during this last step of RT, the learners discuss and agree on the hypotheses. Later on, they evaluate their hypotheses on the basis of the following text. (This step is omitted when predicting is meaningless or impossible.)

There are many varieties of this complex form of cooperative learning. Despite the difficulties in the introductory phase, every teacher should practice RT with his or her students because of its high effects. In most cases, teachers invite the students to read out the text to each other after the silent reading at the beginning. When introducing RT it is quite impossible for the teacher to attribute an adequate role to every group member. Some students are not able or not willing to respond. Therefore, the teacher should take the different roles – questioning, summarizing, clarifying, and predicting – and pass them on to the students only later, when they are more familiar with RT. There has to be continuous scaffolding and feedback from the teacher.

> In summary, in the context of RT, strategies are being taught in meaningful contexts, that is, while reading extended text, rather than in isolation using artificial tasks (e.g., "underline the main idea"). In addition, students are encouraged to use the strategies flexibly and

opportunistically; in other words students learn to use the strategies as opportunities arise in which they will assist comprehension, rather than routinely applying the strategies. Finally, the strategies are taught as a means for enhancing comprehension, rather as an end in themselves. (Palincsar, 2013, p. 370)

> **All forms of cooperative learning** described earlier – that is, TGT (Teams-Games Tournament), STAD (Student Teams-Achievement Divisions), TAI (Team Assisted Individualization), Jigsaw Method, and RT (Reciprocal Teaching) – have the overall aim to make students understand that they **can improve their learning when seeking "outcomes that are beneficial to themselves and beneficial to all other group members."**

10.6. A JOINT VENTURE: *OTHELLO*

Noah and Chace, both in the last grade of high school, have to prepare a project for their ELA class. Both like English literature and are really enthused about the idea of their teacher, Mrs. Burton, to work on Shakespeare's *Othello*. They know quite well that their teacher envisions traditional projects, such as describing one of the protagonists or finding out more about Shakespeare's position toward jealousy and racism. But they both want to do something extraordinary. So they team up.

CHACE: Got an idea for our project?
NOAH: Not really. At first I thought of street interviews, but then I dropped the idea.
CHACE: Street interviews?
NOAH: Yes, we could ask people what they know about *Othello*, perhaps before the theatre in the evening.
CHACE: Not that bad. Why did you drop it?
NOAH: It's clear that we would have to analyze the answers. It's not enough to give some examples. The answers must be classified.
CHACE: Sure, not easy. But I think that there is not much to classify, because most people think of a jealous black man. They don't even know that Othello was a respected black general in the Venetian army.
NOAH: And you, what about you? Do you have a better idea?
CHACE: I don't know if it's better, but perhaps more feasible.
NOAH: So let's hear it!
CHACE: I thought of time travel. We could imagine that one of the main figures travels through time with a time machine.

NOAH: Oh, as in the novel by Wells. And to which year do you want to make him or her go?
CHACE: I didn't think of the future, but of the present. Someone who comes right out of Shakey's play to our town.
NOAH: Great! And who did you think of?
CHACE: Iago; he is involved in the whole play.
NOAH: I don't think that this is a good idea. Another villain in our world – not with Mrs. Burton. We must find someone who is more instructive.
CHACE: What do you mean by instructive?
NOAH: For example Brabantio, Desdemona's father. He is not that much involved with the intrigues, and he is a senator – so he can tell us something about the history and the invasion of the Turks.
CHACE: That's really good. And it will be great fun to have a Venetian gentleman in our ranks. Think about his clothing!
NOAH: I think more of his language; Shakey's English has nothing to do with our slang.
CHACE: That's true. But I recently found an online translator. It turns our speak to *Shakespeak*. There will be more than one of these Shakespearean translators.
NOAH: Cool. Let's talk to Mrs. Burton about our idea tomorrow.
CHACE: Wait a moment! What about a joint venture? We can do some interviews, too. Just as an intro. So we can show that people do not know very much about Venice at the time of Othello. Then Brabantio arrives.
NOAH: Really great; I would like very much to do something outside the classroom.

10.7. PBL – PROJECT- AND PROBLEM-BASED LEARNING

In the Anglophone scientific literature, the term "PBL" is interchangeably used as an abbreviation for project- as well as for PBL. Furthermore, most scholars and practitioners do not differentiate between these two forms of cooperative learning. "PBL integrates knowing and doing. Students learn knowledge and elements of the core curriculum, but also apply what they know to solve problems and produce results that matter" (Markham, 2011, p. 38). Among the 138 factors that influence cognitive achievement according to Hattie's study, project-based learning does not even feature. Hattie focuses on PBL, which he characterizes on the basis of Gijbels et al. (2005) in the following way:

1. Learning is student-centered.
2. Learning occurs in small groups.

3. A tutor is present as facilitator or guide.
4. Authentic problems are presented at the beginning of the learning sequence.
5. The problems encountered are used as tools to achieve the required knowledge and problem solving skills necessary to eventually solve the problem.
6. New information is acquired through self-directed learning. (Hattie, 2009, p. 210–211)

These characteristics are to be found in one way or another in all forms of cooperative learning. They are valid for learning projects, too. In contrast to problem-based teaching, where the teacher models all steps toward the solution (Hattie, 2009, p. 210, d = 0. 61, rank 20), PBL in the above sense has very low effects on cognitive outcome. Hattie indicates an effect size of d = 0.15, which corresponds to rank 118 (ibid., pp. 210–211). Hattie admits that there might be greater effects:

> As will be seen, this is a topic where it is important to separate the effects on surface and deep knowledge and understanding. For surface knowledge, problem-based learning can have limited and even negative effects, whereas for deeper learning, when students already have the surface level knowledge, problem based learning can have positive effects. This should not be surprising, as problem-based learning places more emphasis on meaning and understanding than on reproduction, acquisition, or surface level knowledge. (Hattie, 2009, p. 211)

Considering the premises and claims illustrated in the context of cooperative learning in this chapter, the above list reproduced by Hattie on the basis of Gijbels et al. (2005) is not complete. What does "Learning occurs in small groups" mean? Is there a positive relationship between the group members characterized by mutual support and the accountability of all learners for the success of the whole group? Is the teacher as facilitator responsible for the effective cooperation of the students or is his or her role limited to vague coordination? It is not surprising that PBL, in the form described by Hattie on the basis of the six meta-analyses incorporated into his research, is not more effective than traditional instructional methods.

Most premises and claims illustrated in this chapter are valid for project- and PBL as well. There are, nevertheless, some differences to be taken into consideration:

- Project-based learning – with reference to Dewey (see Sections 2.6 and 10.2) – means learning by doing, possibly with all senses. A project in

- which students cooperate is based on different learning processes and outcomes than traditional classroom teaching.
- Depending on the subject, the product, and the targeted outcome of a student project, collaborative learning can also be indispensable (see e.g., *Money and More*).
- Even though the emphasis should be on the students' learning processes, the product that stands at the end of a project is at least of equal importance. If only cooperation leads to the desired product, it is beyond reasonable doubt that social learning is not neglected.
- Learners that engage in a project should have sufficient basic knowledge, skills, and attitudes to rely on. Creativity is furthered best when creative processes are based on existing interrelated concepts in the brain's network.

Example: Money and More

The following project brings together different subject matters, for example ELA (English Language Arts), ESL (English as a Second Language), Politics and Economy, and Visual Arts. *Money and More* refers to the real world. Children and adolescents today are confronted more than ever before with issues about money; therefore a project that refers to different aspects of money contributes to more meaningful and responsible handling of money, besides other domains of knowledge. There are not many subjects that allow for more wide-spanned and various considerations than money. Issues about money are dealt with in a variety of texts and media, for example:

- literary texts (from drama to novel, from comics to graphic novels);
- visual arts (from paintings and sculptures to digitally directed installations);
- non-fictional texts (from informative texts to internet sites, for example advertisement and social networking);
- combinations of word, image, and sound (from movies to music videos).

Besides the previously mentioned goals, the project *Money and More* offers many opportunities to initiate and improve audio literacy, visual literacy, and audiovisual literacy. Since the 1990s the *New London Group* has called for a *Pedagogy of Multiliteracies*, which is indispensable if we want to prepare our students for the challenges of the present and the future (www.newlearningonline.com/multiliteracies; last accessed August 2015):

> In summary, we would define a multiliterate person as someone flexible and strategic in their literacy: able to understand and use literacy and literate practices with a range of texts and technologies, in socially responsible ways, within a socially, culturally and linguistically diverse world: someone able to participate fully in life as an active and informed citizen. (www.curriculum.edu.au/leader/whats_ so_different_about_multiliteracies.18881.html?issue_ID; last accessed August 2015)

My teacher-proofed project consists of five segments, or six if we include assessment. The overall aim of the project does not consist of posters or other products to be shown to a wider public, but in the elaboration of worksheets about special aspects of money. The subjects of the five segments were fixed with the help of the teachers – we teamed up teachers of different subject matters – in Interactive Whole-class Teaching. Every group, of up to four, gathered as much information as possible, discussed it, and elaborated worksheets for the rest of the class.

After the completion of the worksheets (and language focuses), the other groups tried out all worksheets. We discussed and corrected them. In subsequent phases the students presented their project to other classes, which they invited to improve their knowledge and skills about *Money and More*.

In order to give interested teachers and other educational practitioners an idea of the subjects or tasks on which our students of different ages and grades focused, a choice of different issues is now listed.

I. Money in proverbs and quotes

(Language focus 1: Basic vocabulary about money)
Money doesn't smell
Similarities and differences between proverbs and quotes

II. Money and music: anything new?

Lyrics: ABBA, Pink Floyd, and Mea
(Language focus 2: Attitudes toward money)
(Language focus 3: Lyrics and music)

III. What is money?

What we can learn from King Midas
Why a bank is called a bank
Money is a promise
Interest is a legal right
Keynes vs. Hayek

IV. Money in literature and art

Do they show off?
(Language focus 4: Reading and describing pictures)
When money doesn't count
Rolling in money
What about Shakespeare?
Money makes the world go round

V. What does money mean to me?

Questionnaire: Money and me
How to construct, administer, and evaluate a questionnaire

VI. Evaluation

Gathering of experiences

We carried out similar projects about *Media* and *Sports*.

10.8. NEWER RESEARCH INTO PROBLEM-BASED LEARNING

Hattie seems to be aware of the restrictions of his research focus. In the last chapter of his study he states that his synthesis of several hundreds of meta-analyses is eventually nothing more than a "literature review" (Hattie, 2009, p. 227). His overall aim is "to generate a model of successful teaching and learning" (ibid.). His mega-analysis should allow for a new perspective on the existing scientific literature: "My task is to present a series of claims that have high explanatory value, with many (refutable) conjectures" (ibid.)

That Hattie's results are nothing more than meaningful hypotheses is especially true for PBL. This can be seen when looking at newer research. Hattie's most recent meta-analysis of Gijbels et al. dates back to 2005.

In the meantime, important developments have taken place. At Purdue University School of Education in Indiana, United States, a group of educational scientists worked on a project analyzing, synthesizing, and further developing PBL research of the past four decades. In a Special Issue of the *Interdisciplinary Journal of Problem-based Learning*, the effectiveness of PBL is widely discussed (2009, Vol. 3/1). The contributions show clearly that PBL is successful when applied to deepen and interrelate knowledge and skills already acquired (Ravitz, 2009).

The Purdue University project is noteworthy because it further legitimates evidence-based teaching and learning (De Florio-Hansen, 2014a, p. 135; 2014b, p. 145). A remarkable article in the above mentioned issue of the *Interdisciplinary Journal* is entitled *When is PBL More Effective? A Meta-Synthesis Comparing PBL to Conventional Classrooms* (Strobel & van Barneveld, 2009). A meta-synthesis is a qualitative research method integrating qualitative as well as quantitative research. The synthesis is based on systematic reviews and meta-analyses. The two authors opted against a meta-analysis "which would have meant quantitatively synthesizing all effect sizes into a single one" (ibid, p. 46). The main focus of the two scholars is on analyzing and interpreting data in order to elaborate conceptions that show the effectiveness of PBL in different learning contexts. This broadening of the spectrum is overdue, even though the research findings of the Purdue and other similar groups may not be as spectacular as Hattie's barometers. Qualitative synthesizing of significant results will refine scientific results so that teachers can benefit from newer findings in order to improve teaching and learning.

> **Project- and problem-based learning**, summarized under the term PBL, are important **forms of cooperative learning**. Even though PBL may require collaborative learning and give priority to the product, **group cohesion and reciprocal support are of utmost importance.**

REVIEW, REFLECT, PRACTICE

1. What is deliberate practice? How does it differ from guided and interdependent practice included in the first learning cycle?
2. What does this statement from Johnson and Johnson (2013, p. 372) mean: "Within cooperative situations, individuals seek outcomes that are beneficial to themselves and beneficial to all other group

members"? Explain in your own words what teachers should do in order to promote cooperative learning. Discuss your points with others.
3. Choose one of the major forms of cooperative learning (TGT, STAD, TAL, Jigsaw Method) and concretize it for practice. Look for an adequate task in your subject matter and prepare, together with others, work sheets or handouts. If possible try them out in class.
4. Read and discuss chapter 11 (pp. 248–250) of Bransford et al. (2000). *How people learn. Brain, mind, experience, and school.* (National Research Council). Washington, D.C.: National Academy Press. Which of the objectives mentioned by the scholars have been attained, or at least reached in part?

11

Feedback – Reciprocal and Informative

Whereas for many decades feedback for students consisted only of scoring and grading, in recent times different forms of feedback have become increasingly important. Nowadays, educationalists as well as practitioners are convinced that adequate feedback is decisive for learning progress. In this discussion, two main developments have to be considered.

On the one hand, educational research led to a growing corpus of results differentiating between various forms of feedback. As far as experimental research is involved, significant findings show what types of feedback may work in different teaching and learning contexts. On the other hand, standards-based education brought quite different discussions about feedback to the fore. Teachers have to be well informed about these internal and external forms of feedback if they don't want their students and themselves to be torn between two – at times, contrasting – aims of teaching and learning. In my view, Interactive Whole-class Teaching is able to provide helpful compromises between contrasting aims of feedback.

Deliberate practice has to consider and evaluate different forms of feedback, which vary from a sign like *thumbs up* to unspecified praise, from "well done" to a differentiated indication of the steps already taken during the precedent learning processes. So we will take a closer look at different expressions used by teachers to inform students about how to improve their learning.

Recent research is not at all limited to analysis of feedback in order to show which form of information given to the students may work best in a special learning context. It is no longer only for the teacher to provide feedback. In introducing and practicing collaborative and cooperative forms of learning, feedback given by peers is of growing importance. As the majority of this feedback type is false – Nuthall (2007) indicates a deficit rate of about 80 percent – students have to be trained again and again so that peer feedback reaches the positive effects it can have on cognitive achievement and other educational goals.

In my view, a third form of feedback is still more significant: It is the feedback teachers might be able to elicit from their learners. Until students are willing to express what works for them in a particular learning context, a long and arduous route to trust building has to be taken.

It is not anonymous written surveys we have to think of, but communication between individual students and the teacher built on fairness and respect. This helps to diminish the artificial character of classroom discourse and can lead to a relationship between learners and their teacher that really deserves this name.

To sum up: During the lesson, feedback should have three directions: from teachers to students, among the learners, and from students to teachers. There is a fourth type of feedback, but it occurs mostly outside the classroom, even though it refers to teaching and learning. That is the feedback teachers provide themselves reciprocally during professional collaboration. Sometimes professional feedback beyond class is given by a coach. To date there is little empirical research into the effects of teacher collaboration on students' cognitive achievement and other outcomes of learning.

11.1. NEWER RESEARCH INTO FEEDBACK

In general, feedback in the context of teaching and learning is defined as information given about their learning by an agent – for example the teacher, another expert, or a more knowledgeable peer – to individual students or whole learning groups (Timperley, 2013). According to this definition, it is not sufficient to provide the learners with the correct answer or the solution of a given or chosen task. The agent, moreover, should give detailed indications concerning different aspects of students' performance and the concrete comprehension level of the learning content. The agent may be also the student him- or herself. This form of self-assessment, for example, occurs when students look up content or solutions by themselves in order to go ahead with their learning.

This general view of feedback has been modified and enlarged.

> More recently, feedback has become integrated into formative assessment processes [...] so some forms of feedback could more accurately be seen as new instruction. In these situations, feedback takes the form of extending students' understandings and fill gaps

between what is understood and what is aimed to be understood. Whichever way it is thought about, it is most powerful when it addresses faulty interpretations, not a lack of understanding [...]. (Timperley, 2013, p. 402)

In order to make sense of Timperley's statement, we must have a clear idea of formative assessment including *diagnostic testing* (*National Board of Professional Teaching Standards*). As previously mentioned several times, for example in the context of assertive questioning, teachers can improve the learning of their students by adjusting their teaching, if they know where the individual students stand. They have to find out which aspects of knowledge, skills, and attitudes have already entered students' working memory in a more or less stable form, and where misconceptions must be clarified (see Section 8.4).

Formative assessment was introduced into the field of education by Bloom (1968; see also Bloom, Hastings, & Madaus, 1971). In the 1990s, Black and William (1998) elaborated a synthesis of more than 250 studies on formative assessment. Defined in a broad way, formative assessment refers to all activities that teachers and/or students use to conduct in-process evaluation. Formative assessment provides information of student comprehension, learning needs, and progress during the lesson or unit.

In contrast to forms of summative evaluation, formative assessment involves qualitative feedback focusing on details of content and performance. It is most effective when students are enabled to correct and complete their task comprehension by themselves and to extend their ideas and learning strategies. The last aspect refers to students' meta-cognitive awareness of how they learn. Comparisons between the effects of summative and formative forms of evaluation show that formative assessment is much more successful (Marzano, 2003, 2006).

Even though no adaptive teacher could be against this order of ideas, there are several points to consider.

- First, feedback should not be given too early. If it does not operate on a sufficient amount of learning, it is not only useless but in fact detrimental. "Feedback must have something on which to build" (Timperley, 2013, p. 402). Or: No knitting without wool (Wellenreuther, 2013).
- Second, the scaffolding provided during the phases of orientation and presentation is conceptualized for the whole class. No teacher is able to continuously provide formative assessment for individual students in order to detect hidden misunderstandings.

- Third, "new instruction," in the sense of Timperley, should occur when it becomes evident that some students are struggling with main features of new knowledge, skills, and attitudes. A continuous alternation of teaching and re-teaching is not productive. Wait time is also necessary for students' brains to deal with new content.
- Fourth, the best results of feedback are obtained when teachers and students arrive at a sort of natural dialogue about the outcomes of teaching and learning. Undoubtedly, genuine, authentic communication can be furthered by formative assessment, but only if it is not overdone.

Together with Timperley, Hattie synthesized a great number of meta-analyses on feedback. From this mega-analysis they deduced an influential feedback model (Hattie & Timperley, 2007) (see Chapter 11.2). In Hattie's study of 2009, feedback reaches rank 10 (scoring d = 0.71), whereas he indicates a score of d = 0.81 in former summaries of effect sizes (Petty, 2009, p. 87). When it comes to feedback, Hattie loses his missionary tone and states:

> We need to be somewhat cautious, however. Feedback is not "the answer" to effective teaching and learning; rather it is but one powerful answer. With inefficient learners or learners at the acquisition (not proficiency) phase, it is better for a teacher to provide elaboration through instruction than to provide feedback on poorly understood concepts. (Hattie, 2009, p. 177)

Feedback is one of the greatest challenges of effective teaching. It has to correspond to the learning context, the curriculum, the task, and above all it has to be student-centered. Furthermore, feedback has to be provided in such a form that individual students recognize it as a form of support. Feedback can reach students well and improve their learning because it occurs together with other teaching and learning strategies. One is formative assessment; other features are self-reported grades – that is to say, learners' self-confidence on the one hand, and teacher clarity on the other. Finding the right mixture in the respective situation is what Hattie calls "the art of feedback" (Hattie, 2009, p. 177; 2012, p. 129).

> A good point of departure **to improve feedback** is the frequent question from teachers:
> Which students did I provide in today's lesson with a form of feedback from which they really have benefitted?

11.2. THE FEEDBACK MODEL OF HATTIE AND TIMPERLEY

Whereas Hattie is succinct in his study when it comes to explaining research results into most of the 138 factors that determine achievement, he extensively describes the findings about feedback (Hattie, 2009, pp. 173–178). In his teacher resource book he dedicates an entire chapter to this issue: "The Flow of the Lesson: The Place of Feedback" (Hattie, 2012, pp. 115–137). The model of feedback that Hattie elaborated with his colleague is based on more than twenty meta-analyses. The main purpose of feedback, according to Hattie and Timperley, is to be seen in reducing the discrepancy between actual understanding or current performance and the goal(s) to be reached (Hattie, 2009, p. 176).

Feedback is not only integrated into formative assessment (see Section 11.1) and interrelated to motivation (see Section 6.3). There is also a close relationship between feedback and goals inciting students to greater efforts and the use of more effective learning strategies. Locke and Latham explain these connections by contrasting feedback and goals:

> Feedback tells people what is; goals tell them what is desirable. Feedback involves information; goals involve evaluation. Goals inform individuals as to what type or level of performance is to be attained so that they can direct and evaluate their actions and efforts accordingly. Feedback allows them to set reasonable goals and track their performance in relating to their goals, so that adjustments in effort, direction, and even strategy can be made as needed. Goals and feedback can be considered a paradigm of the joint effect of motivation and cognition controlling action (Locke & Latham, 1990, p. 197)

Goals and feedback constitute a paradigm. In their schematic arrangement, the effect of motivation is connected with actions through which the learners evaluate their cognitions. Simply put: goals and feedback act together on motivation and cognition (see also for the following De Florio-Hansen, 2014a, 2014b).

The foundations of Hattie and Timperley's feedback model consist of the answers to three basic questions that learners are invited to ask themselves in order to evaluate and improve their learning. According to Hattie and Timperley, these three fundamental questions indicate the focus of feedback (Hattie, 2012, p. 134):

1. Where am I going?
2. How am I going?
3. Where to next?

Hattie and Timperley consider possible answers to the first question about the targeted goals (Where am I going?) as *feed up*. The students who are able to answer this question know which goals to aim at, taking their subject matter knowledge, their past learning experiences, and their general world knowledge into account. Goals, standards, and objectives are preferably to be fixed on the basis of the Zone of Proximal Development (ZPD) (see Section 1.4). It is a sign of expertise and empathy when the teacher together with the students determines broader goals and more concrete objectives that constitute a challenge for the learners without overwhelming them. Different levels of performance may be indicated. In sum, all students have to be given the opportunity to reach the goals. For this feed up, teachers need a great amount of diagnostic competence – an important term that Hattie and Timperley do not use.

The answer to the second question comes close to traditional feedback (How am I going?). Therefore Hattie and Timperley name it *feed back*. The students are invited to consider their learning progress and to find ways to improve their performance. Scoring and grading their current outcomes is absolutely insufficient because these types of summative assessment proved ineffective with regard to the necessary learning efforts. Various forms of feedback lead to different results. "Those forms of feedback with positive effects provide information to the learner about the tasks, the processes needed to understand or perform the task, and self-regulation of learning. Those much less effective are focused on forms of feedback that do not provide task-related information" (Timperley, 2013, p. 401). Extrinsic or tangible rewards are counterproductive (Deci et al., 1999).

The two educationalists from New Zealand consider the answer to the third question as *feed forward* (Where to next?). It is directed to the near future and offers various opportunities to improve the next steps of learning. "What activities need to be undertaken next to make better progress?" (Hattie, 2012, p. 116).

The answers to the three questions constitute a progression. The feedback starts from the task (To what level did the students understand and perform?), going on to the learning processes (Which strategies are needed to carry out the task? Are there alternative strategies?), arriving at self-regulation (What knowledge has a student to dispose of in order to give an account of his or her learning?) (De Florio-Hansen, 2014a, p. 143).

The answers to these three questions exert great influence on different levels of learning. Hattie uses the term *effect* for this aspect of feedback (Hattie, 2012, p. 134). Whereas the focus indicates the direction of learning in a sequence of time from past to future, the effect considers the aspects of learning influenced by feedback. The learning results operate on four levels:

1. task level;
2. process level;
3. self-regulation level;
4. self-level.

Whereas in general the influence of feedback on the first three levels is positive, the self is often negatively influenced by inadequate feedback.
Timperley explains the reasons (see Section 6.3):

> The final level of feedback to self as a person is only referred to here because of the high frequency of its use in classrooms, particularly in the form of personal praise [...]. The circumstances under which praise might be effective occur when it is directed to the effort, self-regulation, engagement, or processes relating to the task and its performance. (Timperley, 2013, p. 403)

Hattie's succinct conclusion, in my view, is significant:

> In summary, **feedback** is what happens second, is one of the most powerful influences on learning, occurs too rarely, and needs to be more fully researched by **qualitatively and quantitatively investigating** how feedback works in the classroom and learning process (Hattie, 2009, p. 178; my emphasis).

11.3. FEEDBACK GIVEN BY TEACHERS TO STUDENTS

From the findings exposed in the previous chapters (see especially Chapters 8 and 9) it clearly results that general, not task-related, praise is counterproductive. It induces students to rest in their comfort zone in order to not lose the label we have attributed to them. Furthermore, we have learned that most feedback that teachers claim to have given does not reach the students. Perhaps teachers omit to emphasize it so that the students notice it as information about their learning processes, or teachers do not exactly refer to the individual learners they want to reach with their remarks. Most of the time, feedback is not worded in a way from which learners may benefit. So what forms should feedback given by teachers to students take? Hattie mentions different methods of effective feedback:

> Feedback can be provided in many ways: through affective processes, increased effort, motivation or engagement; by providing students with different cognitive processes, restructuring understandings, confirming to the student that he or she is correct or incorrect, indicating that more information is available or needed, pointing to directions that the students might pursue, and indicating alternative strategies with which to understand particular information. (Hattie, 2012, p. 115)

How can we specify and exemplify Hattie's useful advice?

Affective processes refer above all to the teacher–student relationships (d = 0.72). All students should feel equally accepted by the teacher. Educational practitioners have to clarify and underscore, through examples from learner biographies or other narratives, that every student can reach high goals, provided that he or she is self-confident and willing to display effort and engagement. In this context teachers can be of great emotional help. Their feedback is successful when they support individual learners to overcome their particular learning difficulties, paying more attention to progress than to errors and mistakes.

Increased effort, motivation, or engagement should be restored by the teacher when he or she notices during the presentation or the guided and independent practice that individual students have relaxed their attention and their efforts or are completely demotivated. Trying to find out together with the student what his or her difficulties consist of is a better method than a warning or even blame. Quite often teachers can improve effort, engagement, and motivation by presenting concrete examples, interesting stories, or riddles. Furthermore, the example of teachers should not be underestimated. How can we expect effort, engagement, and motivation from our students if we lack the required characteristics?

Providing different cognitive processes means re-teaching when we notice, through assertive questioning or in another way, that part of our teaching did not reach the learners. When we decide to present or model indispensable features of knowledge, skills, or attitudes, it is seldom worthwhile to re-teach in the same way we originally taught. In most cases it does not lead to success when teachers, for example, repeat a grammar rule rewording it in a different way, or invite the students to read the rule in their textbooks. Re-teaching is more successful when we offer examples or visualizations of the new learning content. Students benefit even more from this revising when they participate in the construction of examples or other aids.

Restructuring understanding occurs when learners are given the opportunity to reconsider concepts or schemata they already know. Let us take an example. The students have to formulate a written complaint because they have received from an internet trader a pair of sneakers that does not correspond to their order. Beside the fact that we can provide the learners with a worked example of a complaint or a list of the main points to consider, we can also refer to a complaint by a guest talking to a restaurant manager read in a short story. Either way, it is important to focus on the main aspects of a complaint, adding particularities when the structure is understood.

Correct or incorrect: The main factor in this context is the classroom climate. Not only teachers are responsible for a supporting learning atmosphere; to a certain extent the learners also have to contribute to classroom cohesion and respectful behavior toward the teacher and their peers. What has this consideration got to do with correct or incorrect answers of the learners? Feedback is successful when teachers or peers say what they mean. They must feel free to state that an answer is incorrect in an unambiguous way. Otherwise feedback does not lead to improved outcomes. As previously mentioned repeatedly, errors must be welcome as an opportunity for further learning. It takes a long time for all students to be convinced that there is nothing wrong with misconceptions or misinterpretations as long as they pay attention and feel motivated to learn. It contributes to a beneficial learning atmosphere in the above sense when it is not only the teacher who corrects false interpretations or other errors; all students have to contribute to learning outcomes that can be the basis of further learning.

More information should always be available. The learners must feel free to ask the teacher for further information, for example if they have undertaken research on the internet without finding the necessary piece of information or if they have doubts that the gathered material is sufficient and adequate to solve the task. An example: During close reading of a graphic novel, students are not always aware of the great amount of information that may further and deepen their understanding. In these cases it is up to the teacher to indicate to the students that are in some way at the crossroads of their learning where to look for help.

New directions: As with adults, some students hinder their learning by themselves, because of prejudices or learning habits. They stand in their own way. If teachers are able to detect these preconceived ideas they can lead the learners to more critical and creative thinking so that unexploited possibilities can be used.

Alternative strategies are another means to adapt and extend or even change students' learning paths. Even though the strategies of individual students lead to successful learning, teachers should invite them to try out alternative strategies. Depending on content and task, teachers can discuss with the students possible solution strategies in order to attract the attention of single students to strategies or techniques that they do not frequently apply. Teachers should motivate a change of strategies with a view to future (professional) life, where different modes of solving problems are quite often required.

These **different forms of feedback** lead to successful learning and improved outcome when they are directed to those students who need them. Teachers and expert peers must help these students to make real use of the particular feedback. **More important than frequency is an adequate form of feedback.**

In their feedback model, Hattie and Timperley (2007) differentiate between the influence (called effect) that feedback exerts on different levels of learning, that is on the task, the learning processes, and the self-regulation of the students (see Section 11.2). In his resource book, Hattie points out that feedback is not sufficiently directed to the learning processes and self-regulation of the students (Hattie, 2012, p. 129).

When feedback is not limited to marking and grading and unmotivated praise, teachers and peers mostly focus on task solutions. According to Hattie and Timperley, feedback is more effective when related to the learning processes and student awareness with regard to learning strategies (self-regulation). Therefore Hattie lists questions directed to all three levels of feedback, with major emphasis on processes and self-regulation (ibid.). Most of these questions show Hattie's focus very well – that is, they help to understand his order of ideas. In my view, many of them are less adequate in the flow of the lesson. My own proposals are not exhaustive but are hopefully more learner-friendly.

Questions related to tasks

What does X mean to you?
Can you show me the single steps you took to solve the problem?
Explain why you took this step at that point?

Questions related to the processes

Did you think of alternative strategies?
Why did you choose this strategy or technique?
Could you profit from further information?

Questions related to self-regulation

Did you have doubts about a step taken to achieve the task?
Did you seek help? In what way? Why not?
What support would you have needed?
How did you control your learning during your work on the task?

> **Feedback is more effective** when teachers (and expert peers) answer the following questions **with particular attention to individual students or groups of learners:**
>
> - What does the feedback refer to? To the task, the learning processes, or the self-regulation?
> - Which form of feedback is adequate when taking the needs and interests of particular learners into account?
> - In what phases of teaching and how frequently does feedback make sense in a specific learning context?

11.4. PEER FEEDBACK

In scientific reports as well as in popular resource books, we often come across statements about the high effects of peer feedback. Feedback among learners is considered effective for at least two reasons. First, it is a question of communication. The modes and tones used by peers when they talk to each other are often easier to understand than teacher talk. Second, peers have similar problems when it comes to achieving particular goals and resolving learning problems.

On the whole, these may be valuable arguments for peer feedback. Why are peers sometimes more successful when providing feedback to a classmate? In tandem or in small groups, peers are confronted only with one or two classmates, whereas teachers have to correspond to a greater number of students that (might) need help. In most cases, members of small groups work on the same tasks. It is easier for them to find out where a group member begins to struggle, whereas the with-it-ness of teachers does not offer the same insights.

So, in my perspective, teachers do a good job? Mostly, yes! But what if teachers explained the goals, learning intentions, and success criteria in a more comprehensible way? What if teachers learned to better present and model new learning content? Why not ask questions that are more learner-like and less science-related? The function of peer feedback should not consist of compensating for insufficient teaching.

If teachers see learning through the eyes of their students – another of Hattie's mantras (2009, p. 238) – they are able to improve their feedback so that it reaches more and more learners. In this order of ideas, peer feedback has other important functions. As previously mentioned, small group learning scores d = 0.49 and reaches rank 48 (Hattie, 2009, pp. 94–95), while cooperative learning occupies rank 63 with a score of d = 0.41 (Hattie, 2009, pp. 212–214). We should not forget that Hattie's study is limited to measurable cognitive achievement, neglecting emotional aspects and social learning.

In his ample and benchmark research into small group work and other forms of cooperative learning, Nuthall (2007) shows that *The Hidden Lives of Learners* mainly consists of three different worlds: the official world of the teacher, the influential world of peers, and the private world of the students, which is determined by their experiences. Using a sophisticated methodology consisting of a combination of quantitative and qualitative methods, Nuthall points out as one of his significant findings that about 80 percent of all feedback occurring in classrooms is peer feedback. He underscores that most of this peer feedback is false (Hattie, 2012, p. 131). It is erroneous with regard to the tasks or other aspects of learning content.

What we can deduct from Nuthall's research results is the obligation for teachers to train their students before inviting them to provide feedback to their peers. Peer feedback furthers learning outcomes when several conditions are met. Students have to use appropriate verbal behaviour. Statements such as "That's incorrect" or "Couldn't you pay attention?" are inappropriate, if not detrimental. Students have to be trained in assertive questioning, for example "What did you do when . . .?"

Furthermore, they have to internalize appropriate behavior. One of the best ways to prepare students for providing effective feedback to peers is worked examples in the form of videos. Nevertheless, training students to be able to give effective peer feedback is a long process.

Gan, one of Hattie's doctoral students, carried out an RCT on the basis of Hattie and Timperley's feedback model using the questions regarding the task, learning processes, and self-regulation. Gan provided the experimental group with somewhat transformed questions and pieces of information regarding the level to which they refer, whereas the control group limited its feedback to the correct task solution and some form of praise. Gan (2011) showed that the described form of assertive questioning is more effective than simple indication of the correct solution. Nevertheless, Hattie (2012, p. 134) opts for "deliberate instructional support" of peer feedback until learners are able to provide it in an acceptable way.

Why invest time and effort in training students in adequate peer feedback? Peer tutoring is not only effective in furthering cognitive achievement. Its positive results, in my perspective, consist much more in enabling students to work together with others in constructive ways. Being able to collaborate in order to improve group cohesion or to cooperate in order to reach better products is a key qualification in our world. Peer feedback is often seen in the limits of better learning outcomes – peer tutoring reaches rank 36 and scores d = 0.55 (Hattie, 2009, pp. 186–187). It is true that well-trained students achieve more. More important, in my view, is the fact that peer tutoring's emotional support is underestimated. Moreover, its positive effects on students' attitudes are underestimated because of a lack of appropriate research.

In her overview of a great number of meta-analyses that assess the influence of feedback, Timperley (2013, p. 402) does not explicitly refer to peer feedback. Timperley's conclusion completes Hattie's summary, quoted at the end of Section 11.2.

> The research on feedback presents an unsolved dilemma. Potentially, feedback can have high effects on student learning and achievement when it helps students reduce the discrepancies between current understanding and performance and goals. Yet the most common forms of feedback in classrooms, test marks and personal praise, are those least likely to produce these effects. Shifting these teacher behaviours appears to be very difficult. The key question needs to shift from "What kinds of feedback are effective?" to "How can we encourage teachers to use kinds of feedback known to be effective?" (Timperley, 2013, p. 404)

> During work in small groups, **teachers cannot eliminate peer feedback**. It occurs as such because feedback is frequent in the life contexts of children, adolescents, and adults. Therefore **adequate training is of utmost importance** not only for classroom learning but also with regard to future professional and private requirements. If it is effectively practiced, both **tutee and tutor benefit from peer tutoring**.

11.5. LOVE IS NOT ALWAYS BLIND

The parents of Thomas, who is in grade 8, have chosen for their son a renowned high school which offers, among other electives, the opportunity to learn foreign languages. As his father is of German origin, his parents want him to start in grade 9 with German, a language Thomas knows already quite well.

They are astonished that Thomas puts up no resistance when it comes to filling out the registration form. During several discussions in the preceding weeks, Thomas has always maintained his opinion that it would be better to learn a foreign language other than German – perhaps French or Spanish. His parents cannot explain Thomas' shift of opinion, but they are satisfied with his new choice.

Thomas himself does not reveal to them what caused his change of mind. Some days ago the principal, Mr. Shepherd, talked to him in the hallway, convinced that Thomas would choose German due to his father's origin. During this short talk the principal mentioned that Mrs. Barski would teach German in the new group, formed of students from different classes. Mrs. Barski, an attractive young woman, is among the school's most popular teachers. Thomas has sometimes talked to her in German in the schoolyard.

Two months after the beginning of the German lessons, Mrs. Barski invites the students to tell her frankly what, in their view, did not go well. She reserves a certain amount of time each week for what she calls "feedback for the teacher." Nothing happens, even when she herself mentions certain possible shortcomings during previous lessons. On the contrary, some students try to comfort her by telling her that, for example, a math test before the German lesson was the main cause of their lack of attention and effort. But Mrs. Barski does not give up.

She installs a *Schülersprechstunde*, a weekly students' consultation hour, without any success. No student ever shows up. So the teacher invites Thomas to come to her next consultation hour, and Thomas does accept. Afterwards the classmates want to know how Thomas managed to get out of this difficult situation. Without any hesitation, Thomas tells them about his conversation with Mrs. Barski.

First she wanted to get general feedback about her teaching. Thomas answered: "It's ok, all going quite well." As Mrs. Barski replied that Thomas' statement was trivial and meaningless, Thomas countered that these were her exact words. Mrs. Barski could not stifle a laugh. In fact, she expressed her feedback mostly that way in order to avoid discouraging the learners. So she invited him again to express his critique frankly, but to remain fair.

To the great surprise of his peers, Thomas criticized the teacher, openly summarizing his points of critique:

"Sometimes we lose too much time with less important things like bureaucracy and so on."

"Many need much more time. You mostly pick those who put their hands up and you call them too fast."

"You continuously praise us. During the last lesson you praised me three times for nothing special."

"Could you, please, tell me finally what I can do to improve?"

Some of the peers do not believe that Thomas really said this. Others are convinced that Thomas will have to bear negative consequences for his frankness. At the beginning of the next lesson, however, the teacher talks about Thomas' criticism. She is willing to consider most points in order to help the learners to better achieve. Never before has a teacher talked to them in that way. From then on more and more students have the courage to frequent Mrs. Barski's *Schülersprechstunde* or to give her feedback on other occasions. Thomas is still more enthused about his teacher. Love is not always blind.

11.6. FEEDBACK GIVEN BY STUDENTS TO TEACHERS

In the course of this chapter it was pointed out several times that feedback has to be informative. It always should be related to something concrete, for example different steps on the way to problem solving, the choice of useful strategies and techniques, and/or the meta-cognitive awareness of personal progress.

Furthermore, feedback – thus the title of this chapter – should be reciprocal. Reciprocity does not refer only to peer feedback; it is even more significant when we think of student–teacher relationships. In other words, feedback is most effective when it is not only a case of teachers supporting their learners by providing feedback; students have to respond to teachers' assertive questioning with frank and fair answers if they want to benefit from teacher support.

Learners could even turn teacher feedback to more advantage for their learning if they can find the courage to tell their teacher, at the right moment, why they, in their view, cannot identify with the goals or the learning intentions. Students should be eager to clarify the criteria to meet for success. They should learn to profit from teachers' assertive questioning during the orientation and the presentation phase in a respectful way that makes teachers understand why something is not clear or why it remained too vague for them. The effort to provide this reciprocal feedback from teachers to students and vice versa has to be on both sides – the teacher and the learner.

Teachers have to relentlessly encourage the students to provide feedback about their individual learning processes, and even the needs and interests of their tandem or team partners. In many cases we are still far away from such confident and meaningful communication in classrooms. In the meantime, researchers have elaborated and provided various forms of written surveys for students and sometimes even for teachers in order to find out how the learners perceive important steps and aspects of teaching in different subject matters. Even though these surveys are completed anonymously, many teachers are against the questionnaires, mainly for three reasons:

1. The results can be altered by opportunistic students who want to support the teacher even though they are not identified. This behavior occurs sometimes when scholars carry out empirical research. There are participants who try to help the researcher by marking those options that, in their opinion, correspond best to the desired results.
2. There are still many teachers, other education professionals, and parents who cherish a traditional image of the teacher. If he or she does not know what to do, who else should know it? How could he or she pretend that the students tell him or her what to do? Do patients tell their doctors what to do?
3. Teachers might feel obliged to correspond to some of the requests even though they are not convinced of the adaptations or changes. It is beyond doubt that every teacher can improve (part of) his or her teaching strategies or even the whole program, but this should happen on their own initiative. Furthermore, the results of written questionnaires do not remain hidden to colleagues.

Above all, the most elaborated and sophisticated written survey does not provide teachers with any information about the learning processes and achievement of individual students. Teachers can gather the necessary information through short conversations with (single) students during or after particular learning activities. Providing formative evaluation of entire programs is even more effective (Hattie, 2009, p. 181, d = 0.90, rank 3). It is beyond doubt that teachers should see learning through the eyes of students. Of equal importance is that teachers see themselves as learners, willing to seek negative evidence and to see the effects of their teaching on all learners. It would be best if all persons involved in educational processes understand themselves as learners and search for reciprocal feedback – that is, from student to teacher and from teacher to teacher.

> **What is the shortest word in the English language that contains the letters: abcdef? Answer: feedback. Don't forget that feedback is one of the essential elements of good communication.** (Anonymous)

REVIEW, REFLECT, PRACTICE

1. Why should feedback be reciprocal and informative?
2. What does formative assessment mean? Give a definition in your own words. What is the role of feedback in formative assessment? Discuss your findings with others.
3. What does "no knitting without wool" mean in the context of feedback?
4. Describe the feedback model of Hattie and Timperley (2007). What is its focus? What is its effect? In your view, is this model useful for teaching and learning? Why? Why not?
5. Which are the main objectives of peer feedback? Why is student training so important? How could you proceed in order to train the learners to provide peer feedback? Find some examples related to your respective subject matter and, if possible, try them out in class.
6. Why does Timperley (2013, p. 404) call research on feedback an unsolved dilemma?
7. Read the blog review of Nuthall's *The hidden life of learners* (2007) by Andy Warner
   (https://andywarner78.wordpress.com/2014/05/17/the-hidden-lives-of-learners-by-graham-nuthall/; last accessed August 2015).
   Why does Warner end up recommending Nuthall's book?

Concluding Remarks: Standards Need More Evidence

My concluding remarks consist mainly of questions. Another book would be required to illustrate the answers, because up to now educational standards and evidence-based education have been discussed separately. How is it possible that those who preach evidence-based teaching do not look for scientific evidence of educational standards? Would it not be more reasonable to elaborate standards which are based on reliable research and not only on the suggestions of experts or policy makers? Why are performance standards not tested out with poor, low-level students in order to find out if these learners ever could reach them? The following considerations will hopefully bring us closer to answers. At least they are food for thought.

What does standardization of schools mean? Standardization has been introduced into industrial production and the field of services to guarantee that products and services all over the world correspond to the same requirements. When booking a four-star hotel you can expect similar equipment, facilities, and services in Aberdeen and in Shanghai. Not only hotels but also schools are standardized. In most countries, schooling is regulated in the same way: There are classes composed of students of approximately the same age. In general, teachers are professionally trained. Knowledge and skills are distributed along different subject matters. Quite often content is fixed by curricula, and there are timetables to be respected. Standards are instruments to create institutions which regulate the exchange among human individuals. In short: every characteristic that determines a school as an institution is to be considered a standard (Herzog, 2013, p. 4).

What are educational standards? There is a wide range of standards referring to teaching and learning, for example curriculum standards, learning standards, pupil achievement standards, instructional standards, teaching standards, proficiency standards, competence standards, and outcome standards. Before having a closer look at the most important educational standards and their possible influences on student outcome, we should remember the example of the coffee machine in Section 3.5. Even though the coffee drinker has an undeniable influence on the machine by filling it up with water and coffee, he does not direct or even regulate the machine as a system. This is done by a built-in algorithm. When we consider, furthermore, the effect of the coffee on the consumer, we must admit that there is no direct connection between the machine and the coffee drinker.

Teaching and learning are in a similar relationship. Teaching does not govern learning, because teaching and learning occur in two different systems. There is no direct influence of teaching on learning. This can be easily demonstrated: The same teaching leads to different results depending on numerous characteristics of the learners. Sometimes students learn a lot in lessons given by average teachers because they are highly motivated and interested in subject matter content. Others do not benefit at all from thoroughly planned and presented knowledge and skills. Learning occurs through learning. Undoubtedly, teachers can help students to improve their learning processes through effective teaching. The idea that the existence of some sort of standard leads to successful learning should be reconsidered. Standards may constrain teachers and students to reach better test scores, nothing more.

Which standards may further teaching in such a way that student learning is initiated and improved? Diane Ravitch (1995, 2010), who has long experience with the US standards movement, proposes the following categorization:

1. *Content standards* describe in a clear and (subject matter-) specific form what teachers should teach and what students should learn, which is to say, knowledge, skills, and attitudes. These standards should be acquired by all students through particular learning strategies that teachers initiate and promote through adequate teaching. Just as, with the coffee machine, there is no output without input, in classrooms there are no learning outcomes without content input that is fine-tuned to students' possibilities.
2. *Opportunity-to-learn standards* guarantee that the necessary resources are available. Opportunity-to-learn standards refer primarily to qualified teaching professionals as well as to teaching and learning materials. These personal and material resources create the conditions which contribute to an improvement of all students' learning.

3. *Performance standards* ensure that the learners can achieve the targeted goals under the conditions of their particular learning contexts.

"Performance standards," according to Ravitch (1995, pp. 12–13), "describe what kind of performance represents inadequate, acceptable, or outstanding accomplishment." Whereas curricular standards indicate what has to be taught and learned, performance standards specify how much of the prescribed content should have been acquired in particular subject matters at a certain point of time, for example at the end of grade 6 or grade 10.

What are performance standards used for? The main purpose of performance standards is control. Students and teachers can assess their teaching and learning outcomes. Schools give an account to parents and the wider public. Above all, performance standards allow school boards and policy makers to monitor the education system. Nevertheless, the insights that interested people gain through respective testing are very limited. Tests measure only the main outcomes in subject matters considered to be relevant for international assessment studies such as TIMSS and PISA. The tests refer to a limited part of the targeted goals; quite often only surface knowledge is tested because it can be easily measured and scored. Even if deeper knowledge is subject to appropriate tests, performance standards measure nothing other than performance. The significant difference between the displayed performance and the often higher competence that remains hidden is not taken into account.

Is there a relationship between education systems that are based on performance standards and students' test scores in international assessment studies? To date there is no serious empirical proof which may underpin any kind of dependence. There are nations that score very high in international surveys without obliging teachers and students to adopt and adapt performance standards. An example is New Zealand, whose students attained extraordinary results at the beginning of the millennium. Since educational standards were introduced in 2009, New Zealand's rankings have been close to average. For example, "In the 2013 rankings, New Zealand slipped from seventh to 13th in reading, from seventh to 18th in science and from 13th to 23rd in maths" (Campbell, 2013). Others, on the contrary, reach only low results even though teachers and learners follow well-elaborated standards.

A significant example is the United States. Despite a movement of three decades which has seen different generations of thought-through standards coming to the fore, U.S. students' performance in reading (rank 17) and science (rank 20) was close to the OECD average in 2012, whereas they ranked below average in mathematics (rank 27). Over time there have been no significant changes.

In their recent publication, *50 Myths and Lies that Threaten America's Public Schools*, Berliner, Glass, and Associates (2014) dedicate an entire part to the myths about education systems. The authors describe in detail the many factors that influence student performance, among the most important of which is the poverty rate. It seems clear to them that even a good education system in a "big heterogeneous country like the United States" cannot produce the same results as Finland, whose success in education may be "due to its remarkably low poverty rate for children" (ibid., p. 11). "In the end, when you hold constant all the variables that affect school achievement (variables like family income, family members with college degrees, health care, equity for women, treatment of minorities, and the like), you find that it is much more difficult than it seems to distinguish the best from the worst schools" (ibid., p. 12).

A question that the authors should have asked is: Why spend so much effort and time on the development of performance standards when, for example, opportunity-to-learn standards for the underprivileged would probably lead to better results? Why do educationalists and policy makers always discuss Finland? Have they ever thought about the poverty rate in Poland, a country that has reached high ranks in the last PISA surveys?

In the view of many reviewers and bloggers, one of the greatest shortcomings of Hattie's study is that he does not take societal conditions into account. In an online contribution entitled *Academics put heat on half-baked reactions*, this criticism is summarized by a group of scientists from Massey University, New Zealand under the leadership of Snook:

Student background and social context are important

The commentary raises a number of concerns, including that social effects and background context are ruled out.

> "(This) is not a book about what cannot be influenced in schools – thus critical discussions about class, poverty, resources in families, health in families and nutrition are not included – but it is NOT because they are unimportant, indeed they may be more important than many of the issues discussed in this book. It is just that I have not included these topics in my orbit," Hattie says.

The commentators however are very concerned about this attitude.

"Hattie acknowledges the important role of socio-economic status and home background... but chooses to ignore it. This is his choice: but it is easy for those seeking to make policy decisions to forget this significant qualification," they say. (PPTA News, April 2009, p. 4).

How can educational standards be assessed? This question implies the willingness of policy makers to submit performance standards to scientific scrutiny. In my view, a good way would be to assess student performance in different subject matters at the end of decisive grades. Which averages do students in different societal contexts reach? Is it probable that these averages can be attained by all students? Empirical research, firstly descriptive and gradually more and more experimental, should lead to standards that really improve learning.

When consulting a book like Marzano et al.'s (2013) *Using Common Core Standards to Enhance Classroom Instruction and Assessment*, many teachers may ask: Is there any evidence that these Common Core State Standards (CCSS) improve student outcome? In a paragraph called *Assessing the CCSS*, the authors (ibid., p. 69–71) describe the methods by which two consortia produced formal assessments, not to state students' improvement before and after the introduction of the standards, but in order to find out if certain test formats are adequate for assessing the CCSS. If the purpose of educational standards is to help all students to improve their learning and to attain better results, standards have to be subject to evidence-based research.

Are standards in accordance with significant results of evidence-based education? This question is closely related to the missing evidence of governmental standards in general. Even in detail, the CCSS do not relate to scientific results. Troia and Olinghouse (2013), in a theoretically grounded content analysis, show that "Typical writing instruction and assessment in the United States generally does not reflect evidence-based practices. [...] Out of 36 evidence-based writing instruction and assessment practices, the CCSS signal less than half of these in any given grade..." (ibid., p. 343). To avoid conflicts for teachers that may cause undesired effects for learners, it should at least be guaranteed that standards are in accordance with evidence-based research.

In what way should educational standards be evaluated?

It has to be evidenced if and how standards influence the learning processes and the outcomes of all students.

References

Ackerman, P. L. (2013). Engagement and opportunity to learn. In J. Hattie & E. M. Anderman (Eds.), *International guide to student achievement* (pp. 39–41). London/New York, NY: Routledge.

Adams, G. L., & Engelmann, S. (1996). *Research on direct instruction: 20 years beyond DISTAR*. Seattle, WA: Educational Achievement Systems.

Anderson, C. A., Carnagey, N. L., Flanagan, M., Benjamin, A. J., Eubanks, J., & Valentine, J. C. (2004). Violent video games: Specific effects of violent content on aggressive thoughts and behavior. *Advances in Experimental Social Psychology, 36*, 199–249.

Anderson, J. R., Reder, L. M., & Simon, H. A. (1996). Situated learning and education. *Educational Researcher, 25*(4), 5–7.

Anderson, L. W., & Krathwohl, D. R. (Eds.). (2001). *A taxonomy for learning, teaching and assessing: A revision of Bloom's taxonomy of educational objectives*. New York, NY: Longman.

Anonymous. (2013). *Visible learning for teachers: Maximizing impact on learning*. By John Hattie (Routledge, 2012). The Main Idea Net: Current book summaries, pp. 1–12. Retrieved from www.TheMainIdea.net

Arnold, I. (2011). John Hattie: Visible learning. A synthesis of over 800 meta-analyses relating to achievement. *International Review of Education, 57*, 219–221.

Atkinson, E. (2000). In defence of ideas, or why 'what works' is not enough. *British Journal of Sociology of Education, 21*(3), 317–330.

Ausubel, D. P. (1968). *Educational psychology: A cognitive view*. New York, NY: Holt, Rinehart, and Winston.

Bandura, A., & Schunk, D. H. (1981). Cultivating competence, self-efficacy and intrinsic interest through proximal self-motivation. *Journal of Personality and Social Psychology, 41*(3), 586–598.

Baron, J., Boruch, R., Crane, J., Ellwood, D., Gueron, J., Haskins, . . . Zoll, N. (2003). *Identifying and implementing educational practices supported by rigorous evidence: A user friendly guide*. U.S. Department of Education. Retrieved from www.asu.edu/educ/epsl/EPRU/articles/EPRU-0312-46-OWI.pdf

Bennett, R. E. (2011). Formative assessment: A critical review. Assessment in education: Principles. *Policy and Practice, 18*(1), 5–25.

Bereiter, C. (2002). *Education and mind in the knowledge age*. Mahwah, NJ: Lawrence Erlbaum Associates.
Berliner, D. C. (2002). Educational research: The hardest science of all. *Educational Researcher*, 31(8), 18–20.
Berliner, D. C., Glass, G. V., & Associates (2014). *50 myths & lies that threaten America's public schools: The real crisis in education*. New York, NY/London: Teacher College, Columbia University.
Biesta, G. J. J. (2007). Why 'what works' won't work: Evidence-based practice and the democratic deficit in educational research. *Educational Theory*, 57(1), 1–22.
　(2010). Why 'what works' still won't work: From evidence-based education to value-based education. *Studies in Philosophy and Education*, 29, 491–503.
Biggs, J. B., & Collis, K. F. (1982). *Evaluating the quality of learning: The SOLO taxonomy (structure of the observed outcome)*. New York, NY: Academic Press.
Black, P. & William, D. (1998). Assessment and classroom learning. *Assessment in Education: Principles, Policy and Practice* 5/1, 7–74.
Bloom, B. S. (1956). *Taxonomy of educational objectives*. Boston, MA: Allyn & Bacon.
　(1968). *Learning for mastery*. Los Angeles, CA: University of California Press.
Bloom, B. S., Hastings, T., & Madaus, G. (1971). *Handbook of formative and summative evaluation of student learning*. New York, NY: McGraw-Hill.
Borich, G. D. (1995). *Effective teaching methods: Research-based practice* (7th ed.). Boston, MA: Pearson.
Borman, G. D., Hewes, G.M., Overman, L. T., & Brown, S (2003). Comprehensive school reform and achievement: A meta-analysis. *Review of Educational Research*, 73, 125–230.
Bransford, J. D., Brown, A.L., & Cocking, R. R. (2000). *How people learn: Brain, mind, experience, and school (National Research Council)*. Washington, DC: National Academy Press.
Brophy, J. E. (2000). *Teaching* (Educational Practice Series, Vol. 1). Brussels: International Academy of Education and International Bureau of Education. Retrieved from www.ibe.unesco.org
　(2006). History of research on classroom management. In C. Evertson & C. S Weinstein (Eds.), *Handbook of classroom management: Research, practice, and contemporary issues* (pp. 17–43). Mahwah, NJ: Lawrence Erlbaum Associates.
Bruner, J. (1960). *The process of education*. Cambridge, MA: Harvard University Press.
　(1996). *The culture of education*. Cambridge, MA: Harvard University Press.
Campbell, G. (2013). *Gordon Campbell on New Zealand's PISA education rankings*. Retrieved from www.scoop.co.nz; last accessed August 2015
Cardelle-Elawar, M. C., & Corno, L. (1985). A factorial experiment in teachers' written feedback on student homework: Changing teacher behavior a little rather than a lot. *Journal of Educational Psychology*, 77, 162–173.
Carlo, M.S., August, D., McLaughlin, B., Snow, C., Dressler, C., Lippman, D., ... White, C (2004). Closing the gap: Addressing the vocabulary needs of English language learners in bilingual and mainstream classrooms. *Reading Research Quarterly*, 39(2), 188–215.

Cash, A. H., & Hamre, B. K. (2013). Evaluating and improving student–teacher interactions. In J. Hattie & E. M. Anderman (Eds.), *International guide to student achievement* (pp. 119–121). London/New York, NY: Routledge.

Clark, R., Nguyen, F., & Sweller, J. (2006). *Efficiency in learning: Evidence-based guidelines to manage cognitive load.* San Francisco, CA: Pfeiffer.

Cochrane, A. L. (1972, 1999). *Effectiveness and efficiency: Random reflections on health services.* London: The Royal Society of Medicine Press.

Coe, R. (2002). It's the effect size, stupid: What effect size is and why it is important. Paper presented at the British Educational Research Association Annual Conference, Exeter, England, 1–18.

Coe, R., Aloisi, C., Higgins, S., & Elliot Major, L. (2014). *What makes great teaching? Review of the underpinning research.* Durham University, U.K.: The Sutton Trust.

Coffield, F., Moseley, D., Hall, E., & Ecclestone, K. (2004a). *Learning styles and pedagogy in post-16 learning: A systematic and critical review.* (LSRC reference) Retrieved from www.lsda.org.uk/research/reports

(2004b). *Should we be using learning styles? What research has to say to practice.* (LSRC reference) Retrieved from www.lsda.org.uk/research/reports

Cohen, J. (1988). *Statistical power analysis for the behavioral sciences (2nd ed.).* Hillsdale, NJ: Lawrence Erlbaum Associates.

Cornelius-White, J. (2007). Learner-centered teacher–student relationships are effective: A meta-analysis. *Review of Educational Research, 77*(1), 113–143.

Davies, P. (1999). What is evidence-based education? *British Journal of Educational Studies, 47*(2), 108–121.

Deci, E. L., Koestner, R., & Ryan, M. R. (1999). A meta-analytical review of experiments examining the effects of extrinsic rewards on intrinsic motivation. *Psychological Bulletin, 125*, 627–668.

De Florio-Hansen, I. (Ed.) (2011). *Towards multilingualism and the inclusion of cultural diversity.* Kassel, Germany: Kassel University Press.

(2014a). *Lernwirksamer Unterricht: Eine praxisorientierte Anleitung.* Darmstadt, Germany: Wissenschaftliche Buchgesellschaft (WBG).

(2014b). *Fremdsprachenunterricht lernwirksam gestalten: Mit Beispielen für Englisch, Französisch und Spanisch.* Tübingen: Narr.

(2015). *Standards, Kompetenzen und fremdsprachliche Bildung: Beispiele für den Englisch- und Französischunterricht.* Tübingen: Narr.

Deutsch, M. (1949). A theory of cooperation and competition. *Human Relations, 2*, 129–152.

(1962). Cooperation and trust: Some theoretical notes. In M. R. Jones (Ed.), *Nebraska symposium on motivation* (pp. 275–319). Lincoln, NE: University of Nebraska Press.

Dewey, J. (1900). *The school and society.* Chicago, IL: University of Chicago Press.

(1916). *The school and society (2nd ed.).* Chicago, IL: University of Chicago Press.

(1938) *Logic: The theory of inquiry.* New York, NY: Henry Holt and Company.

Diao, Y., Chandler, P., & Sweller, J. (2007). The effect of written text on comprehension of spoken English as foreign language. *The American Journal of Psychology, 120*(2), 237–261.

Dweck, C. S. (1999). *Self-theories: Their role in motivation, personality and development*. Philadelphia, PA: Psychology Press.
(2006). *Mindset: The new psychology of success*. New York, NY: Random House.
(2012). *Mindset: How you can fulfill your potential*. London: Constable and Robinson.
Evertson, C. M., Emmer, E. T., Clements, B. S., & Worsham, M. E.(2004). *Classroom management for elementary teachers*. Boston, MA: Allyn & Bacon.
Fraser, B. J., Walberg, H. J., Welch, W. W., & Hattie, J. (1987). Syntheses of educational productivity research. *International Journal of Educational Research, 11*, 145–252.
Freiberg, H. J. (2013). Classroom management and student achievement. In J. Hattie & E. M. Anderman (Eds.), *International guide to student achievement* (pp. 228–230). London/New York, NY: Routledge.
Fuchs, L.S., Fuchs, D., Compton, D. L., Wehby, J., Schumacher, R. F., et al. (2015). Inclusion versus specialized intervention for very-low-performing students: What does access mean in an era of academic challenge? *Exceptional Children, 81*(2), 134–157.
Gan, M. (2011). *The effects of prompts and explicit coaching on peer feedback quality* (Unpublished doctoral dissertation). Retrieved from https://researchspace.auckland.ac.nz/handle/2292/6633
Gijbels, D., Dochy, F., Van den Bossche, p., & Segers, M.(2005). Effects of problem-based learning: A meta-analysis from the angle of assessment. *Review of Educational Research, 75*(1), 27–61.
Goetz, T., & Hall, N. C. (2013). Emotion and achievement in classrooms. In J. Hattie & E. M. Anderman (Eds.), *International guide to student achievement* (pp. 192–195). London/New York, NY: Routledge.
van Gog, T. (2013). Time on task. In J. Hattie & E. M. Anderman (Eds.), *International guide to student achievement* (pp. 432–434). London/New York, NY: Routledge
Gorard, S. (2013). *Research design: Creating robust approaches for the social sciences*. London: Sage.
Haas, M. (2005). Teaching methods for secondary algebra: A meta-analysis of findings. *NASSP Bulletin, 89*(642), 24–46.
Hartley, J. (2012). Review: Visible learning for teachers. *British Journal of Educational Technology, 43*(4), E134–E136.
Hattie, J. (1992). *Self-concept*. Hillsdale, NJ: Lawrence Erlbaum Associates.
(2009). *Visible learning: A synthesis of over 800 meta-analyses relating to achievement*. London/New York, NY: Routledge.
(2012). *Visible learning for teachers: Maximizing impact on learning*. London/New York, NY: Routledge.
Hattie, J., & Anderman, E. M. (Eds.). (2013). *International guide on student achievement*. London/New York, NY: Routledge.
Hattie, J., & Timperley, H. (2007). The power of feedback. *Review of Educational Research, 77*(1), 81–112.
Hattie, J., & Yates, G. (2014). *Visible learning and the science of how we learn*. London/New York, NY: Routledge.

Heath, C., & Heath, D. (2007). *Made to stick: Why some ideas survive and others die*. New York, NY: Random House.

(2010). *Teaching that sticks* (www.heathbrothers.com/download/mts-teaching-that-sticks.pdf), 1–12.

Herzog, W. (2013). *Bildungsstandards: Eine kritische Einführung*. Stuttgart, Germany: Kohlhammer.

Higgins, S., & Simpson, A. (2011). Visible learning: A synthesis of over 800 meta-analyses relating to achievement. By John A. C. Hattie. *British Journal of Educational Studies*, 59(2), 197–201.

Hunter, Madeline Cheek (1976). *Improve Instruction*. El Segundo, CA: TIP Publications.

Iversen, S. A., & Tunmer, W. E. (1993). Phonological processing skills and the reading recovery program. *Journal of Educational Psychology*, 85, 112–125.

Johnson, D. W., & Johnson, R. (1989). *Cooperation and competition: Theory and research*. Edina, MN: Interaction.

(2005). New developments in social interdependence theory. *Psychology Monographs*, 131(4), 285–358.

(2013). Cooperative, competitive, and individualistic learning environments. In J. Hattie & E. M. Anderman (Eds.), *International guide to student achievement* (pp. 372–374). London/New York, NY: Routledge.

Johnson, D. W., Johnson, R., & Holubec, E. (1994). *Cooperation in the classroom*. Edina, MN: Interaction.

(2008). *Cooperation in the classroom (7th ed.)*. Edina, MN: Interaction.

Johnson, D. W., Maryama, G., Johnson, R., Nelson, D., & Skon, L. (1981). Effects of cooperative, competitive, and individualistic goal structures on achievement: A meta-analysis. *Psychological Bulletin*, 98(1), 47–62.

Kang, S. H. K., McDermott, K. B., & Roediger, H. L. III. (2007). Test format and corrective feedback modify the effect of testing on long-term retention. *European Journal of Cognitive Psychology*, 19, 529–558.

Kim, J. S. (2006). *The influence of class size research on state and local education policy*. Brooking Papers on Education Policy.

Kingston, N., & Nash, B. (2011). Formative assessment: A meta-analysis and a call for research. *Educational Measurement: Issues and Practice*, 30(4), 28–37.

Klahr, D., & Nigham, M. (2004). The equivalence of learning paths in early science instruction: Effects of direct instruction and discovery learning. *Psychological Science*, 15(10), 661–667.

Kounin, J. S. (1970). *Discipline and group management in classrooms*. New York, NY: Holt, Rinehart, and Winston.

Kuncel, N. R., Crede, M., & Thomas, L. L. (2005). The validity of self-reported grade point averages, class ranks, and test scores: A meta-analysis and review of the literature. *Review of Educational Research*, 75(1), 162–181.

Kyun, S., Kalyuga, S., & Sweller, J. (2013) The effect of worked examples when learning to write essays in English literature. *The Journal of Experimental Education*, 81(3), 385–408.

Lemov, D. (2010). *Teach like a champion: 49 techniques that put your students on the path to college*. San Francisco, CA: Jossey-Bass.

Liem, G. A. D., & Martin, A. J. (2013). Direct instruction. In J. Hattie & E. M. Anderman (Eds.), *International guide to student achievement* (pp. 366–368). London/New York, NY: Routledge.

Locke, E. A., & Latham, G. P. (1990). *A theory of goal setting and task performance.* Englewood Cliffs, NJ: Prentice Hall.

Markham, T. (2011). Project based learning. *Teacher Librarian, 93*(2), 38–42.

Marzano, R. J. (1998). *A theory-based meta-analysis of research on instruction.* Aurora, CO: Mid-Continent Regional Educational Lab.

Marzano, R. J., Pickering, D., & Pollock, J. E. (2001). *Classroom instruction that works: Research-based strategies for increasing student achievement.* Aurora, CO: Mid-Continent Research for Education and Learning (MRL).

Marzano, R. J., Yanoski, D. C., Hoegh, J. K., & Simms, J. A. (2013). *Using common core standards to enhance classroom instruction and assessment.* Bloomington, IN: Marzano Research Laboratory (MRL).

Maslow, A. H. (1970). *Motivation and personality (3rd ed.).* New York, NY: Harper Collins.

McComas, W. F. (1998). The principal elements of the nature of science: Dispelling the myths. Adapted from the chapter in W. F. McComas (Ed.), *The nature of science in science education* (pp. 53–70). Dordrecht, the Netherlands: Kluwer Academic Publishers.

Mosteller, F. (1995). The Tennessee study of class size in the early school grades. *The Future of Children, 5*(2), 113–127.

Mosteller, F., Light, R. J., & Sachs, J. A. (1996). Sustained inquiry in education: Lessons from skill grouping and class size. *Harvard Educational Review, 66*(4), 797.

Nuthall, G. A. (2007). *The hidden lives of learners.* Wellington, New Zealand: New Zealand Council for Educational Research.

Oakley, A. (2002). Social science and evidence-based everything: The case of education. *Educational Review, 54*(3), 277–286.

Olson, D. R. (2004). The triumph of hope over experience in the search for 'what works': A response to Slavin. *Educational Researcher, 33*(1), 24–26.

Paivio, A. (1969). Mental imagery in associative learning and memory. *Psychological Review, 76*(3), 241–263.

(1971). *Imagery and verbal processes.* New York, NY: Holt, Rinehart, and Winston.

Palincsar, A. S. (2003). Collaborative approaches to comprehension instruction. In A. S. Sweet & C. E. Snow (Eds.), *Rethinking reading comprehension* (pp. 99–114). New York, NY: Guilford Press.

(2013). Reciprocal teaching. In J. Hattie & E. M. Anderman (Eds.), *International guide to student achievement* (pp. 369–371). London/New York, NY: Routledge.

Palincsar, A. S., & Brown, A. (1984). Reciprocal teaching of comprehension-fostering and comprehension-monitoring activities. *Cognition and Instruction, 1*(2), 117–175.

Palmer, J. A. (Ed.) (2001). *Fifty modern thinkers on education: From Piaget to the present day.* London/New York, NY: Routledge.

Palmer, P. J. (1997, 2007). *The courage to teach: Exploring the inner landscape of a teacher's life.* San Francisco, CA: Jossey-Bass.

Petty, G. (2009). *Evidence-based teaching: A practical approach (2nd ed.)*. Cheltenham, U.K.: Nelson Thornes.

Piaget, J. (1952). *The origins of intelligence in children*. New York, NY: International Universities Press.

   (1970). *Science of education and the psychology of the child*. New York, NY: Orion Press.

   (1971). *Genetic epistemology*. New York, NY: W. W. Norton.

Polanyi, M. (1966). *The tacit dimension*. Chicago, IL: The University of Chicago Press.

Popper, K. (1963). *Conjectures and refutations*. London: Routledge.

Raji Codell, E. (1999). *Educating Esmé: Diary of a teacher's first year*. Chapel Hill, NC: Algonquin Books.

   (2009,). *Educating Esmé: Diary of a teacher's first year* (2nd ed.). Chapel Hill, NC: Algonquin Books.

Ravitch, D. (1995). *National standards in American education: A citizen's guide*. Washington, DC: Brookings Institution Press.

   (2010). *The death and life of the great American school system: How testing and choice are undermining education*. New York, NY: Basic Books.

Ravitz, J. (2009). Introduction: Summarizing findings and looking ahead to a new generation of PBL research. *Interdisciplinary Journal of Problem-Based Learning*, 3(1), 411.

Renkl, A. (2005). The worked-out examples principle in multimedia learning. In R. E. Mayer (Ed.), *The Cambridge handbook of multimedia learning* (pp. 229–245). Cambridge MA: Cambridge University Press.

Ripley, A. (2010). What Makes a Great teacher? The Atlantic, issue January/February 2010

Rockwood, H. S. III (1995a). Cooperative and collaborative learning. *The National Teaching and Learning Forum*, 4(6), 8–9.

   (1995b). Cooperative and collaborative learning. *The National Teaching and Learning Forum*, 5(1), 8–10.

Rohrer, D., & Pashler, H. (2010). Recent research on human learning challenges. Conventional instructional strategies. *Educational Researcher*, 39(5), 406–412.

Rosenshine, B. (1985). Direct instruction. In T. Husen & T. N. Postlethwaite (Eds.), *The international encyclopedia of education* (Vol. 3, pp. 1395–1400). London/New York, NY: Routledge.

Rosenshine, B., & Meister, C. (1994). Reciprocal teaching: A review of research. *Review of Educational Research*, 64(4), 479–530.

Rosenshine, B. V. (1979). Content, time and direct instruction. In P. L. Peterson & H. L. Walberg (Eds.), *Research on teaching* (pp. 28–56). Berkeley, CA: McCutchan.

Roth, G. (2011). *Bildung braucht Persönlichkeit: Wie Lernen gelingt*. Stuttgart, Germany: Klett-Cotta.

Scheerens, J., & Bosker, R. J. (1997). *The foundations of educational effectiveness*. Oxford, U.K.: Pergamon.

Schoen, D. (1984). *The reflective practitioner: How professionals think in action*. New York, NY: Basic Books.

Scott, C. (2013). The search for the key for individualized instruction. In J. Hattie & E. M. Anderman (Eds.), *International guide to student achievement* (pp. 385–388). London/New York, NY: Routledge.
Seidel, T., & Shavelson, R. J. (2007). Teaching effectiveness research in the past decade: The role of theory and research design in disentangling meta-analysis results. *Review of Educational Research, 77*, 454–499.
Shavelson, R. J., & Towne, L. (2002). *Scientific research in education* (National Research Council). Washington, DC: National Academies Press.
Slavin, R. F. (1995). *Cooperative learning: Theory, research and practice (2nd ed.)*. Boston, MA: Allyn & Bacon.
Snook, I., O'Neill, J., Clark, J., O'Neill, A.-M., & Openshaw, R. (2009). Invisible learnings? A commentary on John Hattie's book: *Visible learning*. A synthesis of over 800 meta-analyses relating to achievement. *New Zealand Journal of Educational Studies, 44*(1), 93–106.
Sousa, D. A. (2011). *How the brain learns (4th ed.)*. Thousand Oaks, CA: Corwin.
Strobel, J., & van Barneveld, A. (2009). When is PBL more effective? A meta-synthesis of meta-analyses comparing PBL to conventional classrooms. *Interdisciplinary Journal of Problem-Based Learning, 3*(1), 44–58.
Sweller, J. (1988). Cognitive Load during Problem Solving: Effects on Learning. *Cognitive Science* 12/2, 257–85
  (2006). How the human cognitive system deals with complexity. In J. Elen & R. E. Clark (Eds.), *Handling complexity in learning environments: Theory and research* (pp. 13–25). Amsterdam, the Netherlands: Elsevier.
  (2011). Cognitive load theory. In J. Mestre & B. H. Ross (Eds.), *Cognition in education* (Vol. 55, pp. 37–76). Oxford, U.K.: Academic Press.
Taylor, K., & Rohrer, D. (2010). The effects of interleaved practice. *Applied Cognitive Psychology, 24*(6), 837–848.
Thurstone, L. L. (1925). *The fundamentals of statistics*. London: MacMillan Norwood Press.
Timperley, H. (2013). Feedback. In J. Hattie & E. M. Anderman (Eds.), *International guide to student achievement* (pp. 402–404). London/New York, NY: Routledge.
Torgerson, C. J., Porthouse, J., & Brooks, G. (2005). A systematic review and meta-analysis of controlled trials evaluating interventions in adult literacy and numeracy. *Journal of Research in Reading, 28*(2), 87–107.
Troia, G. A., & Olinghouse, N. G. (2013). The common core state standards and evidence-based educational practices: The case of writing. *School Psychology Review, 42*(3), 343–357.
de Vaus, D. (2001). *Research design in social research*. London: Sage.
Vygotsky, L. S. (1934, 1999). *Thought and language*. Cambridge, MA: MIT Press.
  (1978). *Mind in society. The development of higher psychological processes*. Cambridge, MA: MIT Press.
Wang, M. C., Haertel, G. D., & Walberg, H. J. (1993). Toward a knowledge base for school learning. *Review of Educational Research, 63*, 249–294.
Wellenreuther, M. (2004). *Lehren und Lernen – aber wie? Empirisch- experimentelle Forschung zum Lehren und Lernen im Unterricht*. Hohengehren, Germany: Schneider.

(2014). *Lehren und Lernen – aber wie? Empirisch- experimentelle Forschung zum Lehren und Lernen im Unterricht* (7th ed.). Hohengehren, Germany: Schneider.

White, W. A. T. (1988). A meta-analysis of the effects of direct instruction in special education. *Education and Treatment of Children, 11*(4), 364–374.

Wijnia, L., Loyens, S. M. M., & Derous, E. (2011). Investigating effects of problem-based versus lecture-based learning environments on student motivation. *Contemporary Educational Psychology, 26*(2), 101–113.

Wood, D., Bruner, J., & Ross, G. (1976). The role of tutoring in problem solving. *Journal of Child Psychology and Psychiatry and Applied Disciplines, 17,* 89–100.

Index

Adams, Gary l, 97–99
advance organizers, 11
Anderman, Eric, 90
Arnold, Ivo, 97
assertive questioning, 126, 151–154
   five steps of, 152

Baron, Jon, 58–59
   Identifying and Implementing Educational Practices Supported by Rigorous Evidence, 58–59
Berliner, David C., 50, 56, 218
   50 Myths and Lies that Threaten America's Public Schools, 218
Biesta, Gert J. J., 61
Biggs, Jeremy B., 104–106
   levels of learning outcome, 106
   Structure of the Observed Learning Outcome (SOLO), 104, 106
Binet, Alfred, 13, 35
Bloom, Benjamin S., 104
   taxonomy of educational objectives, 104–106
Borich, Gary D., 102
brain hemispheres, 106
   influence on learning, 106–107
Bransford, John D., 197
   How People Learn, 197
Brophy, Jere E., 140, 143
Brown, Ann L., 188
Bruner, Jerome, 19–21
   Man: A Course of Study (MACOS), 20
   The Process of Education, 19–20
   Toward a Theory of Instruction, 19

Campbell Collaboration, 46, 60, 68
class size, 91
classroom climate, 139–140
classroom management, 139–143
   definition of, 139
   rules and routines, 137

Cochrane Collaboration, 46
Cochrane, Archie L., 46
   Effectiveness and Efficiency: Random Reflections on Health Services, 46
Coe, Robert, 68, 118, 120–121
   six components of great teaching, 120
   What Makes Great Teaching, 120
cognitive development of children, 12
   four stages of, 13–14
Cognitive Load Theory. *See* Sweller, John
Cohen, Jacob, 68
   Statistical Power Analysis for the Behavioral Sciences, 68
collaborative learning, 175–176
Collis, Kevin F., 104–106
concept mapping, 113
conceptual learning, 113
concluding the lesson. *See* lesson conclusion
constructivism, 17
   constructivist approaches, 137
content knowledge, 120–121
cooperative learning, 18, 175–176, 189–190
   major forms of, 182–190
   research into, 179–182
correlation studies, 41

deduction, 31
deep learning, 113
deliberate practice. *See* practice of presented knowledge and skills
descriptive research, 27–28
Dewey, John, 41–43, 61–62, 176–178
   democratic forms of education, 177
   laboratory school, 177
   learning by doing, 177
   Logic. The Theory of Inquiry, 43
   School and Society, The, 177
   Sources of a Science of Education, The, 61
didactic teaching, 137
Direct Instruction. *See* Hattie, John

Index

disruptive behavior, 137
dual-coding theory, 29
Dweck, Carol S., 108–109
   theory of motivation, 109–110, *See also* growth mindset, *See also* fixed mindset

education, 20–25
   definition of, 25
   evidence-based, 47
   standards-based, 198
educational standards
   assessment of, 219
   definition of, 215
   evidence-based standards, 219
   scientific evidence of, 215
   types of, 216
effect size, 65–69
   barometer of, 82
   calculation of, 66–67
empirical evidence, 49, 51
Engelmann, Siegfried, 97, 99
   Direct Instruction System for Teaching Arithmetic and Reading (DISTAR), 99
evaluation. *See* feedback
evidence, grades of, 50
examples. *See* teaching examples
experiment/experimentation, 37–41
explanation, 111–112
explanatory research, 28, 30

falsifiability, 29
feedback
   formative feedback, 166, 171, 199
   forms/types of feedback, 198
   from students to teachers, 212–214
   from teachers to students, 204–208
   peer feedback, 208–211
   research into, 199–201
   summative feedback, 200
fixed mindset, 109
Freiberg, H. Jerome, 139

Glass, Gene V., 64, 68, 218
growth mindset, 109–110
guided practice. *See* practice of presented knowledge and skills

Hattie, John, 71, 75, 80–83, 94–100, 122–124, 127, 142, 181, 188, 192, 201, 210
   Direct Instruction, 95–100, 115
   Feedback-Model of Hattie and Timplerey, 202–204, *See also* feedback
   goals, challenging, 122
   International Guide to Student Achievement, 90–92
   limitations of, 80, 84–87
   positive affective outcomes of, 137
   seven major steps of, 97–100
   summary of results, 82
   Visible Learning for Teachers. Maximizing Impact on Learning, 87–90, 97
   Visible Learning. A synthesis of over 800 meta-analyses relating to achievement, 65, 79–92, 97
Heath Brothers (Heath, Chip & Heath, Dan), 132–136
   Made to Stick, 133
   principles of effective teaching, 133–136
   Teaching that Sticks, 133
hemispheres of the brain. *See* brain hemispheres
Herzog, Walter, 55, 215
hooks, examples of, 131–133
Hunter, Madeline Cheek
   Lesson Plan Design, 102, 117
hypothesis, 28

independent practice. *See* practice of presented knowledge and skills
individualized instruction/individualized learning, 95, 138
induction, 31
instruction, quality of, 121
interactive dialogue, 151–152, 154
Interactive Whole-Class Teaching, 119, 137, 139, 145, 151, 156, 185
internalization, processes of, 16
interventions in teaching and learning, measurement of, 54–56
intuition, 20

Jigsaw Method, 183, 186–187, 190
Johnson, David W., 179–182
Johnson, Roger T., 179–182

Kim, James S., 52–53
   Influence of Class Size Research on State and Local Policy, The, 52
Kounin, Jacob S., 141

Language Acquisition Device (LAD), 19
learning atmosphere/climate. *See* classroom climate
learning processes, 102–104
learning styles, 106–107
   influence on learning, 106–107
learning to learn, 102
Lemov, Dough, 22–24
   Teach Like a Champion, 22
lesson conclusion, 173
Lesson Plan Design. *See* Hunter, Madeline Cheek
lesson planning, 119
   five steps of, 121–122
   summary of lesson planning, 128
lesson starting, 119

four steps of, 130–131
summary of lesson starting, 135
Liem, Gregory A., 137
lifelong learning, 174

Martin, Andrew J., 137
Marzano, Robert J. (Marzano Research Laboratory, MRL), 61, 73–77, 79, 103, 181, 200, 219
  Classroom Instruction that Works: Research-based Strategies for Increasing Student Achievement, 77
  Theory-Based Meta-Analysis of Research on Instruction, A, 73–77
  Using Common Core Standards to Enhance Classroom Instruction and Assessment, 77, 219
medicine, evidence-based, 45–47, 50
mega-analysis, 65
mental representation, stage model of, 21
mentalese, 103
meta-analysis, 64–67, 69
  definition of, 64
  six steps of, 64–65
mistakes
  positive attitude toward, 109, 112, 155
Model of Effective Teaching (MET), 102, 110–113, 137, 139, 185
  summary of steps one to nineteen, 157–158
  thirty steps of the MET, 110–113
modeling, 144
Mosteller, Frederick, 51–53, 60, 91
  Tennessee Study of Class Size in the Early Grades, 51
motivation, 107–110

Nuthall, Graham, 209, 214
  The Hidden Lives of Learners, 209

Oakley, Ann, 58
Othello, 190–191

Paivio, Allan, 29
Palincsar, Annemarie Sullivan, 188, 190
Pashler, Harold, 69
PBL. *See* project-based learning, *See* problem-based learning
Pearson, Karl, 64
peer influences, 149–151
Petty, Geoff, 61, 74, 91, 95, 103–104, 106, 126, 187–188
Piaget, Jean, 12–16
planning the lesson. *See* lesson planning
Polanyi, Michael, 57
  Tacit Dimension, The, 57
Popper, Karl R., 96
practice of presented knowledge and skills, 157

deliberate practice, 175
guided practice, 157, 164–166, 169–170
independent practice, 157, 170–173
types of practice, 157–160
presentation of knowledge and skills, 138, 143–144
  five steps of, 143–144
  interactive presentation, 138
primary studies, 64–65, 67
problem-based learning, 176, 191–193
  research into, 195–196
Program for International Student Assessment (PISA), 35, 217
project-based learning, 18, 177, 191–193
  premises of, 192–193
  project-/problem-based learning, summary of, 196
psychometrics, 35–37

qualitative research, 98
quantitative research, 98
quasi-experiments, 40
questioning. *See* assertive questioning

Randomized Controlled Trial (RCT), 39–40, 51–54
Ravitch, Diane, 216
Reciprocal Teaching (RT), 183, 187–190
  strategies of, 188–190
reliability, 38
Reliability, 38
research
  definition of, 11
  educational, definition of, 11, 56–57
  evidence-based, 49–51, 58–61
  types of, 27–28
research design, 32–35
research methods, 32–35
Ripley, Amanda, 116
  What Makes a Great Teacher, 116
Rohrer, Doug, 69–70
  Recent Research on Human Learning Challenges Conventional Instructional Strategies, 69

scaffolding, 18, 21, 94
schema, concept of, 14
Schoen, David, 20
science
  definition of, 10
  educational, definition of, 22
scientific model, 28
scientific theory, 28–30
Seidel, Tina, 69–71
  Teaching Effectiveness Research in the Past Decade: The Role of Theory and Research Design in Disentangling Meta-Analysis Results, 69–71

Shavelson, Richard, 25, 40, 69–71
short term memory, theories about learning, 119
short-term/working memory, limits of, 157, See also *Cognitive Load Theory*
small group work, 178–179
Snook, Ivan, 218
sociocultural theory, 17
Socrates, 49
Socratic inquiry, 49
spaced versus massed practice, 119
special education, research into, 17
spiral curriculum, 19
standardization of schools, 215
standards. *See* educational standards
starting the lesson. *See* lesson starting
student background, 218–219
Student-Teacher Achievement Ratio (STAR-Project), 52–53
Student Teams-Achievement Divisions (STAD), 183, 185, 190
Sutton Report, 118, *See also* Coe, Robert
Sweller, 138
    borrowing principle, 138
    Cognitive Load Theory, 138
    learning principles, 138
    randomness as a genesis principle, 138
systematic reviews of research, 63

tasks, graded, 169
teacher
    as activator, 95
    as facilitator, 95
    characteristics of great teachers, 115–117
    clarity, 115, 124, 201
teaching examples (in order of occurrence)
    A Choice of Hooks, 131–133
    A Lot of Prejudice, 135

A Test of Reading Literacy: The Miser and his Gold, 160–164
Describing the Iceberg-Model of Culture, 165–166
Know Thy Students, 166–169
Making Punctuation Visible, 134
Money and More, 193–195
Take It Easier, 184–185
Talking About Preferences and Hobbies, 124–125
Teachers Can Make a Difference, 140–143
Toward a Better Understanding of Cultural Differences, 145–149
Team Assisted Individualization (TAI), 185–186, 190
Teams-Games Tournament (TGT), 183–185, 190
theory of social construction, 16, *See also* sociocultural theory
Thurstone, Louis Leon, 35
Timperley, Helen, 199–201, 210
Towne, Lisa, 25, 40
transfer of knowledge and skills, 171–172
Trends in International Mathematics and Science Study (TIMSS), 35, 217

Validity, 38–39
variable, dependent, 38
variable, independent, 38
Vygotsky, Lev S., 16–19

Wellenreuther, Martin, 94, 115, 141, 187–188
with-it-ness, 142–143
work in small groups. *See* small group work
worked examples, 112, 119, 144–145, 165–166, 209
world knowledge of students, 127

Zone of Proximal Development (ZPD), 18, 94

Printed in the United States
by Baker & Taylor Publisher Services